Witnesses to the Baptist Heritage

While designed as a companion volume to *Turning Points In Baptist History*, this book is an excellent companion to any introduction to Baptist history. One finds here, also, some biographies new to this kind of work, as well as some promising new biographers. Kudos to both Mike Williams and MUP for their continuing superb work in Baptist historiography.

—Walter B. Shurden, Minister at Large, Mercer University

These brief biographies recount memorable stories of men and women who have lived out their devotion to Baptist principles. The authors, specialists who cherish their Baptist heritage, describe multiple legacies vital to Baptists, including preaching, missions, theology, justice and religious liberty. This volume offers a splendid introduction to the rich diversity of Baptist thought and practice and is ideally suited for both church study and the university classroom.

—Bill Pitts, Professor of Church History, Baylor University

Before anyone ever again stereotypes, discusses, or argues about Baptists in America, they should be required to read WITNESSES TO THE BAPTIST HERITAGE. This book spells out that heritage in words too simple to misunderstand. Within Baptist life there is so much diversity that all attempts to generalize misstate the enormous complexity. Hopefully, stereotypes of conformity and uniformity will recede into darkness as the light of complication takes over the narrative, beginning with this book.

—Wayne Flynt, Distinguished University
Professor Emeritus, Auburn University

The editorial genius of Michael Williams has produced an incredible resource for the local church. *Witnesses to the Baptist Heritage: Thirty Baptists Every Christian Should Know* brings together the amazing biographies of influential Baptists written by the most brilliant of Baptist scholars who intentionally keep the congregational life of the church in mind. Who would have thought of incarnating the best of the Baptist story, putting flesh and blood on distinctive Baptist traditions? Preachers, missionaries, educators, social activists, and fighters for religious freedom comprise this treasure trove of inspiration. This work could not come at a more critical time.

Gary Burton, Pastor
Pintlala Baptist Church

When a distinguished Baptist historian enlists a group of highly regarded Baptist authors to write brief biographies on thirty remarkable Baptists who helped shape the Baptist denomination, the result is a must-read book for Baptists…and for all who would gain understanding about the Baptist family of Christians

In a time when many, perhaps most, Baptists know little about Baptist belief and heritage, this book helps provide a remedy for such a sad and even destructive condition. As George W. Truett, one of the thirty persons included in this volume, declared, "Not to have such knowledge is for our churches to be harmed in every way."

    One of the best ways to gain understanding of truths, beliefs, and doctrines is through stories of persons. These thirty well-written biographies by extraordinary scholars guide the reader into doctrinal understanding through persons who formulated and lived by these beliefs.

Why these thirty? Many of us may find that some our favorite Baptists have not been included. Anticipating this question, the author provides an excellent rationale for the selection of the thirty Baptists to be featured as well as for the Baptists chosen to write their biographies.

    —William M. Pinson, Jr., Executive Director Emeritus, Baptist General Convention of Texas, Director, Texas Baptist Heritage Center, Distinguished University Professor, Dallas Baptist University

The James N. Griffith Series in Baptist Studies

This series on Baptist life and thought explores and investigates Baptist history, offers analyses of Baptist theologies, provides studies in hymnody, and examines the role of Baptists in societies and cultures around the world. The series also includes classics of Baptist literature, letters, diaries, and other writings. For a complete list of titles in the series, visit www.mupress.org and visit the series page.

—C. Douglas Weaver, Series Editor

Witnesses to the Baptist Heritage

Thirty Baptists Every Christian Should Know

Edited by Michael E. Williams, Sr.

MERCER UNIVERSITY PRESS
MACON, GEORGIA

Endowed by
TOM WATSON BROWN
and
THE WATSON-BROWN FOUNDATION, INC.

P / 519

© 2015 by Mercer University Press
Published by Mercer University Press
1400 Coleman Avenue
Macon, Georgia 31207
All rights reserved

9 8 7 6 5 4 3 2 1

Books published by Mercer University Press are printed on acid-free paper that meets the requirements of the American National Standard for Information Sciences—Permanence of Paper for Printed Library Materials.

ISBN   978-0-88146-548-8
Cataloging-in-Publication Data is available from the Library of Congress

To the best brother and sister anyone could have,

Gary Williams and Alesia Griswold

Contents

Introduction
  Michael E. (Mike) Williams, Sr. | ix

Thomas Helwys (c.1575–c. 1614), *Witness to Church and State*, Freedom of Conscience / John Inscore Essick | 1

John Clarke (1609–1676), *Global Shaper of Religious Freedom*, Religious Liberty / Bruce Gourley | 8

Benjamin Keach (1640–1704), *Worship Innovator*, Ministry / Randall Bradley | 16

Anne Dutton (1692–1765), *Contemplative Baptist Spiritual Director*, Ministry / Michael D. Sciretti, Jr. | 24

Shubal Stearns (1706–1771), *Southern Evangelist Extraordinaire*, Evangelism / Scott Bryant | 31

Isaac Backus (1726–1806), *Champion of Religious Liberty*, Religious Liberty / David Holcomb | 38

Dan Taylor (1738–1816), *Apostle of God's Free Grace*, Evangelism / Michael Dain | 44

Andrew Fuller (1754–1815), *Guardian of Gospel Proclamation*, Missions / Sheila Klopfer | 50

John Leland (1756–1841), *Preacher, Patriot, Baptist Freedom Fighter*, Religious Freedom / Brad Creed | 58

William Carey (1761–1834), *Father of the Modern Mission Movement*, Missions / Terry Carter | 66

Lott Carey (c. 1780–1828), *Father of African-American Missions*, Missions / Bonnie Oliver Brandon | 73

Adoniram Judson (1788–1854), *American Baptist Bridge to the World*, Missions / Delane Tew | 79

Johann Gerhard Oncken (1800–1884), *Catalyst of European Church Planting Movement*, Missions / Gregory Nichols | 87

Isaac Taylor Tichenor (1825–1902), *Father of Cooperative Baptist Missions*, Missions / Michael E. (Mike) Williams, Sr. | 93

Robert Cooke Buckner (1833–1919), *Father of Social Christianity*, Social Justice / Karen O'Dell Bullock | 100

Charles H. Spurgeon (1834–1892), *Baptist Prince of Preachers*, Preaching / Todd von Helms | 108

Lottie Moon (1840–1912), *Pioneer Missionary and Southern Baptist "Saint,"* Missions / Melody Maxwell | 114

E. C. Morris (1855–1922), *Trailblazer for Racial Equality*, Social Justice / Pamela R. Durso | 121

E. Y. Mullins (1860–1928), *Guardian of Voluntary Faith*, Freedom of Conscience / Douglas Weaver | 128

Walter Rauschenbusch (1861–1918), *Pioneer of the Social Gospel*, Social Justice / Glenn Jonas | 136

Helen Barrett Montgomery (1861–1934), *Apostle of "Woman's Work for Woman,"* Missions / Kendal Mobley | 143

George W. Truett (1867–1944), *Preacher to Preachers*, Preaching / Keith Durso | 150

William Owen Carver (1868–1954), *Theologian for a New Era*, Theology / Mark Wilson | 157

James Henry Rushbrooke (1870–1947), *Baptist Peacemaker*, Religious Freedom / Karen O'Dell Bullock | 162

Nannie Helen Burroughs (1879–1962), *Voice for Gender Equality*, Social Justice / Pamela R. Durso | 169

B. B. McKinney (1886–1952), *The People's Musician*, Ministry / Randall Bradley | 176

Thomas Buford Maston (1897–1988), *Southern Baptist Pioneer in Race Relations*, Social Justice / Michael E. (Mike) Williams, Sr. | 183

Herschel H. Hobbs (1907–1995), *Conservative Advocate for Denominational Unity*, Theology / Jerry Faught | 189

Henlee Barnette (1911–2004), *Baptist Activist for Love and Justice*, Social Justice / Aaron Weaver | 195

Gardner Taylor (1918–2015), *Poet Laureate of Preaching*, Preaching / Kelly Pigott | 203

List of Contributors | 210

Notes | 213

Index | 233

Introduction

ALMOST EVERYONE LOVES a good biography. Biography is a great way to tell a story, especially if interwoven with the context out of which the story grows. This book tells part of the Baptist story by using biography as its vehicle.

The importance of biography for understanding history and telling its stories is one of the concepts for this book. Its design originates out of several other ideas as well. One thought is that not enough Baptists or other Christians know the Baptist story or know the key women and men who make up that story. Another idea for this book comes from my own teaching experience. This volume is designed to be a companion to *Turning Points in Baptist History*, edited by Walter Shurden and me and published by Mercer University Press in 2008. As I utilized *Turning Points* in my Baptist history classes, I found that students were especially fascinated by some of the important people of Baptist history and wanted to know more. This collection of short biographies is a partial answer to that fascination.

Yet another concept behind the book originates in how one of my major professors, H. Leon McBeth, influenced many of his students in "doing" Baptist history. As my friend—and author of two chapters of this current volume—Karen Bullock said in her message delivered at Dr. McBeth's funeral, McBeth "valued incisive biographies over generic summaries for the simple reason that a single biography often best captures the essence of an era, much like a snapshot freezes details of a single event or moment in time."[1] He often would ask one of his Ph.D. students in a seminar to summarize his or her presentation on a key Baptist's life and work in a single phrase or word that described that person in a nutshell. This book and the titles of each chapter reflect that concept.

The book is designed to be an introduction to Baptist biographies, longer than a dictionary or encyclopedia article but far shorter than a

---

[1] Karen O'Dell Bullock, "In Memoriam: For Harry Leon McBeth," in *Texas Baptist History* 33 (2013): 79.

full-length biography. Each chapter focuses upon one Baptist and why Christians should know more about her or him. The chapters are not intended to be exhaustive. Indeed, some writers have focused upon just one aspect of these key figures' lives and ministries. The chapters are intended to be written so that students, pastors, and laypeople can read them, gain an introduction to an important Baptist, and whet their appetites to learn more. For this purpose, each biography includes a suggested reading list at the end of each chapter so that the reader hoping to learn more can do additional reading. They are also written in such a way that a historian or scholar will also pick up the book and gain insight from it. Like *Turning Points*, most chapters utilize limited annotation to help the non-scholarly reader but still provide aid for further research for more scholarly readers.

In choosing the authors for the chapters, I purposely sought some women and men due to their area of interest or time period or because they had already done significant research and, in some cases, already published articles, dissertations, or books on their subjects or related areas. Most, though not all, were people I know well and could trust both to do a good job and to meet deadlines. I also wanted to use young—which on this occasion means younger than me—Baptist historians and scholars to write the chapters, while sprinkling in a few more seasoned writers like me. Each of the chapters typically focuses on one major aspect of the person's career while touching on other aspects of the person's life. Some scholars in particular may quibble with the author's or editor's choice. Some may question why key figures like E. Y. Mullins and George W. Truett are categorized in a certain fashion. Others may question why these thirty Baptists and not some others were selected. Others will wonder why more theologians, pastors, and ethicists are not highlighted. Still others will question the heavy concentration of British and American Baptists to the neglect of other significant Baptists in other parts of the world. The answers to these questions lie in several directions. First, as editor I attempted to enlist writers with certain specialties either in the person, time period, or category in which they were writing. This naturally led to some historical persons being chosen to the exclusion of others. Additionally, I opted not to choose some important Baptists like John Smyth and Roger Williams, who, though making major contributions to Baptist life, were not identified as Baptist for the major portions of their lives. I have also chosen not to have chapters on Billy Graham and Martin Luther King, Jr., who, though identified as Baptists, are well known in both the broader context of Christianity and whose contributions transcend even Christian circles. Their stories are well covered in a myriad of other locations. While some theologians and ethicists are covered, we have not attempted to repeat a different version of books James Tull, Timothy George and David Dockery, and Larry McSwain have done in recent years. I also purposely decided—with the exception of Herschel Hobbs, T. B. Maston, Henlee Barnette, and Gardner Taylor—not to include significant Baptists of the 1960s and later. In many cases, the verdict is still out from historians on the long-term contributions of these later significant Baptists.

Additionally, while I have included some Baptists who are better known—like Mullins, Truett, William Carey, Lottie Moon, and Walter Rauschenbusch—I have also mixed them with other Baptists not as well known, like Anne Dutton, Benjamin Keach, Lott Carey, E. C. Morris, and Nannie Helen Burroughs. Regrettably, only one non-British or American Baptist is included, Gerhard Oncken. Certainly other Baptists, both British and American and especially from the nineteenth and twentieth centuries in other parts of the world, deserve to have their stories told in such a fashion. My hope is that other historians will pick up that banner in the years to come. Perhaps there will be a *More Witnesses to the Baptist Heritage* at some point in the future!

As always, I am grateful to Mercer University Press for their continued publication of books on Baptist history and to my colleagues and students at Dallas Baptist University. I am especially grateful to our Dean of the College of Humanities and Social Sciences, Jack Goodyear and his successor as dean, Rob Sullivan; our history department chair, Greg Kelm; and our Provost, Denny Dowd, for their encouragement; and to Kati Griffin, office manager and administrative assistant in the College of Humanities and Social Sciences, for her technical assistance. I am also thankful to DBU President Gary Cook for his continued support of Baptist history and heritage causes. I am always thankful for the love and support of my wife, Robbie, and our three sons, Michael, Josh, and Carey. This book is dedicated to my brother, Gary Williams, and my sister, Alesia Griswold, who have special stars in their heavenly crowns for putting up with being dragged to historical sites on my behalf by our parents when we were growing up, and for me often having my head stuck in some history book throughout our childhood and adolescence.

Thomas Helwys
(c. 1575–c. 1614)

Witness to Church and State
Freedom of Conscience

John Inscore Essick

THOMAS HELWYS STANDS at the headwaters of a Baptist tradition that is now more than 400 years old. Helwys is perhaps most remembered for co-founding, with John Smyth, the first ever Baptist church in Amsterdam in 1609. Given the subsequent history of the people called Baptist, this distinction alone is reason enough for every Christian to become familiar with Thomas Helwys. Yet what makes Helwys an even more compelling Christian figure is his decision to forsake the relative safety of self-imposed exile and return to England as a witness to the budding Baptist heritage, a decision that would cost him his life.

Thomas was born around 1575 into the considerably wealthy and privileged Helwys family of Nottinghamshire, England. Nottinghamshire was no stranger to reforming zeal during this period, for the county produced the likes of Thomas Cranmer, architect of the Church of England's official *Book of Common Prayer*, and many of the "Pilgrims" who would eventually establish a colony in Plymouth, Massachusetts, in 1620. When his father, Edward, died in 1590, Thomas was the oldest son but not yet of age to assume responsibility as executor, so two uncles functioned as temporary caretakers of the considerable Helwys family estate. In 1593 Helwys began his legal education at the famed Gray's Inn in London. Helwys returned to Nottinghamshire in 1595, took up residence on the family estate in Broxtowe Hall, and married Joan Ashmore, with whom he had seven children.[1]

Little is known of Helwys's personal or professional life during the next ten years, but it is clear that in matters of religion he was frustrated with the pace of reform within the English church. Helwys was among those English Christians commonly referred to as "Puritans," a broad and diverse group of people who were convinced that the Church of England, especially its worship as outlined in the *Book of Common Prayer*, was not sufficiently reformed or purged of Roman Catholic excesses. It is possible that his father or his uncle, Gervase Helwys, had been instrumental in Thomas's increasingly Puritan posture towards the established church.² Broxtowe Hall served as a regional gathering place for Puritan sympathizers, though there is no evidence that Helwys was considering breaking with the Church of England at this point. The most influential and radical influence to enter Broxtowe Hall may have been the Church of England clergyman John Smyth. The controversial Smyth was a guest in Broxtowe Hall when he became ill in 1606, and through conversations with Helwys during his convalescence, a friendship formed that marked the beginning of a journey that would see the two men separate from the Church of England and take a relatively short voyage across the North Sea to Amsterdam in pursuit of a true church.³

John Smyth was a man of spiritual restlessness, a trait that probably resonated deeply with Thomas Helwys. Whatever theological uneasiness Helwys and Smyth may have had about remaining in the established Church of England prior to their time together in Broxtowe Hall, the friends soon concluded that they could no longer in good conscience attend its services. Smyth was the first to take the fateful step of formally separating from the Church of England in February 1607; Helwys followed in his footsteps in September.⁴ Untethered now from the church of their birth, Helwys and Smyth sought a church constituted on New Testament principles. Smyth, and later Helwys, joined a Separatist congregation meeting in nearby Gainsborough, Lincolnshire, that seemed, for the moment, to calm their ecclesial anxieties. The move from Puritanism to Separatism was now complete, but stability and peace proved elusive.

Smyth, being a trained theologian and experienced minister, quickly assumed the position of pastor in a congregation that included other unsettled spiritual souls like Richard Clifton and John Robinson. Neither King James I nor the Church of England took Separatism lightly, and arrest and imprisonment awaited those who did not conform to the *Book of Common Prayer*. To avoid trouble, the Gainsborough congregation decided to divide itself into two worshiping bodies, one gathered in Gainsborough under Smyth's leadership and the other gathered in Scrooby, Nottinghamshire under the leadership of Robinson and Clifton. As the threat of persecution increased, however, the Smyth-Helwys group decided in 1607/1608 to migrate to the less restrictive city of Amsterdam in hopes of establishing a true church there.[5] About this time several members of the congregation were arrested by the authorities; Helwys's own wife, Joan, was among them. Joan was eventually released but little else is known of her future movements or involvement. Why Helwys himself was not arrested remains something of a mystery, but it is possible that he had already made his way to Amsterdam in order to make preparations for the congregation's arrival.[6] Fellow Separatist John Robinson later called attention to the fact that Helwys subsidized the group's passage to the continent: "[He] above all, either guides or others, furthered this passage into strange countries; and if any brought oars, he brought sails."[7] His wife's imprisonment notwithstanding, Helwys had every reason to believe that all hindrances to the founding of a true church would be removed in Amsterdam.

Upon arriving in Amsterdam, the Gainsborough congregation did not find the other exiled Separatists there to its liking, so Helwys and company set up residence in a bake house owned by a wealthy Mennonite, Jan Munter. With the migration complete and no threat of persecution, presumably no obstacles for establishing a true church remained. Stability again proved elusive, however, as Smyth's spiritual restlessness resurfaced, this time centered on the question of valid baptism. If the Church of England was not a true church, he reasoned, then any baptism originating within it was not a true baptism. Smyth, Helwys, and the rest of the congregation began to doubt the validity of their previous baptisms and concluded that they had never truly been baptized. Such a conclusion was radical, even among the Separatists, but for this band of English exiles the path was clear: a true church must be constituted on the basis of believer's baptism. For reasons that are somewhat unclear, they chose not to seek baptism from the nearby Waterlander Mennonites. Instead, it was decided that Smyth would first baptize himself by pouring water over his own head, and after that he would baptize Helwys and the rest of the congregation in like manner. So in early 1609 in Amsterdam, Smyth baptized himself (referred to as "self-baptism") before baptizing Helwys and the rest of the congregation. This series of believer's baptisms marked the beginning of the first known Baptist church in history.

Other Separatists thought Smyth's self-baptism to be a scandalous and disorderly act, but Helwys never doubted the validity of his own baptism or Smyth's. For Helwys, the self-baptism constituted both the end of his restless search for a New Testament church and the beginning of a lifelong witness to a Baptist understanding of the Christian faith. Smyth came to see the self-baptism differently. For him, it induced another round of unsettling spiritual questions that caused him to doubt his decision to self-baptize. Smyth's spiritual journey took yet another turn when he, along with the majority of those he had recently baptized, forsook their recent baptisms and sought membership among the Waterlander Mennonites. It seems that the Smyth-led majority belatedly arrived at the conclusion that the Waterlander Mennonite congregation was, in fact, a true church, and a baptism at their hands would be valid. Thus John Smyth, who died in 1612 while awaiting acceptance into the Mennonite church, holds the distinction of being both the first Baptist and the first *former* Baptist.

Helwys and as many as a dozen others upheld the validity of their baptisms and their status as a true church. The Helwys-led Baptist minority excommunicated Smyth and his followers for falling back into the errors of priestly succession. Helwys took it upon himself to defend the young Baptist congregation, and he did so primarily by writing letters and publishing treatises. In 1611, while still in Amsterdam, he published *A Declaration of Faith of English People Remaining in Holland*. *A Declaration* is comprised of a preface that outlines key theological disagreements between Helwys and Smyth and twenty-seven articles of faith. In the preface and the articles, Helwys charted and established a theological and ecclesial trajectory for an incipient Baptist tradition. On ecclesiology, he argued that baptism is the fundamental act of gathering the one church in locally autonomous congregations. Where Christology is concerned, Helwys affirmed the full divinity and humanity of Jesus over and against the opinion held by many Dutch Mennonites that Jesus did not take his human flesh from Mary. On the question of civil government, so long as Christians are not required to violate Christian convictions, he allowed the swearing of oaths and permits Christians to serve as civil magistrates. On the question of atonement, Helwys anticipated later Baptist ambivalence concerning Calvinism when he insisted on original sin but rejected limited atonement.

Helwys and his small, isolated congregation of baptized believers remained in Amsterdam for about two years following the excommunication of Smyth's group. While Helwys never doubted the validity of his baptism or the soundness of his church, he did harbor a growing suspicion that he had mistakenly left England. Fellow Separatist John Robinson attributed Helwys's regret to a series of bad decisions that made return necessary, and it has also been suggested that Helwys was sensitive to Puritan and Anglican accusations of cowardice.[8] Just before departing Amsterdam for England, Helwys published *A Short Declaration of the Mystery of Iniquity* (1612), his most famous and probing treatise. In the closing section of *The Mystery of Iniquity*, he argues that persecution does not justify retreat or flight. If Christians flee persecution, then the gospel has no power. Interestingly, he also confesses that in "great weakness" he had been "misled by deceitful-hearted leaders who have and do seek to save their lives, and will make sure not to lose them for Christ."[9] While John Smyth is not named, it is clear that Helwys has come full circle and disavowed Smyth's justification for leaving England. Convinced that his new Baptist convictions compelled him to go home, Helwys returned as a loyal, but dissenting, subject of the king.

Sometime in late 1612 or early 1613, Helwys, whose wealth at this point is uncertain, and his small band of Baptists returned to England and settled in the sparsely populated and rural area of Spitalfields, just outside the city walls of London. There Helwys and his fellow Baptists founded the first Baptist church on English soil. The church may have been a transplant church of sorts, but it was also a congregation characterized by return and urgency. Nowhere was the urgency more evident than in the Baptist witness of Helwys.

Helwys wasted no time in making his presence known. He immediately went about the business of seeking religious freedom not only for himself, but also for "heretics, Turks, Jews, or whatsoever."[10] In an effort to persuade King James I to embrace such audacious and unprecedented religious freedom, he gave a copy of the recently printed *Mystery of Iniquity* to the king with a handwritten note in the flyleaf: "The king is a mortal man and not God, therefore he has no power over the mortal souls of his subjects, to make laws and ordinances for them and to set spiritual lords over them."[11] This now famous line epitomized his understanding of religious freedom as *the* proper distinction between the temporal and spiritual realms. The king, he argued, had no authority to compel in matters of religion. Helwys's plea for religious freedom fell on deaf ears, however, and in 1613 authorities arrested him and other members of the church and confined them in London's notoriously miserable Newgate Prison. Helwys may have been the first and most distinguished Baptist to arrive in Newgate, but he was certainly not the last. Through the years Newgate welcomed many other Baptist witnesses such as John Murton, Edward Barber, Francis Bampfield, Thomas Delaune, and Hercules Collins, just to name a few.[12] Thomas Helwys never left Newgate, dying as a prisoner there sometime around 1614. Leadership of the congregation fell to John Murton, who also spent much of the remainder of his life as a prisoner in Newgate and died as a prisoner around 1626.

Thomas Helwys was born into privilege but died an imprisoned witness to the Baptist heritage. His legacy includes many "firsts." He was a founding member of the first-ever Baptist church in Amsterdam in 1609. He was a founding member of the first-ever Baptist church on English soil at Spitalfields around 1613. His *Mystery of Iniquity* may well have been the first published document in England calling for complete religious liberty. Who can forget the now 400-year-old assertion that civil authorities are disallowed from punishing "heretics, Turks, Jews, or whatsoever" for their religious convictions? The considerable role he played in helping found the Baptist movement and his stubborn commitment to religious freedom are two of the most obvious reasons all Christians should know about Thomas Helwys.

The arc of Helwys's life also exemplifies the stubbornly submissive nature of the earliest Baptists. This stubborn submission was manifest in his estranged relationship with John Smyth. Following Smyth's lead, Helwys's spiritual journey was characterized by ever-deepening discoveries of what it meant to hear and respond to the gospel. He, like so many other Baptists, Separatists, and Puritans of his period, was always ready and willing to admit that his convictions about the church might be mistaken. In what must have been a difficult string of concessions, Helwys confessed that the church of his birth was not a true church, that his baptism in that church was invalid, that separating from the Church of England was absolutely necessary, that fleeing persecution was acceptable, that the self-baptism of his close friend was absolutely valid, and finally that fleeing persecution was *un*acceptable. These are the decisions of a man unafraid of baptism's truth and its consequences for life and witness. In his life and death, Thomas Helwys bequeathed to the Baptist tradition a stubborn submission to baptism as *the* defining act of gathering God's church.

Suggested Reading

Clayton, J. Glenwood. "Thomas Helwys: A Baptist Founding Father." *Baptist History & Heritage* 8/1 (January 1973): 2–15.
Durso, Keith E. *No Armor for the Back: Baptist Prison Writings, 1600s–1700s*. Macon GA: Mercer University Press, 2007.
Early, Joe, Jr. *The Life and Writings of Thomas Helwys*. Macon GA: Mercer University Press, 2009.
Oxford Dictionary of National Biography, s.v. "Helwys, Thomas (c.1575–c.1614)." New York: Oxford University Press, 2004.
Payne, Earnest A. *Thomas Helwys and the First Baptist Church in England*. 2nd edition. London: The Baptist Union, 1966.

John Clarke
(1609–1676)

Global Shaper of Religious Freedom

Religious Liberty

Bruce Gourley

EMBLAZONED ACROSS THE façade of the Rhode Island state house in downtown Providence are these words: "To hold forth a lively experiment, that a most flourishing civil state may stand and best be maintained with a full liberty in religious concernments." The story behind these words is an epic narrative starring a remarkable man of whom few Americans outside of Rhode Island are aware, a man who was a co-founder of the colony as well as a medical doctor, foreign ambassador, deputy governor, acclaimed author, freedom fighter, and religious trailblazer—in short, a man who is arguably the most important person in Rhode Island's history.

Roger Williams is not his name, although he was a close friend of Williams. Williams obtained the initial charter for his democratic colony of Providence Plantations (later Rhode Island) from the English Parliament in 1643, only to see it voided in 1660 by King Charles II when the English monarchy was restored.[13] The charter revoked, Rhode Island was suddenly vulnerable to assimilation by the bordering theocratic colonies, Puritan states that for the past two decades had tried to snuff out their neighbor's strange experiment in democratic governance and religious liberty.

Standing between the plotting theocrats and the citizens of Rhode Island was Williams's friend, an Englishman by birth who in 1651 returned to his native land as an agent of Rhode Island, charged with defending the colony from her Christian enemies. The 1660 revocation of the colony's charter made the ambassador's mission all the more desperate—and dangerous. Surrounded by powerful adversaries and political intrigue, the odds of his success appeared dim. His adversaries, however, were as wary of the ambassador as he of them, for the man advocating for Rhode Island did so from convictions that were so powerful that should they not be contained; the Puritan's New Jerusalem in colonial America would be endangered.

The friend and ally of Roger Williams against whom the Christian powers of the New World were arrayed was John Clarke, and his revolutionary convictions were those of his Baptist faith and those of the Rhode Island colony: freedom of conscience and religious liberty. For Baptists and for Rhode Islanders, God alone was Lord of the conscience, religious faith voluntary, and separation of church and state necessary to ensure that all persons were allowed religious liberty.[14]

In addition to being pastor of the second Baptist church founded in the New World—the Newport Baptist Church of Rhode Island—Clarke proved a capable, if untrained, diplomat. For three perilous years following the revocation of Rhode Island's original charter, Clarke struggled to obtain a new royal charter from the king. Finally, in July 1663 the Baptist minister's perseverance and determination paid off: King Charles II granted the wishes of Clarke and his fellow Rhode Islanders, signing Clarke's charter that granted religious liberty to all and separated church from state, protecting Rhode Island from the Christian magistrates of her fellow colonies of the New World.[15] Baptist freedom principles triumphed that day, revolutionary principles that would be carved upon the face of Rhode Island's state house and, many years afterward, written into the United States Constitution, the Bill of Rights, and the United Nations' Universal Declaration of Human Rights.

The story of John Clarke comprises much of the second act of the narrative of how Baptist principles of freedom challenged the Western foundations of government-entwined religion and changed the course of nations. Baptist co-founders John Smyth and Thomas Helwys in the Netherlands and England in the decades prior had starred in the opening act, a drama in which Helwys demanded freedom of conscience from King James I, was imprisoned for his heresy, and around 1616 became a martyr for freedom of conscience and religious liberty.[16]

English Separatist Roger Williams, immigrant to the New World, ushered in Act Two. Williams and his family arrived at Boston in 1631.

A lawyer and minister, Williams's evolving and radical religious views, already Baptistic in nature, quickly placed him at odds with the theocratic Massachusetts Bay Colony. Banished from the colony, in 1636 Williams founded Providence Plantations as a refuge for dissenters. Two years later his freedom convictions led him to convert to the Baptist faith and soon thereafter to establish the First Baptist Church of Providence, the first Baptist congregation in the New World. While Williams remained active in the congregation for only a matter of months, Baptist freedom principles flourished in Providence and the tiny sect grew. For his part, Williams remained committed to Baptist principles for the remainder of his life. Shortly after Williams founded Providence Plantations, medical doctor, self-taught theologian, and religious dissenter John Clarke landed in the New World with his family.

Arriving in theocratic Massachusetts Bay in 1637, Clarke found himself in the middle of a nasty religious fight. For the past year, ministers and government officials of the colony had been embroiled in a controversy over the nature of biblical covenant; while most argued for a covenant of works, some came down on the side of grace. The works-oriented faction won the political upper hand in spring 1637, and several of the key proponents of covenantal grace left to never return. One other, Anne Hutchinson, was soon charged with sedition and banished from Massachusetts for insisting that her theological views were the result of divine inspiration.[17]

Clarke, sympathetic to Hutchinson, wrote of his arrival in the midst of this upheaval:

> I was no sooner on shore, but there appeared to me to be differences among them touching the Covenants. And in point of evidencing a man's good estate, some pressed hard for the Covenant of works and for sanctification that be the first and chief evidence. Others pressed as hard for the Covenant of grace that was established upon better promises and for the evidence of the Spirit as that which is more certain, constant and satisfactory witness. I thought it not strange to see men differ about matters of Heaven, for I expect no less upon Earth, but to see that they were not able so to bear with other in their different understandings and consciences...to live peaceably together, whereupon I moved the latter. For as much as the land was before us and wide enough with the proffer

of Abraham to Lot, and for peace sake to turn aside to the right hand or to the left, the motion was readily accepted and I was requested with some others to seek out a place.[18]

Distaste of theocracy and personal convictions of freedom of conscience led Clarke and other dissenters southward to New Hampshire, where a cold winter soon convinced them to relocate yet again. With Williams's assistance, the group settled on the island of Aquidneck in March 1638, founding the town of Portsmouth. Soon, Clarke held worship services there.

Controversy, however, seemed to follow Clarke. Disputes among the town's leaders over matters of religion resulted in his departure in 1639, at which time he and eight others moved to another area of the island and founded Newport. The Baptist minister soon initiated worship services in his newest home. And finally, in Newport, the wandering Clark put down his roots, reconciling with Portsmouth in 1640.

With both Williams and Clarke now settled in the vicinity of one another, the two leaders began to more formally ensconce their shared convictions of freedom of conscience into their communities. While yet believing citizens accountable to God, in 1641 the General Court of Election officially rejected theocracy, and it was "ordered, and unanimously agreed upon, that the government which this body politic doth attend unto in this Island, and the jurisdiction thereof in favor of our prince, is a DEMOCRACY, or popular government."[19] Furthermore, citizens were allowed freedom of conscience "provided it be not directly repugnant to the government or laws established."[20] The General Court also affirmed that "liberty of conscience in point of doctrine, be perpetuated." Herein Jews and Quakers and other dissenters were allowed to settle, the only colony permitting their entry.[21]

Clarke's stature as both a civil and religious leader continued to grow. In 1644 he organized the First Baptist Church of Newport. By then Roger Williams had secured a charter for Rhode Island, allowing the entire colony—now consisting of Providence, Portsmouth, Newport, and Warwick—to rule itself by democratic government. In 1647, the four communities were collectively incorporated under the 1643 charter as "Providence Plantations."

Yet threats to Rhode Island remained. Clarke and Williams worked together to thwart ongoing legal challenges from the theocracies of Massachusetts, Connecticut, and Plymouth, each of which wished to extend biblical rule by annexing Rhode Island. Against this backdrop, Clarke and two other Baptists in 1651 were jailed in Massachusetts, an experience that heightened Clarke's determination to forever secure Rhode Island as a safe haven for persons of any faith or no faith.

With the Baptist faith illegal in Massachusetts, the few adherents who lived in the colony kept hidden their religious convictions. Not so with William Witter, an aged, blind gentleman who lived in Lynn (or Lin) but was a member of Clarke's Newport congregation, some seventy miles distant. Due to his public disavowal of infant baptism, Witter had a history of running afoul of Massachusetts authorities. Now unable to travel but desirous of Baptist preaching, Witter invited Clarke and two other Newport church members, John Crandall and Obadiah Holmes, to lead a worship service in his home.

Even private Baptist worship, however, was not tolerated by Massachusetts authorities. Having quietly journeyed to Witter's house, the three Rhode Island Baptists tried to avoid problems. Trouble, however, was unavoidable. Word had leaked about their visit, and within the small group gathered for worship two constables were present. Once the service began, the three Baptists were arrested.

In Boston Clarke, Crandall, and Holmes appeared in court, where Puritan preacher John Cotton accused them of soul murder for not baptizing infants. John Endicott, the first governor of Massachusetts, went even further. The deniers of infant baptism were "trash" whom he would not allow in his jurisdiction, and Endicott believed they deserved death.[22]

The court subsequently fined the three men, sentencing them to public whipping. Friends paid Clarke and Crandall's fines, securing their release from jail and avoiding the punishment of whipping. Holmes, however, refused the payment of his fine, rejoicing that he was worthy to suffer for the name of Jesus. Following the thirty lashes he received, in front of the gathered crowd he addressed his punishers with the words, "You have struck me as with roses."[23]

A defiant Clarke requested to debate Massachusetts's Puritan clergy regarding the matter of freedom of worship, a petition they denied. Later in 1651, Clarke and Williams traveled together to England, determined to take the debate to the king's court.

In England, Clarke turned to the pen in petitioning for freedom of conscience and religious liberty. Writing furiously, he published *Ill News from New England: or A Narrative of New-England's Persecution; Wherein Is Declared That While Old England Is Becoming New, New England Is Becoming Old* in London in 1652, laying bare to the English public the persecutions suffered by his fellow colonists. His account included his arrest and the whipping of Holmes, as well as other accounts of religious persecution by "soul murdering" Puritan authorities. Playing to English prejudices, as well as his own, Clarke declared that living in New England was like living in Rome.[24]

His accounts of religious atrocities shocked the English, but many found his prescription equally problematic: "It is not the will of the Lord that anyone should have dominion over another man's conscience," Clarke wrote. Human conscience "is such a sparkling beam, from the Father of lights and spirits that it cannot be lorded over, commanded, or forced, either by men, devils, or angels." Pressing his point, Clarke labeled the coercion of conscience as neither biblical, Christian, nor natural. The time had come to abandon the thousand-year-old-plus story of religious faith mandated by theocratic leaders. True religion required voluntary faith.[25]

A twenty-year-old John Locke had not yet stirred the Enlightenment. Locke would follow Clarke and Williams by decades in advocating for freedom of conscience and religious liberty, yet even then the influential thinker's freedom principles were less radical than those of the Rhode Islanders.[26]

Sending a copy of his tract to Parliament, Clarke determined to fight for liberty, freedom and, democracy with all his might. And fight he did. For eleven years the Baptist doctor remained in England as Rhode Island's agent, hovering in the halls of power and sparring with New World theocratic advocates. Clarke's diligence, patience, and powers of persuasion finally paid off in 1663 when King Charles II, against the advice of many, granted the new and controversial Rhode Island Charter penned by Clarke.

The charter in part read:

> that no person within the said colony, at any time hereafter shall be any wise molested, punished, disquieted, or called in question, for any differences in opinion in matters of religion, and do not actually disturb the civil peace of our said colony; but that all and every person and persons may...freely and fully have and enjoy his and their own judgments and consciences, in matters of religious concernments, throughout the tract of land hereafter mentioned, they behaving themselves peaceable and quietly....[27]

The Baptist-centric document was revolutionary and unique. As historian Stanley J. Lemons—Professor Emeritus, Rhode Island College, and member of the First Baptist Church in America at Providence—notes, the charter:

> ...marked the first time in modern history that a monarch signed a charter guaranteeing that individuals within a society were free to practice the religion of their choice without any interference from the government. This freedom was extremely radical in an age marked by wars of religion and persecution of people for religious beliefs.[28]

Securing freedom and democracy for Rhode Islanders, Clarke returned to the colony a hero. Resuming the pastorate of Newport's First Baptist Church, he supported himself by practicing medicine. From 1664 to 1669, he served in the Rhode Island General Assembly, and from 1669 to 1672 was colonial deputy governor. Accounts indicate that his life of civil service, from his arrival in the colony to his later years, was more a reflection of compelling circumstances than personal ambition, to the point that he used his own financial resources to advance the cause of the colony.[29] Remaining at the center of Clarke's vocations of Baptist pastor and civil servant was his commitment to freedom of conscience, religious liberty for all, and church-state separation. He pastored and remained a colonial leader until his death in 1676.

The legacy of John Clarke still remains in Rhode Island, embedded on the statehouse and celebrated and remembered through the Newport-based John Clarke Society of Early American Democracy, a national scholarly organization that promotes and advocates Clarke's Baptistic principles of religious and civil freedoms enshrined in the colony's 1663 charter.[30] Yet the Baptist pastor's influence extends far beyond Rhode Island. The freedom and democratic principles of his 1663 Rhode Island charter are also written into the United States Constitution, the U.S. Bill of Rights, and the United Nations' Universal Declaration of Human Rights.[31] A witness to the Baptist heritage of freedom during his life, John Clarke's freedom legacy has arguably shaped the Western world to a greater degree than any other individual.

Suggested Reading

Backus, Isaac. *A History of New England with Particular Reference to the Denomination of Christians Called Baptists*. 2nd edition. Newton MA: The Backus Historical Society, 1871, 1:125–29, 277–81, 348, 349.

Barrows, C. E. "Dr. John Clarke." *The Baptist Quarterly* 6 (1872): 483–502.

Clarke, John. *Ill News from New England: or A Narrative of New England's Persecution Wherein Is Declared That While Old England Is Becoming New, New England Is Becoming Old, 1652*, London: Henry Hills, 1652: reprint. Baptist Standard Bearer, Inc, 2004.
http://www.particularbaptistlibrary.org/LIBRARY/History/Ill20News,20John20Clark.pdf

James, Sydney. *John Clarke and His Legacies: Religion and Law in Colonial Rhode Island, 1638–1750*. Edited by T. Dwight Bozeman. University Park: Pennsylvania State University Press, 1999.

Nelson, Wilbur. *The Hero of Aquidneck: A Life of Dr. John Clarke*. New York: Fleming H. Revell, 1938.

Benjamin Keach
(1640–1704)

Worship Innovator

Ministry

Randall Bradley

FEW BAPTISTS HAVE lived a life more embroiled in controversy than Benjamin Keach. From his earliest writing, a primer for children, to his final days, his prolific publications and his stances on congregational song, church polity, religious education, religious freedom, remuneration for ministers, and theological issues have earned him the distinction of being referred to as the leading Baptist theologian of his day.[32] Known for his stubbornness and sometimes perceived as a hothead, he was primarily a man who deeply believed the Bible and stood strongly for his convictions, yet he modeled a tolerant spirit and a sense of ecumenicity that provides a model for Baptists leaders today.[33] Having been briefly imprisoned for his writings and witnessing the burning of his books by the authorities, Keach persisted through a tumultuous period and paved a smoother path for others who followed. His impact is still felt today, particularly in the groundbreaking work he did in the area of worship and congregational song.

Benjamin Keach was born on 29 February 1640, in the village of Stoke Hammond, northern Buckinghamshire, to John and Fedora Keach. He was christened a few days later on 6 March. Though described by the first Baptist historian, Thomas Crosby (c.1685–1752), who happened to be Keach's son-in-law, as "genius," his parents were unable to provide an education for him, and he was apprenticed as a tailor.[34] Naturally drawn to study the Bible, at the age of fifteen Keach became convinced that infant baptism was not biblical, and he decided to be baptized upon his own profession of faith and join the majority Baptist group in the area, the General Baptist church in Buckinghamshire.

Serving faithfully in this congregation, his ministry gifts were recognized, and by the time he was twenty years old in 1660, he had assumed a position of leadership in that congregation. In the same year he married Jane Grove of Winslow, with whom he had five children prior to her death ten years later at the age of thirty-one. Three of their children lived to adulthood: Mary, Elias, and Hannah. He remained single for about two years before marrying a widow, Susanna Partridge, whose husband had died after only nine months of marriage. Together they had five daughters: Elizabeth, Susanna, Rebekah, and two named Rachel. They lived together for thirty-two years prior to Keach's death in 1704, and Susanna lived for twenty-three more years.

Beginning at the age of eighteen, Keach preached occasionally at the church in Buckinghamshire and a year later accepted the call from the General Baptist congregation at Winslow. Perhaps because of the persecution he had experienced in Winslow, or sensing greater opportunity, in 1668 Keach sold all of his possessions to have enough money to move to London, where at the age of twenty-eight he became the pastor of a small congregation in Southwark. He remained the pastor of this congregation until his death in 1704 at the age of sixty-four. During his pastorate there, he saw the church grow from a small congregation meeting on Tooly Street to a building that could seat as many as 1,000. Once dissenters were given tolerance, the congregation relocated to Horsely-down, where the building was expanded several times throughout his ministry.

During his first years in London, he embraced Calvinism and became a Particular Baptist. Crosby maintains that in London Keach was exposed to books and learned people, and he carefully considered the distinctions between the General and Particular Baptists, choosing the Particular Baptists out of his own conviction. He espoused the Reformed position throughout the rest of his life.

Keach's first book, *The Child's Instructor*, was written in 1664. Along with serving as a primer for reading, writing, and arithmetic, the book spoke against infant baptism, defended the right for laypersons to preach the gospel, and declared that during the end times the saints would reign with God on earth for 1,000 years. As a result of the controversy this book generated, Keach was tried and sentenced to jail for two weeks without bond. His sentence required him to appear in the gallows for two consecutive Saturdays in Aylesbury and Winslow. There he was forced to stand in the pillory (stocks) during open market. However, while in the pillory at Aylesbury, he preached to the crowds who gathered even while he watched officials burn his book. He later rewrote the book by memory, and it went through more than thirty editions.[35]

Keach continued to be harassed in London, and at one point he was accused of having reprinted *The Child's Instructor*. He was fined twenty pounds, which John Roberts, a medical doctor and close friend, paid.

Keach was a prolific author who wrote fifty-four books and over 1,000 pages of sermons. His books were primarily written in defense of his theological beliefs and his views about church polity.

Although Keach contributed many significant components of church life, his most important and long-lasting influence remains in the area of introducing and solidifying the practice of hymn-singing in regular worship services. The British scholar Horton Davies, in the second volume of his *Worship and Theology in England,* proclaimed that the greatest gift of Particular Baptists to the seventeenth-century church was the introduction of congregational song for which Keach was responsible. After the Reformation, those following Luther's example championed hymn-singing; however, those in the Reformed tradition of Calvin only sang texts found in the Bible—Psalms and Canticles. Even more restrictive were those who followed Zwingli and allowed no singing. While Psalm-singing was widely accepted in seventeenth-century England, hymn-singing was seldom practiced. Psalm-singing fit well into the belief that singing biblical texts was acceptable, while singing texts of human composure was neither biblical nor within the free and spontaneous movement of the spirit acceptable to the dissenters. The dissenters strongly objected to the set forms of prayer as practiced by the Anglicans in the *Book of Common Prayer;* therefore, to sing songs of human composure with a group of worshipers was akin to rote praying from a prayer book. Should non-Christians be present, their singing might pollute worship. Also, what about those with un-tunable voices?[36] While Keach wrote about 500 hymns, his contributions are not in the body of his own work since none are in broad usage today—his significance lies in his bringing the practice of hymn-singing into regular use and his paving the way for hymn-writers such as Isaac Watts and the Wesleys, writers who far outshone Keach's literary aptitude.

Keach introduced hymn-singing in the Horsley-down Particular Baptist Church somewhere between 1673 and 1675, first following the observance of the Lord's Supper, later on days of special thanksgiving or fasting, and finally in weekly worship.[37] There is also evidence that Keach introduced hymns to funeral services during this period. In order to assess the full scale of the opposition to hymn-singing, Vaughn cites that some within Keach's congregation opposed hymn-singing, some within the Particular Baptist community in London opposed hymn-singing, and Keach had already engaged in a bitter debate with Isaac Marlow long before Marlow's initial publication. Eighteen years had passed between the date that Keach claims to have introduced hymn-singing following the administration of the Lord's Supper in 1673 and the date of Keach's publication of *The Breach Repaired* (1691).[38]

Isaac Marlow (1649–1719) was a member of the Mile End Green Church, although his wife and children were listed as members of the Horsley-down Church. He became outspoken against hymn-singing, and the short books he published against Keach's practice of hymn-singing spawned an intense debate that began and ended with pamphlets by Marlow. The first of the pamphlets was *A Brief Discourse*, which appeared in 1790, and the final publication was *An Answer to a Deceitful Book* in 1698. Keach published a book related to the controversy with Marlow, *The Breach Repaired* (1691), and he endorsed *A Sober Reply to Mr. Steed's Epistle Concerning Singing* (1691), which is usually attributed to Thomas Whinnel. While the official controversy over hymn-singing is chronicled in the books exchanged between Keach and Marlow, two of Keach's earlier books, *Tropologia* and *Gold Refin'd*, also address the issue of hymn-singing; therefore, Keach had primed the debate prior to Marlow's initial publication.

On 1 March 1691, a majority of members of the Horsely-down congregation voted to allow singing following the sermon each Lord's Day. However, the controversy that was already entrenched from the bitterness about which all involved had debated did not quickly go away. Following the vote, a small but influential group petitioned to withdraw from the church. Although Keach announced the meeting and its topic one week earlier, the detractors objected not only to the outcome of the vote but also argued that the issue had not been thoroughly debated. Following the local church vote and the dissension that resulted, the singing controversy discussion continued at the General Assembly of Particular Baptists in June, where Thomas Whinnel of Taunton asked the assembly to censure people who wished to withdraw from their churches over the issue of hymn-singing. However, the motion was brought up on the last day of the meeting, and since many members had left early, the issue was ruled out of order. Shortly before the denominational meeting, Keach published *A Sober Appeal for Right and Justice* (30 May 1691), in which he appealed for a committee to be formed with half chosen by Keach and half chosen by Marlow in order to mediate the conflict. Although the assembly ratified the agreement and endorsed the committee of eight men—four chosen by Keach and four chosen by Marlow—the committee did not fulfill its mandate and, sometime after 9 November 1691, disbanded due to conflicts over the ground rules for the committee; Keach wanted the rules to be set as they went, and Marlow wanted the rules agreed upon in advance.[39]

The following year, in June 1692, the Particular Baptist churches again assembled in London and took up the singing issue a second time; however, after heated debate over this and other issues that were brought into the discussion, the dispute left the Baptist group deeply divided and disorganized. No more Particular Baptist assemblies were held after 1693, and the "Particular Baptist organization withered, but hymn singing prospered."[40] Perhaps the issue finally came to an end in 1736 when the Maze Pond Church, which was established by the hymn-singing dissenters, called Abraham West to be their pastor, with hymn-singing as a condition of his accepting their call.

While Keach's contributions in other areas of the church's life are significant and had a lasting impact on decisions for the future, none impacted the church beyond Baptists the way his introduction did, and the eventual wide acceptance of hymn-singing paved the way for what became and continues to be at the core of congregational worship for nearly every Christian gathering.

Keach made significant contributions in many aspects facing the church in his day, and to some degree his positions made wider ripples.

One such issue to which Keach was profoundly committed was religious instruction and education; his first book, *The Child's Instructor*, while a primer also included his position against infant baptism. However, nearly all of his books were intended to educate. Additionally, Keach wrote a number of religious allegories that sought to engage the broader public and encourage reading. While Keach's writings are far inferior to Bunyan's allegories, Keach was also engaged in "conveying heavenly truths through earthly symbols."[41]

Other examples of issues about which Keach crusaded through his writings were the laying on of hands as an ordinance and pay for ministers. Keach maintained that ministers should be paid and supported by their congregations, and he also believed throughout his life that the laying on of hands was an ordinance, an idea that he observed among the General Baptists and retained. In addition to his impact on singing and worship, Keach was involved in all aspects of Baptist life in his time. He signed the 1689 *London Confession*, one of the most important Baptist confessions of all time, defended the Baptist understanding of baptism with great passion, and was the most prolific Baptist writer of the seventeenth century. He was a leader among leaders, and his peers looked to him as their spokesperson when controversy arose—he never shirked passionate debate and intense engagement. However, if change was merited according to his understanding of scripture, Keach was willing to make it.

Without dispute, Keach's greatest contribution was establishing the practice of hymn-singing firmly in the worship gatherings of all congregations who descend from English traditions. Keach spent over twenty years slowly introducing and eventually establishing this practice, yet his own hymns are not considered of high literary value and are no longer used. However, in addition to his persistence, the time was right. According to Copeland, "If England was ready for toleration, it was also ready for songs to be sung in worship that were penned by the hands of men and women of God belonging, not to the ages, but to the age at hand."[42]

Keach's understanding of scripture spurred him to write, "I cannot see how any, who own the Bible and New Testament of Christ to be their rule, can deny it."[43] His ability to assess accurately the day in which he lived, his biblical commitment, and his passionate leadership coalesced, and when the evidence was weighed, the church followed him. History has also affirmed him as well. Again, Copeland's analysis is helpful: "If Keach's establishment of congregational hymn-singing overshadowed all else that he did, it is because the innovation of a practice provides more acclaim or notoriety than the defense of practices already instituted."[44]

Other issues about which Keach engaged were not new, and Keach's contributions were added to those voices who preceded him; however, in the case of hymn-singing, at least in the context of the English Church, his ideas about congregational song were innovative and timely. While some of the other issues about which Keach wrote and debated still persist among Baptists even to this day, congregational singing is not one of them. Keach settled the issue over three centuries ago.

However, at the end of the day, although Keach always debated with passion and conviction, he also demonstrated a conciliatory spirit. When he spoke of those who disagreed with him about the laying on of hands and congregational singing, he urged his congregation to show "Tenderness, Charity, and Moderation to such as differ from you in those Cases…[do] not refuse Communion with them…."[45] Conflict over music's role in worship did not begin or end with Keach, and as long as Christians worship through singing, conflicts will likely continue. However, may we be inspired to follow Keach's example in being patient when change occurs slowly, being persistent in our adherence to our understanding of scripture, being sensitive to the cultural milieu of our current situation, and always embracing tenderness, charity, and moderation.

Suggested Reading

Copeland, David A. *Benjamin Keach and the Development of Baptist Traditions in Seventeenth-Century England.* Lewiston NY: The Edwin Mellen Press, 2001.

Crosby, Thomas. *The History of the English Baptists.* 4 volumes. London: n.p., 1739, 1:185–209, 3:143–47, 4:268–314.

Martin, Hugh. *Benjamin Keach (1640–1704): Pioneer of Congregational Hymn Singing.* London: Independent Press, 1961.

Riker, D. B. *A Catholic Reformed Theologian: Federalism and Baptism in the Thought of Benjamin Keach*, 1640–1704. Colorado Springs: Paternoster, 2009.

Vaughn, J. Barry. "The Glory of a True Church: Benjamin Keach and Church Order Among Late 17th-Century Particular Baptists." *Baptist History & Heritage* 30/4 (1 October 1995): 47–57.

Anne Dutton
(1692–1765)

Contemplative Baptist Spiritual Director

Ministry

Michael D. Sciretti, Jr.

BRITISH BAPTIST ANNE Dutton was a contemplative Baptist laywoman who contributed a transatlantic epistolary ministry of spiritual direction in the eighteenth century. Laypeople and clergy, including leading men and women of the Evangelical Revival, enthusiastically read Dutton's prolific writings because of their spiritual depth and counsel.[46] Throughout the eighteenth and nineteenth centuries, Dutton continued to inspire and encourage Christians as an "eminently pious woman" through her posthumous publications and reprints.[47] Baptist historian Joseph Ivimey called her "the celebrated Mrs. Ann Dutton," stressing that the "fame of her primitive piety, and particularly of her catholic charity, was spread everywhere, so that she received invitations to visit them from persons of all religious parties."[48] Some twentieth-century scholars were not so congenial, bemoaning her "works of mystic piety"[49] and "unpleasant sentimentality."[50] However, scholarship has recently shifted to elucidate important aspects of her "mysticism" and her influence as a key early supporter of the Evangelical Revival.[51]

An analysis of Dutton's voluminous writings reveals that her primary historical contribution was her intentional ministry of spiritual direction to the social-spiritual network of individuals, churches, and communities touched by the Calvinistic wing of the Evangelical Revival.[52] The ministry of the spiritual director is a recognized role in the history of Christian spirituality, but is rarely acknowledged in Protestant or Baptist history. It is even more rare to find any scholarship discussing spiritual direction by female laity. So Anne Dutton provides an extraordinary look at a ministry of spiritual direction by a *Baptist laywoman*.

Anne Williams was born in Northampton, England in 1692 and grew up attending the Independent church at Castle Hill. After a near-death experience in 1705, she experienced conversion and soon became a full member of the church. Even though she experienced her conversion as "the time of my Espousals" and "an Earnest of my eternal Rest in the Bosom of Christ," she struggled with negative, oppressive thoughts. In response, Dutton intuitively began the spiritual practice the contemplative Christian tradition calls "watch of the heart," which she learned at the age of fourteen and used throughout her life and ministry.[53] Once she became aware of some oppressive "thought," Anne would "come to Christ, as a poor Sinner, just as I came at first."[54] This would become a central aspect of her counsel in later years: do not do battle with your thoughts, but instead "venture on Christ afresh."

Two years later in 1707, while coming home dissatisfied from a prayer meeting, a scriptural text "drop'd" into her mind: "*Rejoyce in the Lord alway: And again I say rejoice.*" According to Dutton, the "Word brake in again upon [her] Heart" and directed her to "the true and proper Object of its Joy, even the Lord himself. ...*In* the Lord, not in what you enjoy *from* him, but in what you are *in* him."[55] She interpreted this experience as the "sealing of the Spirit"—a post-conversion, intuitive assurance that she was one of God's chosen. This formative event provided her not only with full assurance of salvation, but also with a foundational lesson in discernment and surrender that it was always possible for her "to foot it by *Faith*, when I had not the Prop of spiritual *Sense* to lean on."

Soon after this event, Dutton read High Calvinist Joseph Hussey's *The Glory of Christ*, which probably facilitated her move in 1710 to John Moore's church College Lane, an open-membership Baptist congregation. By 1713 she became intellectually convinced of the practice of believer's baptism, resulting in her immersion soon thereafter. At this church she met her first husband, Thomas Cattell; the two were married in 1715. The new couple then moved to London where Anne began worshipping with the Calvinistic Baptist church at Cripplegate, pastored by one of Hussey's students, John Skepp. She became a full member in 1718.

In 1719 her first husband tragically died, leaving her a widow at the age of twenty-eight and prompting her return to Northampton. During this "afflictive providence," Anne perceived her "dear Lord Jesus, sweetly call[ing]" her, beckoning her to "take up thy Delights in *me*, converse with *me* as thy *living Husband* at God's right Hand: For *behold, I am alive for evermore!*"[56] She believed God was doing a purgative work in her as she "resign'd into the Will of God, under trying Circumstances!"[57] Back in Northampton she met a young Baptist minister, Benjamin Dutton, and the two were married in 1720. After their marriage, he preached in various locales until the two of them sensed a call to the Great Gransden Church in Huntingdonshire in 1731.

Anne's prolific writing ministry began shortly after Benjamin became the pastor of this church. Her new role as pastor's wife launched her into a ministry that overshadowed her husband's and continued until her death three decades later. In 1734, after her first published work, *A Narration of the Wonders of Grace*, Anne Dutton immediately received negative feedback concerning her writing. Probably because of the opposition she faced (most likely because of her gender as well as her theology), Dutton thought it best to remove her name from the title pages of her writings.[58] Nevertheless, throughout the 1730s a diverse group of English Christians continued to solicit Dutton for spiritual guidance, encouragement, and direction.

By 1740 seven of her works had been published, and she carried on an unpretentious correspondence with individuals across southern England. In the months leading up to 1740 and as the new decade began, Anne corresponded with several leaders of the Evangelical Revival. Her initial interactions with them soon enlarged her ministry of writing that began primarily with poetry, hymnody, and theological discourse, but soon was defined by epistolary spiritual counsel, seemingly at the insistence of men like George Whitefield and Howell Harris.

The 1740s would prove to be her most prolific and fruitful years. Between 1741 and 1743, fourteen more of her works were published. During this same time, John Lewis, Dutton's friend and the editor of *The London Weekly Papers* (the first evangelical magazine), included many of her letters under the anonymous name "From a Friend in the Country."[59] In 1743 Benjamin Dutton traveled to the American colonies to circulate his wife's publications during his preaching tour. By the close of 1743, she corresponded with individuals, churches, and societies on both sides of the Atlantic, as many of her approximately twenty works at this time circulated throughout the colonies. In her role as transatlantic spiritual director, Dutton became one of the earliest Calvinistic British Baptists to support and contribute to the burgeoning Evangelical Revival.

After 1743 Anne's publications slowed slightly, probably because of the difficulties of financing her own works and her increasing input into theological squabbles splintering the Evangelical Revival in England and Wales. In 1747 she received a letter from Whitefield notifying her that Benjamin had died in a shipwreck on his return voyage. She experienced great agony as a result of her second husband's death, agony for her personal state as well as the state of her beloved church at Great Gransden. Widowed and childless, she continued to produce spiritual letters and books. By 1750 an additional fourteen of her works had been published.

After reaching notoriety, she became a vital intermediary in the placement of British Baptist pastors. During her final years, Dutton provided the impetus and editorial skills for the reemergence in England of evangelical periodical literature with the *Spiritual Magazine*, which she helped edit and compile and to which she contributed more of her spiritual letters. At the time of her death, Anne Dutton had become one of the most prolific female writers in the eighteenth century, Baptist or otherwise.[60]

The Duttons' call to the Great Gransden Baptist Church in 1731, which also served as the genesis of Anne's spiritual-direction ministry, provides an entry point into a reflection on her contributions to the Baptist heritage. In this formative event, an evangelical mysticism and vocation merge when a "Word came home to [her] Soul in the great Power of God, *John* xxi, 15. *Lovest thou* ME?—*Feed my Lambs.*"[61] This experience illustrates Dutton's primary spiritual practice—combining scriptural memorization and open receptivity to potential divine impressions—and evinces a kind of experiential Biblicism that employed the "mystical sense" of scripture primarily for her personal comfort, assurance, and direction.[62] Although historians seldom use the words "mysticism" and "contemplative" when referring to Baptists, this is beginning to change, especially with Anne Dutton.[63] The root word of "contemplative" is "temple" (*con-templum*). Thus, a *contemplative* spirituality takes seriously the biblical teaching that a Christian is a "temple of the Spirit" and that God can be experienced in the "holy of holies" of the heart. What happens in that secret place is a "mystery" (*mysterion*, from which we get the word "mystic"). In response to heart-communion with God, the Christian can then assume his or her "priesthood" as a believer and "temple-with" (*con-templum*) the "temple" of creation, embodying the Divine Presence in the world.

In this light, we may consider Anne Dutton as a contemplative Baptist mystic. A fundamental tenet of Baptist spirituality is the possibility of a direct, unmediated experience of God; Anne Dutton personifies how one Baptist encountered God and taught others how to "practice God's presence." She is a Baptist who clearly experienced and communicated what Bernard McGinn describes as "the mystical element in Christianity...that part of its belief and practices that concerns the preparation for, the consciousness of, and the reaction to what can be described as the immediate or direct presence of God."[64] Dutton articulated some of the same experiences as Christian mystics throughout the centuries, at times using the same scriptures, biblical stories, images, and metaphors.[65] Therefore, an awareness of this "ordinary mystic" of the Calvinist Baptist tradition illumines an aspect of the history of Baptist spirituality that has been neglected.

Anne Dutton is also an important Baptist witness to a coherent understanding of the contemplative life, and that any inward mystical experiences should result in outward acts of service. Throughout her spiritual autobiography as well as her popular 1734 work *Walking with God*, Dutton exemplified a democratized, Calvinistic contemplative theology. For a Calvinist mystic, the highest rung of the ladder to God is willing and loving service.[66] Dutton's spiritual autobiography in three parts maps a three-fold contemplative path for her readers: how to experience communion with God, conformity to Christ, and empowerment for Spirit-led service.

Finally, Dutton is an important witness to the Baptist emphases of soul freedom and vocational service. She is one of the earliest examples of a Baptist laywoman who felt called to the ministry of spiritual direction. In the face of great resistance to a woman writing to guide others, Anne Dutton humbly yet firmly defended her divine vocation as a spiritual writer. She considered herself a "private Christian" called to a "public Work" to "preach CHRIST and his Truths...both doctrinally and practically before all."[67] She believed this was the duty of every Christian that for her manifested as a ministry of private teaching, comforting, and edifying.

A contemplative, Calvinistic Baptist laywoman, Dutton believed she had received a vocation to spiritual direction and writing. She grounded her ministry in spiritual formation via Calvinistic congregations and pastors in the early eighteenth century and the lessons she learned through her personal struggles with afflictions. Her Puritan spirituality and the experiential Biblicism reflected in her early writings and letters attracted Calvinist Methodists like Howell Harris and George Whitefield, who in turn expanded her social-spiritual direction network. Calvinist Methodist leaders relied upon her for spiritual confirmation and connected her to struggling evangelical individuals and communities requiring spiritual counsel. The *London Weekly Papers* became another means that disseminated her common spiritual counsel to a vast audience, and her Letter-Books demonstrate her transatlantic influence and the defining elements of her spiritual direction. The individuals and communities that received Dutton's letters all related to her as a spiritual director. To Dutton they came with their transcendence crises concerning communion with God, conformity to Christ, assurance of faith, afflictive emotions, and selfless service. In turn, she instructed and exhorted her correspondents to practice acts of faith, holy ease, and holy resignation to a God she experienced as an Ocean of Mercy. Whether in regard to conversion or assurance, Dutton's consistent message was that all would be well if one could "Come to Christ as a sinner!"

For reasons of historical importance and spiritual insight, Anne Dutton deserves to be read once again—in formative and informative ways, for the spiritual counsel she gives to those who yearn for communion with the Beloved, and for the important example she is of the Christian call to teach, inspire, and heal others. Through her "mystical" experiences, she models the Baptist emphasis on direct, unmediated communion with God, what might be understood as the *inward* dimension of the priesthood of the believer. Through her spiritual-direction ministry (and her tenacious defense that all were called to "preach" Christ), Dutton models the Baptist emphasis on soul freedom that results in a ministry of proclaiming and applying "good news" to individual souls, what might be understood as the *outward* dimension of the believer's priesthood. Indeed, she demonstrates that Jesus' question and exhortation to Peter is addressed to *every* disciple: "Lovest thou ME?—Feed my Lambs."

Suggested Reading

Burleson, Blake, and Michael Sciretti, Jr., editors. *Entempling: Baptist Wisdom for Contemplative Prayer.* Telephone TX: Praxis, 2013.

Dutton, Anne. *A Discourse Upon Walking with God: In a Letter to a Friend. Together with Some Hints Upon Joseph's Blessing, Deut. 33.13, &c. As Also a Brief Account How the Author Was Brought into Gospel-Liberty. In a Letter to a Friend. To Which Are Added, Brief Hints Concerning God's Fatherly Chastisements, Showing Their Nature, Necessity, and Usefulness, and the Saints' Duty to Wait Upon God for Deliverance When Under His Fatherly Corrections.* London: printed by J. Hart and sold by J. Lewis, 1743.

———. *A Letter on the Application of the Holy Scriptures: Shewing How the People of God May KNOW, When Words of Scripture Come into Their Minds, on Any Account, Whether They Are from the LORD, or Not. Written for, and Sent Unto, A Worthy FRIEND and Honourable GENTLEMAN. To Which Are Added, Three Letters Relative to It. As Also, Three Letters on the Application of General Promises. By One Who Has Tasted That the LORD Is GRACIOUS.* London: printed by John Hart and sold by J. Lewis and G. Keith, 1754.

———. *Selected Spiritual Writings of Anne Dutton: Eighteenth-Century British-Baptist, Woman Theologian.* 7 volumes. Edited and compiled by JoAnn Ford Watson. Macon GA: Mercer University Press, 2003–2015.[68]

Sciretti, Michael D., Jr. "'Feed My Lambs': The Spiritual-Direction Ministry of Calvinistic British Baptist Anne Dutton During the Early Years of the Evangelical Revival." Ph.D. dissertation, Baylor University, 2009.

Shubal Stearns
(1706–1771)
Southern Evangelist Extraordinaire
Evangelism

Scott Bryant

SHUBAL STEARNS SERVED as the undisputed leader of the Separate Baptists in North Carolina in the early eighteenth century. Born in Massachusetts in 1706, Stearns's understanding of the experiential nature of the Christian faith was largely influenced by the itinerant preaching ministry of George Whitefield. Whitefield, an Oxford-educated Church of England minister, believed in and preached the importance of a spiritual new birth. This was innovative at the time because the Church of England and the Puritans of the colonies baptized infants into the church and urged the members to take hold of the faith that they had been baptized into, but neither taught nor emphasized the necessity of a new birth.

Whitefield's preaching strategy and his tactics were unusual for the time. Whitefield did not wait for an invitation from a local minister to preach to a congregation, but rather preached to the crowds in markets and in town centers. Whitefield used the techniques of actors from the stage, including dramatic emotions and exaggerated physical actions, in order to attract and keep the attention of the passersby. The colonists had never seen a preacher with the intensity and emotion of Whitefield. He quickly became a sensation that people had to see for themselves in order to determine if the reports and rumors of the dramatic outdoor preacher were indeed true.[69]

As a result of Whitefield's enthusiastic preaching that emphasized the emotional elements of Christianity, many Puritans throughout the colonies began to question the validity of their own faith because it was characterized by serious introspection and reflection and allowed no room for the influence of human emotion. As more and more colonists reflected on their own faith, they also began to examine the faith of the established ministers in their local congregations because these local authority figures practiced and taught a Christian faith free from the influence of human emotion. The colonists in New England did not have choices regarding their church membership, as each community had only one official church and the citizens were expected to be members and to pay the church tax that supported their local congregation. Whitefield's emotional and dramatic style failed to impress the vast majority of the established ministers of the churches throughout New England, and they continued to teach that the Christian faith was best practiced through contemplation and reflection and not based on emotions.

The influence of Whitefield's emotional style eventually prompted church members to question the legitimacy of the faith of the established ministers, and many rebelled to form new congregations that emphasized the new birth and accepted emotions as a legitimate source for religious conviction and conversion. These new congregations were referred to as "Separate" congregations because they separated themselves from the established parish church. Members of the "Separate" congregations were also known as "new lights" because many of the new congregations believed that Whitefield, and others like him, opened their eyes to the true light of the Christian faith. Shubal Stearns was one of the many people who questioned the faith of the local minister and formed a Separate congregation in his hometown of Tolland, Connecticut. The Separate congregation followed the example of Whitefield in emphasizing the necessity of being born again and the importance of emotions in matters of religion. Stearns's examination of the scriptures, coupled with his belief that Christians must experience a spiritual rebirth, prompted him to question the practice of infant baptism because infants could not recognize their sin and be born again. In 1751 Stearns concluded that infant baptism was inconsistent with the belief that followers of Christ be born again. He adopted the Baptist position of believers-only baptism and Separate Baptist minister Wait Palmer baptized him.[70]

Stearns's personal decision to be baptized had a big impact on the Separate congregation that he led. It quickly became a Baptist congregation opposed to the established congregation of the community. Whitefield's ministry that relied on the importance of emotions and feelings had an ongoing influence in the life of the Separate congregations that emerged as individuals and churches began to perceive God's leadership through their emotions and feelings. They understood the emotions and feelings of an individual as a way that the Holy Spirit could prompt, lead, and guide a person and/or a congregation. In 1754 Shubal Stearns became convinced that the Holy Spirit was guiding him to go out west. In order to be obedient to the Spirit's leadership, he and his wife journeyed to Virginia.

Their journey led them to Berkeley County Virginia, where Stearns reconnected with his sister Martha and brother-in-law Daniel Marshall who settled in Berkeley County after they completed missionary work with Native Americans in Pennsylvania. Daniel and Martha Marshall accepted the teaching of believers-only baptism, were immersed, and decided to join with Shubal and Sarah in preaching the gospel in an effort to start a church. They began their ministry in Hampshire County Virginia, but in 1755 they relocated to a frontier region of North Carolina where they formed the Sandy Creek Church.

In their newly established congregation, they emphasized the importance of spiritual rebirth and their sermons connected with the community, and the church began to grow in part because of Stearns's unique preaching style completely new to the community. A contemporary described Stearns's preaching voice as "musical and strong, which he managed as, one while, to make soft impressions on the heart, and fetch tears from the eyes in a mechanical way; and anon, to shake the very nerves and throw the animal system into tumults and perturbations."[71] The community was drawn to hear Stearns preach, and they responded to his sermons with repentance and conversion as they experienced being born again. Stearns enjoyed enormous success very quickly in North Carolina, and his evangelistic efforts, although localized in the Sandy Creek region, rivaled the successful tours throughout the colonies of his idol, George Whitefield. In less than three years, Stearns baptized over 900 people, many of whom joined the Sandy Creek congregation. This evangelistic success also gave rise to additional new congregations in the surrounding region.

Stearns and Marshall influenced others not only through their leadership of the Sandy Creek congregation, but also through others in the area who copied their style of preaching. Both Stearns and his protégés emulated Whitefield's preaching style, which appealed to the emotions of the individual. The Separate Baptist preachers in North Carolina appealed to the emotions of the congregants and emphasized the importance of being born again. The combination of this unique style and the appeal to the emotions of the individual succeeded in attracting converts for Stearns and for his protégés.

In part because of the rapid growth in the congregation, in 1758 Marshall left Stearns and the Sandy Creek Church to become the pastor of a congregation at Abbott's Creek. To maintain a connection between the two congregations, Stearns and Marshall led their congregations to form the Sandy Creek Baptist Association in 1758. The leadership and influence of Stearns and Marshall expanded beyond their local congregations and was evident in the number of ministers sent out from the newly formed organization. The missionary impulse of Stearns and Marshall was evident in the fact that the Sandy Creek Baptist Association began forty-two new congregations and sent out over 125 ministers in its first twenty years of existence. Stearns's influence would eventually far exceed the boundaries of the association as members and ministers of the association moved away from the region, taking with them Stearns's enthusiastic preaching style and his emphasis on the new birth. Marshall ministered for a time in South Carolina and eventually served in Georgia, where he continued to preach and call individuals to repentance.

The formation of the Sandy Creek Baptist Association enabled Stearns to maintain control over the developments in the churches of the organization. The local congregations asked the association to ordain ministers, establish new congregations, and resolve conflicts that emerged within the local congregations. By maintaining control over the ordination of the ministers, Stearns effectively controlled the preaching in the congregations. Some congregations did not have an ordained minister and depended upon the association to send ordained ministers to preside over baptisms and the observance of the Lord's Supper. From 1758–1770, Stearns served as the founding leader of the Sandy Creek Association and used his influential voice to determine who would be ordained and where new congregations would be established.

During Stearns's lifetime, the Sandy Creek Association did not adopt a formal statement of belief, as Stearns adamantly opposed the adoption of any creed or confession. He demonstrated a staunch Biblicism that affirmed scripture as the only tool needed to govern the local church and the newly formed association. His rejection of creeds and confessions prompted him to rebuff overtures from John Gano of the Philadelphia Baptist Association and Oliver Hart of the Charleston Baptist Association, both of whom visited a Sandy Creek Association meeting to discuss the possibility of joining the Baptist associations together. One of Stearns's primary concerns was that both the Philadelphia and Charleston Associations affirmed statements of faith. For Stearns, the Bible was the sole authority for the local congregation and for the association, and to affirm a creed or confession would dilute the authority of the scriptures. Evidence of Stearns's legacy on the association can be seen in the fact that the Sandy Creek Association did not affirm a faith statement of any kind until 1816, more than forty years after his death.

Stearns began to lose his control over the Sandy Creek Baptist Association in 1770, as it decided to divide into three different districts based on their geographic location. The participants' immediate approval of the proposal demonstrated Stearns's waning influence on the group. Stearns failed to prompt a discussion on the matter and to convince the group to stay united under his leadership. The Sandy Creek Baptist Association divided into three groups: one for the Separate Baptists in Virginia, one for the Separate Baptists in South Carolina, and the Separate Baptists in North Carolina remained in the Sandy Creek Association under the leadership of Stearns.

The breakup of the association and Stearns's lagging influence in the association indicated to Stearns that he could be most effective in his local community. The political events of the late eighteenth century, however, influenced the final years of Stearns's ministry, as the political unrest throughout the colonies and pockets of rebellion in the immediate area prompted many citizens to move out of the area. Stearns spent the final year of his life primarily in ministry to the local congregation. He died in 1771.

Stearns was one of the first and most successful itinerant Baptist evangelists on American soil. In many ways, Stearns served as the prototype of a Baptist minister, as he emphasized preaching and evangelism in the rural and largely unsettled Sandy Creek region of colonial North Carolina. He exemplified the Baptist emphasis on the personal experience of spiritual rebirth as he urged people to repent and turn to God so that they could experience grace and be born again. His evangelistic work resulted in dramatic growth that had far-reaching impact in the South. Considered the Father of the Separate Baptists in the South, he is given credit for the lasting impact of his unique preaching style that some contend is still followed today in the Appalachian region.[72]

The meetings of the Sandy Creek Baptist Association were three- to four-day affairs and consisted of fellowship, worship, and plenty of sermons. The drawn-out evangelistic meetings functioned as a preview of things to come in Baptist life, as the camp meeting revivals of the Second Great Awakening in the late eighteenth- and early nineteenth-century followed a similar format and enjoyed similar results with numerous individuals experiencing a spiritual rebirth. Though on the decline in recent years, many Baptist churches across the United States follow the example of the Sandy Creek Association and gather for protracted revival services.[73]

Stearns's formation of the Sandy Creek Baptist Association in 1758 also exemplified an element of Baptist polity, as the rapid growth of the congregation led to the formation of new churches that wanted to remain in relationship with one another. When the association divided into three distinct districts in 1770, the new associations continued to follow the model that was established by the Sandy Creek Baptist Association, as they maintained cooperative relationships between congregations demonstrated and modeled by Stearns's Sandy Creek Association. One aspect of the Sandy Creek Association that was not adopted by many subsequent associations was maintaining control over who could be ordained to the ministry. Eventually, the vast majority of Baptist associations returned the authority of ordination to the individual congregations. For Stearns, the association functioned as one big fellowship composed of different local congregations. The refusal to allow the association to adopt a confession of faith or a creed demonstrated a Baptist principle of affirming a high view of scripture and the rejection of manmade documents. This position is affirmed by some Baptists today and remained a widely held view by many Baptists well into the twentieth century. The Biblicism of the Baptists is what separated them from other Protestant groups that affirmed various creeds and or confessions of faith.

Stearns's legacy is found in his fervent evangelistic efforts and his intense preaching that called the audience to conversion. His successful ministry prompted others to emulate him and effectively spread his influence across the South as members and ministers of the Sandy Creek Baptist Association moved throughout the region. His strident Biblicism and rejection of manmade creeds and confessions are also legacies of Stearns that remain evident in many Baptist congregations today. For Stearns, the Bible served as the authority for faith, and he understood the command of scripture to say that he was to go and proclaim the gospel. The Bible said it, and so Stearns did it.

Suggested Reading

Kidd, Thomas S. *The Great Awakening: The Roots of Evangelical Christianity in Colonial America*. New Haven CT: Yale University Press, 2007.

Morgan, David T. "The Great Awakening in North Carolina, 1740–1775: The Baptist Phase." *The North Carolina Historical Review* 45/3 (July 1968): 264–83.

Sparks, Elder John. *The Roots of Appalachian Christianity: The Life & Legacy of Elder Shubal Stearns*. Lexington KY: University Press of Kentucky, 2001.

Stout, Harry S. *The Divine Dramatist: George Whitefield and the Rise of Modern Evangelicalism*. Grand Rapids MI: Eerdmans, 1991.

Isaac Backus
(1726–1806)

Champion of Religious Liberty

Religious Liberty

David Holcomb

BAPTISTS PLAYED A crucial role in the struggle for religious freedom in eighteenth-century America. Long subjected to religious taxation as well as civil penalties for their nonconformist theology and opposition to established churches, Baptists often found themselves at the forefront of the advocacy of liberty of conscience and separation of church and state. A key, if not *the* key, figure among eighteenth-century Baptists was Massachusetts pastor Isaac Backus. Backus is most noted for his opposition to religious taxation in Massachusetts, particularly in his role as agent of the Warren Association. Yet Backus also made many important contributions to Baptist identity as a pastor, theologian, and historian. During his career, Backus traveled over 67,000 miles, preached over 10,000 sermons, and published more than thirty-five tracts and pamphlets, numerous letters, petitions, and sermons, as well as his noted three-volume *A History of New England with Particular Reference to the Denomination of Christians Called Baptists*. By the time of his death in 1806, Backus gained a reputation as one of the most influential figures in American religious life in the eighteenth century, despite his "lack of any formal education and his almost continual role as a dissenter."[74]

Backus was born in Norwich, Connecticut in 1726. Raised in the local Congregationalist church, Backus attended public schools at a young age though his formal education ultimately would be quite limited. Influenced by the revivals of the Great Awakening, Backus and his family converted and joined the "New Light" Congregationalists during his teen years. "My heavy burden was gone," Backus wrote of his conversion experience, "and my joy was unspeakable."[75] Evidently,

Backus was genetically predisposed to the dissenting tradition. His grandfather left the Congregational Church due to the church's influence in politics and the lack of religious freedom, and his mother spent thirteen days in jail for refusing to pay her church taxes. By 1745, Backus and other "New Lights" formed a Separate congregation in Norwich, and in 1746 Backus responded to a call from God to become a minister: "So I was enabled then to give up my soul and body afresh to God, to serve him in preaching the Gospel."[76] After a year of itinerant preaching in New England, Backus began his first pastorate at a Congregationalist church in Titicut, Massachusetts. Here he challenged the Standing Order by defending the church's right to call its own pastor, a conflict that eventually led to the creation of a Separate congregation. It was here he and his fellow Separates refused to pay the local church tax as well. When encountered by a local official seeking to collect a religious tax of five pounds, "I told him that they were going on in an unscriptural way to support the gospel, and therefore I could do nothing to countenance them in such a way." Backus escaped jail when a local figure paid his tax, yet others were imprisoned. Backus continued to come into conflict with Massachusetts officials committed to the "use of the sword to support religious teachers," and in doing so, quickly emerged as a leader among Separates in Massachusetts.[77]

Backus's church in Titicut soon faced internal conflict over the issue of baptism. As a growing number of members began to advocate believer's baptism, the church began to experience tensions over whether infant baptism should continue to be practiced. Backus struggled to maintain unity in the church, but was ultimately persuaded that the "Baptist principles" of believer's baptism was most consistent with scripture and submitted to baptism in 1751. Backus eventually concluded that the church "had become so broken and divided as to be incapable of acting as a body," and left Titicut to establish a Baptist church in Middleborough, Massachusetts.

It was from this pastorate that Backus became a leading spokesperson for the Baptist cause, seeking, as William McLoughlin has argued, to achieve a level of acceptance and respectability among the Congregationalist stronghold. From here he traveled widely, preached tirelessly, and wrote extensively, seeking to bring together as well as defend Baptists throughout New England. His advocacy, supported in part by Baptists from the Philadelphia Baptist Association, led to the creation of Rhode Island College (later Brown University). The original college charter reflected the theological convictions of its founders, such as Backus, by declaring "that into this liberal and catholic institution shall never be admitted any religious test, but on the contrary, all the members here of shall forever enjoy full, free, absolute, uninterrupted liberty of conscience."[78] Backus became integrally involved in the institution, serving for more than thirty years on its board of trustees.

Baptists in Massachusetts also formed the Warren Association as a way of expressing, in a corporate fashion, Baptist cooperation and concerns. Once assured that the association would not violate the autonomy of individual congregations, Backus and his Middleborough Church joined the association and Backus quickly assumed a key leadership role on the Grievance Committee. This was the platform through which the association expressed its opposition to religious taxation—including the requirement that separate churches obtain certificates of exemption from church taxes.

This effort prompted Backus to pen perhaps his most famous defense of religious liberty and the separation of church and state in 1773. Titled, *An Appeal to the Public for Religious Liberty against the Oppressions of the Present Day*, Backus articulated the Baptist position on religious liberty in a statement that, according to William McLoughlin, "deserves to rank with Williams's *Bloody Tenent* and Madison's *Remonstrance* as one of the great American expositions of this principle."[79] In it Backus called for "the true difference and exact limits between ecclesiastical and civil government." With regard to religious taxation, Backus concluded: "I before declared that the Scripture is abundantly clear for a free support of ministers, but not a forced one." Such religious taxation violated religious conscience and "tends to destroy the purity and life of religion," Backus further warned. It also had deleterious effects upon civil society in that "coercive measures about religion tend to provoke emulation, wrath, and contention."[80] Unfortunately, Backus's arguments did not persuade Massachusetts to abandon religious taxation; nonetheless, it was an influential tract that, according to

William McLoughlin, declared "independence of Separate Baptists against the ecclesiastical tyranny of the Standing Order."[81]

In 1774, Backus and fellow Baptists met with Massachusetts delegates to the Continental Congress urging relief from religious taxation. According to Backus, "I told them that it is absolutely a point of conscience with us; for I cannot give in the certificates they require without implicitly acknowledging that power in man who made which I believe belongs only to God." John and Samuel Adams countered that the Congregational establishment in Massachusetts was "slender" and that any abuses Baptists faced lay at the feet of the General Court and Baptist "enthusiasts." Notwithstanding the delegates' promises to seek greater relief for the Baptists from religious taxation, John Adams made it clear that the Baptists "might as well expect a change in the solar system" as to expect the Congregationalists "would give up their establishment."[82]

Backus aimed his next efforts at the Massachusetts Assembly, to whom he penned a letter drawing a parallel between religious taxes and the British tax on tea. Drawing upon the patriotic fervor of the day, Backus proclaimed that Baptists "heartily unite" in the cause to oppose taxation without representation. However, he argued that civil authorities levying religious taxation "is as much out of their jurisdiction as it can be for Britain to tax America."[83] This melding of political and religious liberty became an important strategy for Backus, who in 1779 was invited to submit a draft of a proposed Bill of Rights to the new Massachusetts Constitution. In it Backus called for removing a clause authorizing religious taxation, even a general assessment to "make suitable provision" for Christian teachers. "Christianity is a voluntary obedience to God's will," Backus concluded, "and everything of a contrary nature is antichristianism."[84]

Isaac Backus's prominence in Massachusetts led to his election as a delegate to the Massachusetts Ratification Convention for the new U.S. Constitution. Backus viewed this opportunity as a way to ensure religious liberty would be guaranteed to the new nation. Interestingly, while many Baptists opposed the new Constitution because it did not contain explicit guarantees of religious liberty and the separation of church and state, Backus supported the Constitution, believing that the "exclusion of any heredity, lordly power, and of any religious test" were sufficient protections. The No Religious Test Clause found in Article VI of the Constitution specifically drew Backus's support: "Many appear to be much concerned about it, but nothing is more evident, both in reason, and in the holy scriptures than that religion is ever a matter between God and individuals."[85]

While extensively involved in ministry and advocacy, Backus somehow found time to write his *A History of New England with Particular Reference to the Denomination of Christians Called Baptists*. First published in 1777, the eventual three-volume work "did much to define the theological identity of the Baptist movement in his region."[86] In many ways his work served as an apologia for the Baptists, but as such he reintroduced Roger Williams and Obadiah Holmes to the Baptist narrative in New England. His retelling of their stories helped galvanize the identity of Baptists as staunch defenders of religious liberty and the separation of church and state.

While Backus never strayed from his advocacy of religious liberty and the separation of church and state, he focused his later years upon doctrinal disputes and evangelism. He challenged the Arminian trends in some Baptist congregations and the spread of universalism in other churches. Backus was particularly sharp in his condemnation of the Shakers, whom he felt "totally perverted the Christian faith."[87] In general, Backus was concerned with what he perceived to be a general "indifference to religion" in New England. Backus would maintain an active preaching and writing schedule until his death in 1806.

Backus's legacy, particularly on the issue of the relationship of church and state, has led to a good deal of examination by scholars. Some have argued that Backus would not necessarily identify with modern-day "strict separationists," as his "evangelical Calvinism" led him to seek a "sweet harmony" between church and state. While Backus clearly viewed church and state as two separate institutions, he did understand Christianity to be essential to civic virtues and good government. As a result, Backus did not oppose general oaths of office, Sabbath laws, or state-supported chaplains.[88] Consequently, some scholars have argued that Backus's separationism did not go as far as his Baptist contemporaries John Leland, Thomas Jefferson, or for that matter,

Roger Williams. William McLoughlin has noted, however, the "Separationism that we now associate with the (Baptist) tradition was still unresolved among the Baptists even at the time of Backus's death." Nonetheless, he concludes that Backus's "pragmatic middle-ground" on church-state issues, "not the more consistent positions of Jefferson and Williams," have "prevailed in practice throughout American history."[89]

Backus's legacy must also be understood in light of his time and geographic context. Backus's quest to gain not only religious freedom, but also greater respectability and standing for Baptists, occurred in a state where Congregationalism enjoyed its privileged legal status until 1833. More importantly, however, is that Backus's fundamental principles of separation of church and state, protection of individual conscience, and voluntary support of religion laid the groundwork for a viable church-state arrangement when the United States became much more religiously and ethnically pluralistic than what Backus experienced during his lifetime. Ultimately, Backus's legacy is best characterized by his persistent advocacy of religious freedom. As Anson Phelps Stokes declared, "No man of his generation devoted his time and thought more consistently and unselfishly to the cause of religious freedom."[90]

Suggested Reading

Coker, Joe L. "Sweet Harmony vs. Strict Separation: Recognizing the Distinctions Between Isaac Backus and John Leland." *American Baptist Quarterly* 16 (September 1997): 241–49.

Grenz, Stanley. *Isaac Backus—Puritan and Baptist.* Macon GA: Mercer University Press, 1983.

Maston, T. B. *Isaac Backus: Pioneer of Religious Liberty.* Rochester NY: American Baptist Historical Society, 1962.

McLoughlin, William G. *Isaac Backus and the American Pietistic Tradition.* Boston: Little, Brown, 1967.

———. *Soul Liberty: The Baptists' Struggle in New England, 1630–1833.* Hanover: Brown University Press, 1991.

Dan Taylor
(1738–1816)

Apostle of God's Free Grace Evangelism

Michael Dain

DAN TAYLOR, A Yorkshire General Baptist leader, is readily identifiable as the founder of the New Connection of General Baptists, a group of churches that separated from the established English General Baptists in 1770. Taylor was instrumental to the success of this evangelistic renewal movement among eighteenth-century General Baptists. Taylor, however, is not nearly as well known as earlier General Baptist leaders like John Smyth or Thomas Helwys. Nor is he as recognizable as the later General Baptist leader John Clifford, who led the General Baptists into the Baptist Union in 1891. Dan Taylor, however, deserves a place among those influential Baptists.

Dan Taylor was born in the Yorkshire village of Northowram on 21 December 1738.[91] Taylor's father was a coalminer and the young boy followed his father into the mines as early as age five. Largely self-taught, Taylor had a love for books and reading, which he cultivated throughout his life. In his teen years, Taylor began listening to Methodist evangelists, often walking several miles with his brother to hear George Whitefield or John Wesley preach.[92] Taylor came to faith through the influence of the Methodist class meetings he attended and continued his association with the Methodists until 1762, though not uncritically.[93]

Dan Taylor left the coal mine at age twenty-four and began preaching to a small group meeting in the village of Wadsworth. In that same year, Taylor had become convinced of the truth of believer's baptism after having read Dr. William Wall's *The History of Infant Baptism*. Taylor sought to be baptized by some Particular Baptist ministers he knew, only to be rebuffed because of his belief in a general atonement. By spring 1763, Taylor had discovered a group of General Baptists and they baptized him. Taylor returned to Wadsworth and his small church, now associated with the Lincolnshire General Baptist Association, and he began attending their annual meetings. Taylor hoped to find kindred spirits among the Lincolnshire General Baptists, but they did not share his evangelistic zeal or fervent worship. Taylor's orthodox Christology, hymn-singing, and enthusiastic evangelism soon caused conflict with the older group.[94]

Taylor and a few other General Baptist ministers met in London in summer 1770 after deciding to withdraw from the Lincolnshire Association and form a "New Connection" of General Baptists.[95] This New Connection continued to grow as Taylor provided leadership over the next forty-six years. Taylor pastored the church in Wadsworth until 1782 when he was called to Halifax. Two years later Taylor moved again, this time to London to serve the General Baptist church in Whitechapel. Taylor remained the pastor of the London church until his death in 1816.

Despite a lack of formal education, Dan Taylor served General Baptists as the editor of the *General Baptist Magazine* beginning in 1798, and as the principal of the General Baptist Academy from 1798 until 1813. Taylor continued to communicate with the Old General Baptists, attempting to bring the groups closer together. The older body continued to consider the new churches as a part of the General Assembly. The New Connection churches pulled away from assembly life after 1803.

Taylor's pastoral duties kept him active and busy. He also had an active and busy family life as well. He married four times. His first wife, Elizabeth Saltonstall, bore him a total of thirteen children, of whom a son and five daughters survived him. Taylor was active with pastoral responsibilities even in summer 1816, just months before his death. After a short illness, Dan Taylor died 26 November 1816.

The New Connection of General Baptists owed its founding and early growth to the efforts of Dan Taylor. Because of the singular contribution of Taylor, a recent historian of the New Connection determined that the group would most appropriately be called "the Tribe of Dan."[96] Taylor likely never envisioned the impact he would have when he and the small group meeting at Wadsworth formed a new church. Taylor came to faith from the influence of the early Methodist revivals that were sweeping England at the beginning of the eighteenth century. His association with Methodism and his early attempts at preaching very nearly landed him a position as a Methodist itinerant. Taylor, however, had already begun to form his own religious opinions, and he determined to be neither a Calvinist nor a Methodist.

After much discussion, Taylor and his small band determined that they were Baptists. This group soon discovered that there were other Baptists who shared their belief in a general atonement, and in spring 1763 Taylor began to meet with the General Baptist association in nearby Lincolnshire. As mentioned above, after only two years Taylor discovered that there were significant differences between his theological convictions and the old General Baptists with whom he had begun to cooperate.

The old General Baptists were mired in theological debates concerning the deity of Christ and the meaning of the atonement.[97] Many General Baptists accepted views that compromised the full deity of Jesus and the necessity of the atonement. These views often led to Unitarianism. Taylor was not a university-trained theologian and was not caught up in the rationalistic philosophies of the day. He combined the zeal of the evangelical revivals with a commonsense approach to doctrinal issues. Taylor was convinced that among the older General Baptist congregations, the "great and essential doctrines of the gospel were neglected, if not opposed" by ministers of the older churches.[98]

By 1770, Taylor and other orthodox ministers from the Leicestershire area churches determined to form a new association more congenial to their views. Ministers from London, Kent, Essex, Lincolnshire, and Leicestershire met in London on 6 June 1770 and organized the "New Connection" of General Baptists. This group published a confession of six "Articles of Religion" defining their doctrinal stances in contrast to the older Baptists. Taylor composed the articles that were adopted by the whole.

Article three dealt directly with the disputed points between the factions. Here Taylor affirmed that Jesus Christ was both "god and man, united in one person." While that belief might be hard to explain,

Christians were "bound by the word of God" to accept the doctrine.[99] With regard to the atonement, the document affirmed that Jesus suffered to make full atonement for all, a free gift offered to those who believed.

With Taylor's leadership the New Connection experienced rapid growth. From seven churches in 1770, the movement claimed thirty-one by 1786. Taylor was the undisputed leader and worked hard to advance the cause. He wrote polemical works engaging the various controversies of his day, including hymn-singing. He produced a catechism for children and various works on baptism, worship, and church discipline. Over forty-six years of active ministry, Taylor published some forty-five tracts and numerous associational letters, and participated in many ordinations for new minsters. His publications ranged from published sermons to longer doctrinal pieces like his *Fundamentals of Religion in Faith and Practice*, published in 1775 and revised in 1802.[100]

Taylor worked strenuously to preserve the orthodoxy of the New Connection. He refused to allow ministers to fall back into the old ways. Ironically, he had previously rejected the almost dictatorial control that John Wesley exercised over his Methodist itinerants, and yet was often charged with being too strict on "disputed matters."[101] The New Connection churches flourished, but within two generations of the separation in 1770, the old General Baptists had practically disappeared.

Dan Taylor bequeathed to the New Connection of General Baptists a significant legacy. Had Taylor not resurrected the denomination, there would have been little possibility for a Baptist Union at the end of the nineteenth century because the General Baptists would have ceased to exist. Taylor displayed three important characteristics that flowed into the ethos of General Baptist life. First, Taylor led a return to a simple Biblicism that had been lost in the cold, rationalistic hermeneutic of the General Baptists at the beginning of the century. Next, Taylor was an advocate for an evangelistic imperative. Taylor believed that Christians had a responsibility to invite sinners to repent and turn to Christ. Lastly, Taylor displayed and promoted an experiential religion—a religion of the heart, not the head.

Dan Taylor's Biblicism is evident not only in the New Connection Articles of Religion, but also in his other published works. The Lord has indulged humans "with a clear revelation of himself and his will concerning man," said Taylor in his treatise *Fundamentals of Religion*.[102] The scriptures reveal God's will and should be "read, preached, and heard under a deep sense of his supreme authority, immaculate purity, and inflexible justice."[103] Furthermore, the scriptures reveal the way of salvation and the love and grace of God to "sinful and miserable man."[104] Whatever humans needed for salvation and happiness is found in the simple message of the Bible.

From his earliest religious inclinations, Taylor was a "warm advocate" of the idea that "Christ died for every man."[105] This evangelistic zeal remained a part of Taylor's ministry throughout his lifetime. One of the primary issues that gave rise to the formation of the New Connection was the lack of evangelistic zeal and "gospel preaching" among the older churches.[106] Taylor asserted that the writers of the biblical texts never hesitated to encourage sinners to repent. The "sacred writers" did not speak of salvation as a doubtful or hazardous thing; instead, they called sinners to repent and assured them that salvation required only their believing.[107]

Taylor bequeathed to the New Connection the heartfelt religion of the evangelical revival. The lives of true believers were to be characterized by love, kindness, and the pursuit of "purity and holiness."[108] This heart religion worked its way into the worship, evangelism, and even the structures of the New Connection churches. Some Yorkshire New Connection churches began to hold Experience Meetings, something Taylor had brought from his Methodist background. These meetings allowed converts to share their personal experiences and help others with personal devotion and spiritual growth.[109]

Dan Taylor brought a renewed doctrinal orthodoxy and spiritual vitality to the General Baptist denomination. As a child of the Evangelical Revival, his simple Biblicism and experiential religious faith proved to be just the antidote for the malaise of the older established General Baptist churches. Taylor was well known among both his General and Particular Baptist contemporaries and perhaps could be better known today than he is.

Suggested Reading

Rinaldi, Frank W. *The Tribe of Dan, The New Connexion of General Baptists 1770–1891: A Study in the Transition from Revival Movement to Established Denomination.* Milton Keynes, UK: Paternoster Press, 2008.

Taylor, Adam. *Memoirs of the Rev. Dan Taylor.* London: printed for the author, 1820.

Taylor, Dan. *Fundamentals of Religion in Faith and Practice.* Leeds: printed for the author, 1775.

Andrew Fuller
(1754–1815)

Guardian of Gospel Proclamation

Missions

Sheila Klopfer

ANDREW FULLER, A Baptist pastor, theologian, and the first secretary of the Baptist Missionary Society, devoted his life to evangelical renewal and missions. It is in these two related areas that he left a most impressive and enduring mark. Fuller was born on 6 February 1754 in Wicken, Cambridgeshire England. His parents, Robert, Sr. and Philippa, were both raised Baptists. The Fuller family attended a little Particular Baptist church at Soham, where the young Andrew would one day become pastor. The Particular Baptists, known for their Calvinist theology, among other things, affirmed a limited or "particular" atonement that Christ died only for the elect. They differed from the General Baptists, who held a more Arminian theology and taught a "general" atonement that Christ died for all. Particular Baptists first emerged in the early seventeenth century and increased in number. By about 1750, however, they fell into an extreme form of theology known as High Calvinism, popularized by two London Baptist pastors, John Brine and John Gill. Fundamentally, it taught the belief that because of total depravity, the unconverted could not repent and believe the Gospel. They argued that faith was not the duty of all; instead, the Holy Spirit gave a supernatural gift only to the elect.[110] Thus, since it was the Spirit's work to persuade the elect, it was unnecessary and, according to some High Calvinists, even wrong for preachers to extend an open offer of the Gospel to all.

Not all Baptists agreed with High Calvinism, and a theological controversy, dubbed the "Modern Question," preoccupied Baptist life for the early part of the eighteenth century.[111] It was in this context that

Andrew Fuller proved most influential. Baptists asked such questions as, was it the duty of all people who heard the Gospel to repent, believe, and be saved? Should the Gospel of salvation be offered to all? Is a minister obligated to offer an open call to all to exercise faith and repentance? John Eve, the pastor of Soham Baptist, where Fuller attended as a child, was a High Calvinist. Fuller later recalled that Eve "had little or nothing to say to the unconverted."[112] As a young teenager, Fuller struggled with his sin and guilt for an extended period of time, waiting for a "warrant of faith" or an inner persuasion from the Holy Spirit that he was one of the elect. He was taught to believe that a sinner could not simply trust the Gospel message, but needed an internal sign of his election. In the young Fuller's case, he agonized for three years under a heavy burden of guilt upon his conscience until, at the age of fifteen, he experienced the warrant of faith and "found rest for [his] troubled soul."[113] He later came to believe that this long distressful time of waiting for conversion was unnecessary.

Beginning in the 1730s, in the midst of controversies regarding the "Modern Question," British and American religious life began to be transformed by a series of Protestant revivals that gave birth to modern Evangelicalism. Two of the central revivalist figures were John Wesley and George Whitefield, founders of Methodism. They preached in the open field, inviting people to seek new birth in Christ. The revivals, spreading back and forth across the Atlantic from Britain to America, rejuvenated religious life. But until the mid-1770s, most of the Particular Baptists refused to take part in the revivals, proudly describing themselves as a "garden enclosed."[114] With their introverted ecclesiology, refusal to offer the Gospel openly, and resistance to the revivals, it is no wonder that Particular Baptists were on the numerical decline in the early eighteenth century. Estimates suggest that between 1715 and 1750, the number of Particular Baptist churches in England fell from 220 to nearly 150. When the young Fuller was baptized at the age of sixteen in 1770, he had grown up in such an insular congregation at Soham that he had never seen a baptismal ordinance performed until just a month before his own baptism.

Within five years of Fuller's baptism, he felt a call to the ministry that eventually led to a lifelong vocation as a Baptist pastor and theologian. In 1771, a conflict between the Soham pastor and the congregation erupted, eventually leading to Eve's resignation. Apparently Eve made a comment suggesting that, although the unregenerate had no power to do good, they did not have the power to obey the will of God in their outward actions. This theology did not suit the High Calvinists in the congregation who believed that, because of human depravity, it was not the "duty" of the unconverted to believe the Gospel. After Eve left, Fuller periodically, albeit reluctantly, filled the pulpit. Over time Fuller grew more comfortable and quite proficient preaching. After one of his sermons, several young people were converted. It seemed clear to the congregation that God had endowed Fuller with pastoral gifts. He accepted the call, and they ordained him in 1775. What they did not know was that, even at this early date, Fuller was beginning to believe that it was within one's power to believe and respond to the Gospel, a position that, as it developed and grew in his theology, would not sit well with the High Calvinists at Soham.

Two significant events happened in 1775 that helped to shape Fuller's evangelical theology. First, Soham applied to join the Northamptonshire Association of Particular Baptist churches, an association that responded positively to the evangelical revivals. Many of the Particular Baptists in this association were committed to an older Calvinism that was less inclined to withhold a proclamation of the Gospel to the unconverted. Through that association, Fuller developed lifelong friendships with Robert Hall, John Sutcliff, and John Ryland, Jr., Baptists who would later be influential in founding the Baptist Missionary Society. The second event involved a trip that Fuller made to a little secondhand bookstore in London. In it, he ran across and read a pamphlet written by the Congregationalist Abraham Taylor titled, *The Modern Question Concerning Repentance and Faith* (1742).[115] This work argued in defense of the appropriateness of making a Gospel appeal to the lost. The sections of Taylor's argument that were most persuasive to Fuller were the ones in which he identified scriptures in which John the Baptist, Christ, and the apostles invited unbelievers to repent and believe.

During his eight years as pastor of Soham Baptist church, Fuller's life and theology changed drastically. In 1775, he married Sarah

Gardiner, a member of the Baptist church at Soham. Together they had eleven children, only a few of which lived to adulthood. Soham Baptist was unable to offer much of a salary so the Fullers lived in extreme poverty, which eventually took a huge toll on their family. Theologically during this period, Fuller's personal commitment to High Calvinism continued to weaken. Eventually as his theology became more evangelical, he began to offer a direct appeal to the Gospel from the pulpit. This created difficulties in the Baptist church at Soham. The High Calvinists in the congregation opposed his evangelical preaching style. As Fuller grew unhappy, his pastor friends, Sutcliff and Ryland, suggested he seek a pastorate elsewhere. They recommended Kettering, which was not only more centrally located in Northamptonshire, it was also more disposed to evangelical theology.

In 1782 Fuller accepted the call to pastor Kettering Baptist Church. This move proved to be a good fit for more than thirty-three years. Because of the congregation's more moderate Calvinism, he felt free to preach the Gospel, concluding his sermons with stirring appeals to faith. Under his pastorate, the church grew steadily; they enlarged the meetinghouse twice to accommodate the new members. While the Kettering years were often good ones, Fuller also encountered great difficulties. His first wife, Sarah, died in 1792 on the same day that she gave birth to their eleventh child, who survived only a few weeks. Two years later Fuller married Anne Coles, and three of their six children also died in infancy. Fuller's greatest grief was his eldest son, Robert, who became estranged from the family when he entered the navy and rejected the Christian faith. The heartfelt letters that Fuller wrote to his son reveal the pain and anguish that he experienced over his prodigal son. When Fuller heard that Robert died at sea in 1809, he wept from the pulpit. Along with family troubles, Fuller's diaries also reveal his struggle with spiritual depression. He continued to have questions regarding the assurance of his salvation, a carryover from his High Calvinist upbringing. On top of all these hardships, he had a heavy traveling itinerary that often took him away from home for three months at a time. The burdens of being a Baptist pastor and theologian were not easy.

During his years at Kettering, two things stand out as most influential to Fuller's contribution to Baptist life. The first was the publication of his work, *The Gospel Worthy of All Acceptation* (1785), which espoused an evangelical Calvinism that became so popular among Baptists, it was commonly known as "Fullerism." It has been identified as one of the most influential Baptist books of the century, well known to Baptists in Britain as well as America. Not only did it provide a more evangelical focus on Particular Baptist life, it also helped pave the way for the formation of the Baptist Missionary Society (1792), the second of Fuller's enduring legacies.

While the evangelical theology that Fuller espoused in *The Gospel Worthy* was uniquely his own, it is indebted to a number of influential sources. First, as a child Fuller read John Bunyan's *Grace Abounding to the Chief of Sinners* and *Pilgrim's Progress*.[116] Although Bunyan was a Calvinist, he affirmed the free offer of salvation to all, a view that tempered the High Calvinism that was preached from the pulpit at Soham. Another influential source in Fuller's theological development was Taylor's *The Modern Question*, the evangelical Calvinist pamphlet that Fuller found in the London bookstore in 1775. In *The Gospel Worthy*, Fuller utilized the same scriptural arguments that were found in Taylor's work and personally acknowledged Taylor's work as influential.[117] Probably the most significant formative source in the development of Fuller's theology was Massachusetts Congregationalist pastor Jonathan Edwards's *Freedom of the Will* (1754).[118] Edwards distinguished between humanity's natural and moral inability to obey God, arguing that humans were only helpless in responding to the gospel because of their moral inability. In other words, they had the natural ability and "could" respond to the Gospel, but refused to only because of their moral inability.

In *The Gospel Worthy*, Fuller leaned heavily on Edwards's argument, which allowed him to hold together Calvinism and evangelistic preaching. On one hand, Fuller agreed with the Calvinists that regeneration was solely a work of the Holy Spirit, and apart from God's electing grace, humans would not choose to follow the Gospel. But on the other hand, he agreed with Edwards that it was in the moral power of the sinner to respond to the Gospel message. As such, he argued, it was the duty of the pastor to preach the Gospel and the duty of all to believe. This argument, in defense of the duty of faith to the Gospel, was central to *The Gospel Worthy* and to Fullerism, which was so influential to Particular Baptist life. This theology enabled churches to share the Gospel freely and participate in the revivals. As a result, Particular Baptists began to experience growth during the second half of the eighteenth century.

Along with his influential contributions to evangelical theology, Fuller is most often remembered as one of the founders of the "Particular Baptist Society for Propagating the Gospel Among the Heathen" (1792), commonly referred to as the Baptist Missionary Society (BMS).[119] A number of Baptists in the Northamptonshire Association were responsible for the creation of the BMS. One of the key figures was William Carey, the first missionary of the society. In 1792 he published his famous pamphlet, *An Enquiry into the Obligations of Christians to Use Means for the Conversion of the Heathens*, and preached his "Expect Great Things, Attempt Great Things" sermon at the annual association meeting. When it seemed as if another year would pass by without any action among the Baptists in the association, Carey encouraged Fuller to submit a resolution at the business meeting calling for the formation of the BMS. The motion passed, and a group of fourteen Baptists met at the home of Widow Martha Wallace in Kettering to establish the framework of the society. They collected money and pledges in Fuller's snuff box. William Carey agreed to be the one to go to India, and his friend Fuller was elected secretary, a position he served diligently for the next twenty-two years until his death.

Fuller worked tirelessly for the BMS, "holding the ropes" for the Baptist missionaries in India, a metaphor related to the image of mining. He travelled long distances speaking personally to Baptists, wrote letters of correspondence, and raised financial support. Through it all, he helped Baptists throughout Britain to see the importance of combining their resources to support foreign mission work. Along with trips around England, he made multiple trips to Wales, Ireland, and Scotland. All the while, he continued to pastor the church at Kettering and to publish theological treatises. Fuller's exhaustive pace worried his congregation and pastoral friends, who feared for his health. They encouraged him to slow down, but he continued his work faithfully. Just a year before his death, when his health was already deteriorating, it is estimated that he travelled as much as 600 miles in one month alone.[120] Finally, on Sunday morning 7 May 1815, as he listened to his Kettering congregation worship in the sanctuary next door, Fuller died at the age of sixty-two. When news of his death reached India, the missionary William Ward commented that in the promotion of missions, no living person would be able to fill his shoes.

While certainly Fuller was not the only or the most important figure in the development of modern Baptist missions, he has been likened to the glue that held the BMS together. Not only did he provide significant theological direction, but he was also the first secretary, and provided crucial administrative guidance. And certainly his evangelical theology prepared the way for Baptists to commit to sharing the Gospel outside the Western world. The organization of the BMS was the first organized foreign mission society to emerge from the Evangelical revivals of the eighteenth century. A year before his death, Baptists in America adopted a similar style of approach as they formed the Triennial Convention to support foreign missions in Southeast Asia. The method adopted by the BMS, in which multiple Baptist churches joined collectively to fund foreign missions, marked a new era in the Baptist mission movement that continues to this day. The two together, Fuller's insightful Calvinistic evangelical theology and his unrelenting support of missions, form the core of his enduring legacy in Baptist life, theology, and practice.

Suggested Reading

Brewster, Paul. *Andrew Fuller: Model Pastor and Theologian*. B & H Studies in Baptist Life and Thought, edited by Michael A. G. Haykin. Nashville TN: B&H Publishing Group, 2010.

Grant, Keith S. *Andrew Fuller and the Evangelical Renewal of Pastoral Theology*. Studies in Baptist History and Thought 36. Eugene OR: Wipf and Stock Publishers, 2013.

Haykin, Michael A. G., editor. *"At the Pure Fountain of Thy Word": Andrew Fuller As an Apologist*. Waynesboro, GA: Paternoster, 2004.

Morden, Peter J. *Offering Christ to the World: Andrew Fuller (1754–1815) and the Revival of Eighteenth-Century Particular Baptist Life*. Studies in Baptist History and Thought 8. Waynesboro GA: Paternoster, 2003.

Ryland, John, Jr. *The Work of Faith, the Labour of Love, and the Patience of Hope, Illustrated; in the Life and Death of the Rev. Andrew Fuller.* 2nd edition. Charleston: Samuel Etheridge, 1818.

John Leland
(1756–1841)

Preacher, Patriot, Baptist Freedom Fighter

Religious Freedom

Brad Creed

WHEN THE TWENTY-six-year-old Baptist preacher presented himself to the council of elders for ordination to the gospel ministry, it was his second ordination. His first, conducted a few years earlier, had been done without the laying on of hands by the "presbytery of elders." The circumstances surrounding the original ordination caused difficulties with local Baptist preachers and created friction within his congregation. At the urging of others, he begrudgingly agreed to a "proper" ordination by a council of elders who plied him with questions and laid hands of blessing on his head. John Leland submitted to the authority of the elders but in a manner that asserted his dogged independence and his aversion to empty formalism. According to eyewitness accounts, the council's questioning included this exchange:

> Moderator: "Brother Leland, do you not believe that God chose his people in Christ before the foundation of the world?"
>
> Leland: "I know not, brother, what God was doing before he began to make this world."
>
> Moderator: "Brother Leland, do you not believe that God had a people before the foundation of the world?"
>
> Leland: "If he had, brother, they were not our kind of folks. Our people were made out of dust, you know, and before the foundation of the world there was no dust to make them out of."
>
> Moderator: "You believe, Brother Leland, that all men are totally depraved?"

John Leland

Leland: "No, brother, if they were they could not wax worse and worse as some of them do. The devil was no more than totally depraved."[121]

Incidents like these reveal why John Leland was an unforgettable character. His endearing eccentricities and freewheeling style engendered popularity among the Separate Baptists of Virginia and New England. With his sharp wit, keen mind, and amazing gift for communication, Leland was one of the most popular, effective, and sometimes controversial Baptists in America during his time. He is best known as a champion for religious liberty. During his fourteen-year sojourn in Virginia as an itinerant evangelist and pastor, he played a key role in the progress of religious freedom in that state. Along with other Baptist leaders, he successfully petitioned the Virginia Assembly to end the incorporation of the Protestant Episcopal Church and the state-sponsorship of religion.

One event, in particular, that revealed John Leland's influence was his role in Virginia's ratification of the United States Constitution. When the Constitutional Convention put the issue to the states in 1788, the General Committee of Baptists in Virginia concluded that the new Federal Constitution did not make "sufficient provision for the secure enjoyment of religious liberty." [122] The ensuing deliberations brought the state of Virginia into national focus. Baptists had been virtually unanimous in backing James Madison as a delegate to the Constitutional Convention, but when he equivocated on adding a Bill of Rights, they canvassed against ratification and launched a grassroots campaign to elect Leland as their region's delegate to the national convention. Fearing the defeat of the Constitution in his home state and sensing the vulnerability of his own political career, Madison returned from Philadelphia to win Leland and the Baptists over to his side.

Reliable sources, historical records, and a strong oral tradition affirm that Leland and Madison held a momentous meeting in a grove of trees near the town of Orange, Virginia sometime in March 1788. A roadside park today along U.S. Highway 20, the "Constitution Highway," commemorates the historic meeting.[123] With Madison's personal pledge to advocate for a Bill of Rights once the states ratified the Constitution,

Leland withdrew from the race, endorsed Madison, and rallied support from Virginia Baptists. Madison kept his promise and became the principal author of the Bill of Rights, with a First Amendment stipulating that "Congress shall make no law respecting an establishment of religion, or prohibiting the free exercise thereof." The Baptists of Virginia led by Leland were key players in the ratification of the Constitution and in the adoption of a Bill of Rights that became the supreme law of the land. To them, the Bill of Rights was a legal expression of their historic witness for religious liberty, which protected not only their rights but also the rights of all to worship without state interference or threat of punishment.

After a momentous fourteen-year ministry in Virginia, Leland returned to New England and continued his ministry as preacher, evangelist, pamphleteer, and advocate for religious liberty. He had labored with Virginia Baptists in the proclamation of the gospel and advocacy for religious liberty, but he parted company with them over slavery, which he opposed. After returning to his native Massachusetts, he served as a pastor in the Berkshire Hills for most of his remaining days. Never one to believe in the incompatibility of piety and politics, he continued his advocacy for public and ethical issues and even served two terms in the Massachusetts legislature as a representative from his district. His landmark treatise, "The Rights of Conscience Inalienable," written on his return from Virginia in 1791, endures as one of the most effective and impassioned appeals in history for religious freedom. The subtitle of this weighty work, adorned with Leland's colorful imprint, is "The High-Flying Churchman, Stripped of His Legal Robe, Appears a Yaho."[124]

Over the next three decades, Leland toiled to strip away the entitlements of established churches and their clergy throughout New England. With his sharp pen, he whittled away at the remaining vestiges of state-controlled religion in Connecticut, which crumbled in 1818 when the state fully accepted the provisions of the First Amendment. Other states followed course until only Massachusetts held fast and refused to surrender. As he had done in Virginia and Connecticut, Leland fervently assailed the religious establishment with his pamphleteering and sermonizing. In a legislative referendum, citizens voted nearly ten to one to annul centuries-old statutes, so 1833 marks the year when the last remnant of the standing order of state-established religion in the United States fell, never to rise again. Sixty years earlier, a delegation of New England Baptists headed by Isaac Backus met with a subcommittee of the Continental Congress in Philadelphia to protest the discrimination they endured and to advocate for the separation of church and state. John Adams dismissed them as misguided enthusiasts with the retort that they "might as well expect a change in the solar system as to expect they would give up their establishment."[125] John Leland doubted that the laws of nature would change, but he contended that the nature of the law should. His leadership and influence incalculably altered the "political solar system" of the United States on religious liberty.

Even though he earned a reputation as a champion of religious liberty, Leland understood himself fundamentally as a preacher of the gospel. After spending his teenage years in "evening frolicking, follies, and diversions," he was converted at age eighteen in a revival meeting conducted by noted evangelist Elhanan Winchester. Baptized in June 1774, the church he joined licensed him to preach. As others began to discern his gifts, he was rarely without an invitation for evangelistic preaching or to discourse on biblical revelation. In 1775, he left New England for an eight-month preaching tour in Virginia. Upon his return home, he married Sallie Devine, and just a few months before the colonies declared independence from Great Britain, the newlyweds relocated to Virginia where Leland ministered for the next fourteen years.

Baptists in Virginia grew rapidly despite persecution. Anglican clergy publically and legally opposed them, local authorities threw them in jail, and their fellow citizens harassed them. Leland himself encountered this resistance. While he was preaching in a meeting, a violent intruder burst into the room armed with a gun and headed straight towards Leland with the intent to kill. Before the assailant could attack, a brave member of the congregation tackled him, wrestled him to the ground, and disarmed him. The hero of the moment was none other than the preacher's wife, Sallie Leland! She was a "stand-by-your-man" kind of woman before the song was popular. While John Leland eventually won the argument for religious liberty in Virginia, it is hard to imagine that he ever won an argument at home.

Leland's ardor for preaching the gospel, like his wife's instinct to protect him, was unquenchable. He traveled more miles up and down, back and forth across the American colonies, than did George Whitefield, the "Grand Itinerant" of the First Great Awakening. At the age of seventy, with seventeen years of life yet to live, Leland registered in his memoirs that he had preached over 8,000 sermons, baptized 1,524 converts, and mentored and served with almost 1,000 Baptist preachers. He mastered the skill of networking in an age when travel was slow, correspondence was limited to letters, and communication was face to face. He kept an active preaching and writing ministry until the very end of his life, and preached his last sermon on January 1841 at eighty-seven years of age in North Adams, Massachusetts, only six days before he died.

Preaching with importunity aimed for personal decisions was the key to his effectiveness. Attuned to the popular mind of his day, he possessed the rare ability to discourse on almost any subject in a style and manner that would captivate the imagination and win the hearts of his listeners. He often infuriated those whose religious perspectives were different than his own, especially the members of the established clergy. Leland was remarkably effective with the common people—yeomen farmers, shopkeepers, manual laborers, mothers with their domestic responsibilities—the people who so often had been marginalized and excluded from traditional places of worship. He composed hymns in a style that enabled worshippers to express a deeply personal faith nurtured in the womb of revival piety. By giving a voice to the people through sermon and song, he rejected intermediaries that might come between the earnest seeker and the Word of God, whether church hierarchies, educated but spiritually defunct ministers, and even creedal statements that he considered a "Virgin Mary between the soul and God."[126] He preached with fervor and confidence because he trusted the Holy Spirit's power to enable the simplest believer to read the Bible and comprehend clearly the love of God the Father through His Son, Jesus Christ.

Leland, however, was no quietist who tended only to the business of saving souls. He was active in the public square and in politics beyond the struggle for religious liberty and tackled the burning political and ethical concerns of his day. He admonished fellow citizens to go to the ballot box, and he publically supported Jefferson, Madison, and Jackson in their bids for the presidency. He weighed in on slavery, human rights, tariffs, an elected judiciary, and even opposed efforts by Congress to pass laws regulating the delivery of mail on Sunday. Leland tenaciously resisted any attempt to pass laws that, in his estimation, were rear-guard actions to reverse the gains of disestablishment. Though active politically, he reassured his fellow Baptists that it was not his intention "to drop the ministerial vest and assume the politician's garb."[127] His fundamental calling was to preach, but he believed in public service, and through his political involvement and by serving two terms as a state representative in Massachusetts, he created a synthesis between his piety and politics.

Leland did not find piety and patriotism at odds. As long as one's ultimate loyalty lay with Christ, a Christian could love his country and participate in the political process. On New Year's Day 1802, Leland displayed his patriotism prominently. The citizens of Leland's community, Cheshire, Massachusetts, to celebrate Thomas Jefferson's electoral victory over John Adams, sent the new president an unusual gift: a mammoth cheese weighing more than half a ton. Local dairy farmers, along with their wives, constructed a huge mold and contributed copious amounts of milk from their herds to make the cheese. The town selected Leland to chaperone the cheese all the way to Washington as it traveled by sled, by wagon, and by sloop. By the time it reached Baltimore, the ripening cheese was strong enough to walk the remaining distance to Washington. Jefferson personally received the gift while standing in the doorway of the White House with cordial expressions of gratitude. Leland presented the gift, boasting that no Federalist cows contributed milk for the project and stated in a letter to the President that the cheese was crafted without the assistance of a single slave.[128]

John Leland, however, believed that there was no such thing as a "Christian nation," certainly not the kind of "New Israel" envisioned by the Puritans of Massachusetts or the carefully guarded status quo of the Anglican clergy of Virginia. In Leland's view, God's blessing would fall upon the nation that provided freedom for all to worship, not the nation that reflected the dogma of a moral majority of religious leaders. Genuine conversion, true salvation, and authentic Christian faith depended on a free and unforced commitment to Christ. Leland's advocacy for religious liberty was not simply freedom from religion that oppressed dissenting faiths, but freedom for religion that led to eternal faith. What mattered above all was not a Christian nation, but Christian *people*. To him, the quest for full religious liberty was a preamble to authentic New Testament faith, a type of "pre-evangelism" that would not only strengthen the nation but also bolster the cause of Christ. The source of his views on religious liberty was not politics but the gospel of Jesus Christ. Religious freedom is rooted in the gift of God's grace that liberates from sin and death. State-sponsored religion bound the human conscience, but true religion was possible if humans were given the freedom to follow their convictions, even if their convictions led them to an expression of faith that was false. Leland asked, "If a man worships one God, three Gods, twenty Gods, or no God—wherein does he injure the life, liberty or property of another?"[129] These were not crimes to be punished by the state. All citizens should be granted full religious liberty and not mere toleration, a "despicable" idea, since it supposed that "some should have a pre-eminence above the rest; ...all should be equally free, Jews, Turks, Pagans, and Christians."[130] By advocating for religious liberty and its political corollary, the separation of church and state, John Leland was a luminary in the witness of the Free Church, a successor to men such as Balthasar Hubmaier, Thomas Helwys, Roger Williams, and Isaac Backus.

The life and ministry of John Leland serves as a paradigm for watershed developments in American religion that continue to define the ethos of the nation. His memory glowed in anecdotes told with affection and in humorous recollections generations after his death. A popular story in a children's book, "Elder Leland's Ghost," written in 1895, reports harmless sightings along country lanes of an ethereal apparition with a Bible tucked under one arm and green baize travel bag in his other hand. Leland's sparkling personality, keen wit, unforgettable sermons, ministerial wisdom, and legacy in the cause of religious freedom were so memorable, it was as though he was still there among the people he served and who admired him. Today, when someone submits to believer's baptism upon a personal confession of faith in Christ, Leland is there. When a populist politician comes onto the scene and stirs up the grassroots, Leland is there. When a follower of Jesus Christ as a matter of conscience and principle opposes government-sponsored prayers in the public school and also advocates for the right of students to gather voluntarily to pray, Leland is there. During his long and rich life, John Leland stood at the intersection of dynamic religious and political forces that forged a distinctive American identity. Sometimes at that intersection, he directed the traffic.

Suggested Reading

Creed, J. Bradley. "John Leland and Sunday Mail Delivery: Religious Liberty, Evangelical Piety, and the Problem of a 'Christian Nation.'" *Fides et Historia* (Summer/Fall 2001): 1–11.

Hatch, Nathan O. *The Democratization of American Christianity.* New Haven: Yale University Press, 1991.

Ragosta, John A. *Wellspring of Liberty: How Virginia's Religious Dissenters Helped Win the American Revolution and Secured Liberty.* New York: Oxford University Press, 2010.

William Carey
(1761–1834)

Father of the Modern Mission Movement

Missions

Terry Carter

WILLIAM CAREY, CALLED the "Father of the Modern Mission Movement," stands as one of the most significant missionaries in modern mission history. Even though the number of converts he produced in his life's work might seem insignificant, the long-term results and influence of his efforts are mind-boggling. The impact of his Bible translation work alone sets Carey apart as a giant in mission history. This is true in spite of the fact that William Carey probably lacked stellar preaching ability, frequently struggled with family issues, and experienced problems with the very missionary organization that sent him to the field. His story is mixed with struggle and phenomenal accomplishment.

Carey was born into a pious Church of England family that required him to attend church regularly. His father, Edmund Carey, wove cloth and taught school to eke out a modest living. Young Carey possessed a keen interest in nature and botany and frequently led his siblings on nature walks. As a young boy, he hungered for knowledge and read voraciously. His reading list seldom included religious titles but focused on adventure. Carey read of Captain Cook's travels and enjoyed the religious adventure of *Pilgrim's Progress* by Bunyan.[131] Even though Carey received the normal but minimal education for his social class, he taught himself subjects he deemed important. As early as the age of twelve, he memorized the Dyche's *Latin Vocabulary* in order to utilize the language. Carey later borrowed books to study Greek, received help from John Sutcliff to master Hebrew, and even learned to read Dutch and French.[132] He possessed a unique linguistic ability.

Eighteenth-century English society demanded Carey learn a trade to make a living, and at age fourteen he apprenticed with a cobbler named Clarke Nichols. This proved to be a life-changing event due primarily to the influence of an older apprentice named John Warr. Warr convinced Carey to attend a non-conforming church, resulting in his conversion and a spiritual journey that led the young cobbler to the Particular Baptist church and a future missionary career that would influence millions around the globe.[133]

In 1781 Carey married Dorothy Plackett (Dolly). Dorothy, uneducated and closely tied to home and extended family, would prove a great test to Carey's future career choice. Hardly able to make a living as a cobbler, Carey opened a school for the village children to supplement the income. He continued his involvement in the Baptist church, where he met Andrew Fuller and John Ryland, Jr. These men became two of his closest friends and their theology would deeply influence him. Andrew Fuller, having grown up in a hyper-Calvinist church, challenged the predominant theology and championed a new evangelical type of Calvinism that allowed the offering of the gospel to the lost and paved the way for William Carey's later call to missions. Carey, influenced by Fuller, Ryland, John Sutcliff, Jonathan Edwards, and others, acquired the new modified Calvinism sometimes called "Fullerism."

Carey added preaching to his work as a cobbler and teacher. In 1786 he attended a Baptist meeting in Northhampton moderated by John Ryland, Sr., a staunch hyper-Calvinist. Hyper-Calvinists believed the Great Commission was intended only for the original apostles and did not apply to the eighteenth-century church. The young Carey shocked the group when he asked "whether the command given to the apostles to teach all nations was not obligatory on all succeeding ministers to the end of the world, seeing that the accompanying premise was of equal extent." The "accompanying premise" was verse 18, stating that all authority on heaven and earth had been given to Christ. Ryland, Sr. scolded him, saying that "when God wants to convert the heathen, he will do it without your help or mine."[134] Carey sat but did not remain silent for long, already concluding that a hyper-Calvinism that rejected evangelism and missions was not biblical.

Perhaps the most life-defining year for Carey was 1792. In this year, he published the answer to his own questions at Northhampton. Carey wrote *An Enquiry into the Obligations of Christians to Use Means for the Conversion of the Heathen.* This piece explained the universal and timeless intent of the Great Commission, surveyed missions history including stories of groups like the Moravians, and presented a population analysis of the world estimating 731 million. Of those, Carey supposed 420 million lived in "pagan darkness." These people needed the gospel so Carey called for mission efforts and mission support, arguing that moderate-income Christians give ten percent, churches subscribe a penny a week, and the wealthy give more.[135]

Particular Baptist associations met twice a year and the 1792 meetings proved historic on many levels, not only for Particular Baptists but evangelicals in general. In the spring meeting, William Carey preached from Isaiah 54:1–2. Called the "Deathless Sermon," Carey challenged Particular Baptists to "Expect Great Things, Attempt Great Things." It was a call to missions and Carey hoped for the formation of a missionary society to support the evangelization of the world. The association decided to consider the idea of a mission society and revisit it during the fall meeting.[136] The October meeting was held at Andrew Fuller's church in Kettering. At this meeting, The Particular Baptist Society for Propagating the Gospel Amongst the Heathen, later shortened to the "Baptist Missionary Society," commenced.

Carey offered himself as one of the first missionary candidates and the society selected him, along with John Thomas, a doctor who had returned from India.[137] Although Carey knew in his heart God was calling him to go to India as a missionary, Dorothy possessed no such call. She refused to take her children away from England and family. William Carey prepared to go without her but a delay caused by improper paperwork allowed him and Thomas to make one last attempt to convince her. Dorothy conceded only after her sister, Kitty, agreed to accompany them to India.[138] For Dorothy, this marked the start of the most difficult time of her life. The sea journey to India presented a treacherous challenge for the entire family. Dorothy and Kitty often chided William for exposing them to such hardship. Carey penned a record of this journey and his first years as a missionary in a daily journal.

In it the difficulties of the voyage and the initial missionary life in India are chronicled. Daily posts sometimes consisted of only a few words of despair, but Carey's growth and understanding of the new life as a missionary are now priceless. The journal remains a critical piece of literature for mission history.[139]

Upon arriving in India in 1793, the missionaries first settled in Calcutta, but due to Thomas's misuse and miscalculation of funds, Carey soon elected to find a less expensive place to live and to provide more access to those he came to evangelize. The situation was even more difficult due to the refusal of the British East India Company and the government to allow missions to the native population, fearing it would upset a delicate social balance and cause unrest. Carey moved his family to some extremely inhospitable locations outside of Calcutta. Fortunately, they eventually made their way to Debhatta, having heard a plot of land and a cottage were available for free. This worked out well for the family due to the generosity of Charles Short, who would later marry Kitty.[140] Then due to the influence of John Thomas on George Udney, Carey received news of an indigo plantation in Mudnabatti in need of a supervisor. This prompted yet another move, but provided the family with a solid means of support while allowing Carey to learn the language, utilizing a tutor and preaching his first sermons.[141] The acquisition of the spoken language and the daily grind of life in Mudnabatti proved to be challenging tasks.[142] Crisis ensued with the death of the Careys' youngest son, Peter. This loss sent Dorothy into an emotional and psychological downward spiral, eventually rendering her emotionally unbalanced. She blamed her husband and even tried to kill him.[143] The mission field claimed its victims in many ways.

Carey realized the immense difficulty of trying to survive financially, spiritually, and physically alone in the backcountry of India. British pressure to abstain from any mission endeavor with the native population continued. Community and a more mission-friendly environment were needed to enhance the work. Finally, help arrived through William Ward (a printer) and John Marshman (an educator), along with their families. Carey and his family joined them in the Danish-controlled area of Serampore. This became the permanent station for the mission team. Danish sovereignty allowed mission work and offered protection. This move proved a double blessing as the Danish Governor Bie welcomed the families with open arms.[144] He became a friend and protector.

In 1800, after arriving in Serampore, Carey and his colleagues experienced a victory. On 28 December 1800, Carey baptized his eldest son, Felix, and the first native convert, Krishna Pal.[145] In the Serampore mission station, all the families lived together, supporting each other and the work. Carey focused his attention on numerous Bible translations in order to provide the truth to the varying language groups in India and surrounding countries. William Carey translated or supervised the production of full or partial copies of the Bible in forty languages.[146] This stands as one of Carey's most important contributions to missions. The printing press also served as a revenue support for the mission by printing copies of important Indian literature to sell. Serampore under the protection of the Danish government became the sending point of missionaries throughout India and other countries.

William Carey became such a proficient linguist that in 1801, when Ft. William College in Calcutta needed a Bengali teacher, they looked to Carey. Traveling weekly from Serampore to Calcutta, he brought in new income for mission projects and became acquainted with important British officials while mingling with upper-class Hindus.[147] He later drew on those relationships to push some of his most important concerns. From the beginning, Carey witnessed and agonized over horrible injustices that he observed in India and hoped to eradicate. One of those was the practice of *suttee* (*sati*), often forced on involuntary widows, which involved the burning of Hindu women on the funeral pyre of their husbands. Carey spoke and wrote against this practice and finally saw its legal prohibition.[148] The caste system also offended Carey's sense of justice, but it proved too permanently imbedded into the society. Carey and his colleagues worked around it by aiding those natives who converted to Christianity and lost caste in the process.

Even as a self-educated missionary, Carey possessed a passion for providing education for the Indian population. This was especially important for converted natives who could effectively carry the gospel to their own people. In 1821, the missionaries established Serampore College, which educates even today.[149] Carey believed in indigenous missions and theological training for native clergy who played a key role in that effort. The mission trained and sent out itinerant native preachers to preach the gospel. Perhaps due to this practice, Christianity, although a small percentage of the Indian population, remains active in India.[150] Carey's sons also took up roles on the mission field. Felix, the eldest, served in Burma. Unfortunately, his work was tragically interrupted by the loss of his family at sea and then his own moral failure. William, Jr. first supported William Ward as a bookbinder and then took his place on the mission field in places like Dacca. Jonathan studied to be a lawyer in Calcutta but still took on the role of treasurer for the Serampore mission. Jabez, the youngest son, married and spent time in Amboyna, Ajmere, and Rajputana. Carey often wrote to him with advice concerning both the mission work and his marriage. The Carey name impacted India on several fronts.

William Carey bears the title "Father of the Modern Mission Movement." He trumpeted the call for a mission movement and then modeled its fulfillment. He accomplished this despite serious personal and professional struggles. Dorothy's story is tragic and sad. She never wanted to accompany her husband and yet Carey pressed the matter until she complied. She died broken, secluded, and an emotionally scarred woman.[151] Carey remained faithful to her, refusing to send her away to an institution when she became emotionally and psychologically unable to function. Following Dorothy's death, Carey married two more times—Charlotte Rumohr and Grace Hughes. These appeared to be good marriages, with the partners sharing his urgency for mission work. Family issues always presented Carey with challenges and stress. As mentioned, William and Dorothy lost Peter early in the mission work and the grief never allowed them to live in peace. Felix took a horrible turn for the worse after losing his wife and children. Jabez faithfully served as a missionary but Carey believed he did not control his wife well. He often criticized and advised Jabez on that count. Carey battled the Baptist Missionary Society and its missionaries as they attempted to exercise more control over the mission in Serampore. Eventually in 1827, the Serampore mission withdrew from the society.[152] Certainly, this was a sad day when the society no longer related to its first missionary. In addition, life in India took its toll. Carey and his family suffered through many diseases, accidents, injuries, and heartache, but he remained in India, even refusing to take a furlough.

Undoubtedly, the modern mission movement owes a great deal to William Carey. His mission methods and strategies are still incorporated in some fashion by missionaries today. He believed in developing an indigenous Indian church. He committed wholeheartedly to the idea of language missions and vernacular scripture for all people and spent much of his personal time and talent in that task. Carey and his colleagues practiced bi-vocational missions as a means to support the work. They used education effectively to reach the Indian population, even educating young girls, a generally unacceptable practice. Carey sought to live out incarnational missions by relating to the target audience as much as possible. Circumstances tempered that since finances required the mission families to live together in a compound setting. However, his knowledge of the culture and openness to the people served him well.

In a sense, William Carey could be called a "Renaissance man" because his interests spanned many fields. He studied culture, language, nature, botany, and agriculture. He was involved in many organizations that reflected those interests.[153] But his passion, above all else, was to see the lost world come to know Christ. The last words of Carey's *Enquiry* sum up his life focus: "Surely, it is worthwhile to lay ourselves out with all our might in promoting the cause and kingdom of Christ."[154] Carey died in India on 9 June 1834 having never returned to his native England. He sacrificially committed his life to bringing the gospel to the people of India and to the world.

Suggested Reading

Carey, S. Pearce. *William Carey*. London: The Wakeman Trust, 1993.
Carter, Terry, editor. *The Journal and Selected Letters of William Carey*. Macon GA: Smyth & Helwys, 2000.
George, Timothy. *Faithful Witness: The Life and Mission of William Carey*. Birmingham: New Hope, 1991.

Lott Carey
(c. 1780–1828)

Father of African-American Missions

Missions

Bonnie Oliver Brandon

THE ENSLAVEMENT OF Africans did not dispel their respect for spiritual power wherever it originated. Adaptation accounted for the openness of African religions to syncretism with other religious traditions throughout the remote corners of the New World.[155] It was the infiltration of the religious status quo of White slave masters that thrust denominational culture upon African and African-American slaves. Black Baptists in America originated on White Baptists' plantations and in the back or balconies of the White Baptist church.

Lott Carey, although of African descent, was born on American soil, into the shackles of American slavery, and into the spirituality of the Baptist tradition. Noted as the American pioneer of the missionary movement who created a growing interest on the part of African-Americans in the evangelization of Africa and other underdeveloped parts of the world, Lott Carey became the first Black Baptist missionary to Africa.[156] His name would later become synonymous with Baptist world missions and evangelism and represent the Lott Carey Foreign Mission Convention well into the twenty-first century and the annals of Baptist history. Out of the bowels of slavery arose one of its own who answered the call to liberate the people's mind and soul from bondage through the preaching of the Gospel, missions, and evangelism. Lott Carey wrote, "I am an African, and in this country, however meritorious my conduct, and respectable my character, I cannot receive the credit due to either. I wish to go to a country where I shall be estimated by my merits, not by my complexion; and I feel bound to labor for my suffering race."[157]

The Declaration of Independence was signed in 1776, and Lott Carey was born on the estate of slave-master William A. Christian in Charles City County, Virginia circa 1780. Born into American slavery, it would be years before Carey would learn the meaning of liberation. His upbringing, however, did not mirror the past abuse and deliberate separation of family imposed upon slaves for the sake of isolation, capitulation, and profit. He was fortunate enough to be brought up in a rooted two-family household on William Christian's estate.[158]

Lott Carey's unified family consisted of his father, a God-fearing and faithful member of the Baptist denomination; his mother, who apparently was unchurched, but purportedly a believer; and his grandmother and caretaker, Mihala, a devout Christian and Baptist who influenced and shaped Lott's life and belief system. Mihala embodied the essence of Deuteronomy 6:22–24 by remembering to tell her grandson the story of her people's peril and suffering crossing the ocean, their bondage, and the hope of deliverance for her heathen people in the Christless land of Africa.[159] Inquisitively, Carey asked his grandmother, "Do all of them think that the great God lives far away from them and does not love them?"[160]

Mihala answered prophetically in a mission-oriented fashion. She told Lott the people did not know God and that she wished she could go back and tell them about God's love and presence. Because of her age and inability to fulfill her desire, she said, "Son, you will grow strong. You will lead many, and perhaps it may be you who will travel over the big seas to carry the great secret to my people. I will be dust, but my prayers will live that your feet may find the path and after you, others of our race—hundreds."[161] The dice had been cast on young Lott's life. His early Christian education and his grandmother's word would one day become *a light unto his feet and a lamp unto his path*, but not before his fall into the unsavory ways of life.

There is an historical void on Lott Carey's life until 1804, when history resumes its documentation as Master Christian hired Lott out as a slave laborer to the Shockoe Tobacco Warehouse in Richmond, Virginia.[162] Living without parental guidance for the first time at age twenty-four and forgetting his Christian upbringing, Lott became embittered with his new surroundings in Richmond. He was extremely vicious for two to three years and degenerated himself through constant intoxication and profane obscenities.[163] Even in the midst of his debauchery, Lott realized that if he saved a portion of his salary for himself, he could one day buy his freedom.[164]

Carey's first form of liberation came in 1807 while sitting in the balcony at the First Baptist Church of Richmond. During this slave religious service, he felt convicted after hearing a sermon preached by the Reverend John Courtney on Nicodemus from John, chapter three. He accepted Jesus Christ, joined First Baptist Church in Richmond, and tasted his new freedom as a child of God. Being illiterate, not knowing the alphabet, and incapable of expressing his conversion experience, Carey purchased a Bible and immersed himself in learning to read, especially the Nicodemus story that changed his life. This newfound passion for both God's Word and words propelled Lott Carey to learn how to write. Carey's literary education through the Bible was consistent with the learning experiences of the "fortunate few" Black slaves during American slavery.[165] How apropos that the Bible was the only textbook readily available to the Black slaves.

Carey continued to enhance his education through a White deacon, William Crane's "colored tri-weekly" night school, which was organized in 1815. He excelled beyond his religious education and into areas of economics, making possible his advancement to shipping clerk at Shockoe Tobacco Warehouse. Carey was married in Richmond and to this union two children were born. He prudently made and saved his money and, after the death of his wife, purchased his freedom and the freedom of his children in 1813 for the amount of $850. Carey remarried in 1815 as he successfully advanced economically and educationally.[166]

Carey experienced his call to the Gospel ministry soon after his initial conversion. He held meetings with the Blacks of Richmond and exhorted them to repent and flee the judgment to come. The First Baptist Church of Richmond licensed Carey to preach after a significant trial period, and with his determination to be faithful to the call, he ultimately became one of the greatest preachers of American Christianity. Reverend Carey's ministry grew along with his passion to bring others into a relationship with God. His redemption, ambition, and inspiration from William Crane spurred him to go beyond Richmond to Lynchburg and Norfolk.[167]

Crane influenced Lott Carey tremendously. He instilled his passion and interest of the spiritual condition of Africa into Lott, leading Carey's ministerial work at First African Baptist Church to include the acquisition of support to missions in Africa. As a result, in 1815 the Richmond African Baptist Missionary Society was organized by Crane, Carey, and Collin Teague. Historically, First Baptist Church of Richmond became the first church to organize a Black missionary society. The society forged links to the Triennial Convention, thus providing a fraction of the funds that would later enable Carey and Teague to go to Monrovia, Liberia in 1821.[168]

Crane's continual leadership and work with the missionary society and his insistence to the General Missionary Convention served as the impetus for the beginning of Baptist missionary work in West Africa. The former mission seed planted by Carey's grandmother, Mihala, began to stir his growing missionary zeal to go to Africa. He wanted his life's call to be aligned to God's will for his ministry, so he searched his soul for the answer to his burning quest. He reflected over his grandmother's words and Crane's teaching and preparation for him, and intuitively heard the voice of his African brothers and sisters saying, "Come over and help us."[169]

Carey decided to leave all—his job, his pastorate at a Baptist church, and the Richmond African Missionary Society to fulfill his prophetic call. Lott Carey, a pioneer, became one of America's earliest emigrants and the first Black Baptist missionary to Africa. Funding and support were readily given to Carey's missionary endeavor due to William Crane's letters to organizations and conventions, and also to Lott's own popularity with the people—White and Black.[170]

Sailing to Africa with Reverend Carey on the ship, *Nautilus*, from Norfolk were other colonists, a band of six who came together and formed a church under the pastoral leadership of Reverend Carey; Reverend Collins Teague, also a church member, and his family; Joseph Langford; and Lott Carey's wife and children. On 23 January 1821, Lott Carey—the ex-slave, pastor, Black Baptist missionary—and his newly formed missionary church left the shores of America to the distant land of Sierra Leone, West Africa. The voyage, which was born out of an old slave's desire for her African brothers and sisters to hear the Word of God, a seed planted in the heart of a young slave to one day carry out the quest, a passion nurtured by William Crane, and thus, a calling to fulfill, was the "beginning of a new era of missionary expansion by Black Baptists."[171] The *Nautilus* safely arrived in Freetown, Sierra Leone in March 1821. After a smooth sailing voyage, the group encountered various situations throughout their mission. First, there was the political obstinacy of slave-traders and British and American Colonization attempts in West Africa. During Carey's entire time in West Africa, he would be plagued by the "proposed African colonization project of the American Colonization Society and their political, economic, and humanitarian motives."[172]

Reverend Carey kept his missionary cause paramount in spite of the difficulties and obstacles presented to him daily. The death of his second wife after a fatal illness in Fourah Bay, Sierra Leone greatly challenged him. After colony wars and other disputations, Lott and his colony of Americans eventually settled in Liberia at Monrovia. Lott Carey had become versatile in his vocation as preacher and helped to establish and construct schools and churches. Prior to their move, he even had the role of medical doctor thrust upon him. With a unity of purpose, his commitment and character undergirded his multiple ministries of preaching, teaching, and medicine. Lott Carey's missionary style grew out of his commitment to the socialization of Christian theology, which evolved out of his own past experience of slavery to freedom. Lott Carey died in an accidental explosion of ammunition in Liberia, but his work lived on.[173]

Reverend Lott Carey's legacy lives on today in the Lott Carey Foreign Mission Convention headquartered in Washington, D.C. "Its business is to help churches extend the Christian witness to the ends of the earth, and provide financial support and technical assistance to indigenous expressions of evangelism, education, and health"— *through preaching and missions.*

Suggested Reading

Fitts, Leroy. *A History of Black Baptists*. Nashville TN: Broadman Press, 1985.
———. *Lott Carey: First Black Missionary to Africa*. Philadelphia: Judson Press, 1978.
———. *The Lott Carey Legacy of African-American Missions*. Baltimore: Gateway Press, inc., 1994.
Leonard, Bill. *Baptist Ways: A History*. Philadelphia: Judson Press, 2003.
Raboteau, Albert J. *Slave Religion: The "Invisible Institution" in Antebellum South*. New York: Oxford University Press, 1978.

Adoniram Judson
(1788–1854)

American Baptist Bridge to the World

Missions

Delane Tew

THE EXPANSIVE TREE of Baptist international missions has as its taproot the life of Adoniram Judson, Jr. Born on 9 August 1788 into the home of Abigail and Adoniram Judson, Sr., a Congregationalist minister, Judson was nourished by the soil of conservative theology. The struggle within the church between liberal and conservative theology both drove Judson, Sr. out of pulpits and provided him new ones. When it came time for the sixteen-year-old Judson, Jr. to enter college, his father pushed him toward the more conservative Brown University, even though it was Baptist, over what he considered the more liberal Harvard College of the Congregationalists.

Adoniram was an outstanding learner from his childhood, proudly reading a Bible chapter to his father at age three. He thrived in the academic atmosphere of Brown, graduating valedictorian of his class. But amidst his studies, Judson was introduced to ideas inconsistent with his conservative upbringing. He became fast friends with Jacob Eames, a self-proclaimed deist who would later play a key role in Judson's life.

Judson made an effort to settle down after graduation. His accomplishments included opening a school in Plymouth, Massachusetts, and writing an English grammar textbook. But a restless spirit soon overtook him. Within a year he closed his school and set out as a traveler, even joining a band of actors at one point.

Theological thoughts were far from Judson's mind as he announced that he no longer held to the beliefs of his childhood. Influenced by the deism of his friend, he denied both the existence of a personal God and the need for salvation. However, an event took place while he was on the road that changed the course of his life.

One evening he took a room at a small country inn. The innkeeper informed him that there was a dying man in the next room. During the night Judson heard calls of, "God, God, lost."[174] As he was leaving the next morning, he asked about the condition of the sick man. The answer shocked Adoniram. He learned not only that the man had died during the night, but also that the man was Jacob Eames, his college friend. Suddenly the confident, self-assured young man found himself filled with doubts and questioning.

Judson returned home and entered Andover Seminary, where he met several young men who had been part of the "haystack prayer meeting," at which they dedicated themselves to God's service through missions. On 2 December 1808, the twenty-two-year-old Judson committed his life to God's service. Yet, one obstacle lay in Adoniram's way to the international mission field; there was no American organization sending missionaries overseas. The Congregationalists were having their General Association meeting at the Bradford Congregationalist church and agreed to hear a plea from Judson and his haystack friends. The day they were to speak to the association, they lunched in the home of a church deacon, John Hasseltine, whose beautiful daughter, Ann, immediately caught Judson's eye.

Ann was fortunate to have parents who believed in education for girls, an uncommon attitude for the day. John was one of the founders of the Bradford Academy, where his daughter enrolled among the first students when she was thirteen years old. Three years later, as the Second Great Awakening swept through New England, Ann felt a stirring in her heart and committed herself into God's hands. This feeling grew as she graduated from the academy and began teaching in several surrounding towns. In 1809, Ann's commitment to God grew and her heart began to focus on the unsaved of the world. The following year she met Judson as he spoke of his desire to take the Gospel to the heathen.

So it was that Judson left the association meeting with a promise from the Congregationalists to create the Board of Commissioners for Foreign Missions with the goal of supporting Judson on the mission field, and with the image of a beautiful woman in his heart. Adoniram wrote Ann one month later offering a proposal of marriage. After some hesitation—she was, after all, contemplating a life of hardship and perhaps lifelong separation from her family—Ann agreed. Judson, his future helpmate decided, set out to assure some group would give him the support he and Ann would need. His drive sent him to England in 1811 to speak with the London Missionary Society. Although politically relations between America and England were becoming heated, men of faith agreed on the importance of spreading the gospel. Officials of the society said they would be willing to send Judson and his friends as missionaries, but they reserved the right to direct the missionaries' work.

Fortunately for Judson, and for American missions, the Board of Commissioners for Foreign Missions agreed to appoint Judson and three other men as their first missionaries, to work in Burma, Surat, or Penang. The board decided they needed to raise one year's salary for each missionary before departure from the States. Church members, seminary students, and families throughout all of New England contributed to the salary and soon the board had accomplished its goal. On 5 February 1812, Adoniram and Ann were married; the next day Judson was appointed as a Congregationalist missionary. Five other men were commissioned at the same time: they included Samuel Newell, Samuel Nott, Gordon Hall, and Luther Rice. The Judsons and the Newells sailed out of Salem while the others embarked from Philadelphia. Both groups planned to meet in India. Judson was excited to meet the famous William Carey, the English Baptist missionary working in India.

Judson, aware of the theological divide between Congregationalists and Baptists, utilized his time on the trip to teach himself Greek and study the scripture for himself. His study of the language caused Judson to debate many of his long-held convictions, especially the issue of baptism. Congregationalists practiced infant baptism, whereas Baptists held to believer's baptism by immersion. By the time the group arrived in Calcutta, Judson's study convinced him that the Baptist way was biblically based, while Ann, studying on her own, came to the same conclusion. It thus came about that on 1 September 1812, Judson wrote to the Congregationalist board that he could no longer consider himself one of their missionaries nor take their money. Five days later, he and

Ann were baptized. Adoniram and Ann were not alone in this commitment, as Luther Rice also decided to become Baptist. Judson wrote Baptists detailing his decision and requesting that they consider supporting him and Rice. Carey also asked the American Baptists to accept the challenge of making the Judsons their first missionaries.

While in India, the new Baptists chose, despite warnings from Carey, to work in Burma. Suffering a severe ailment, Rice decided to return to America for health reasons and to raise funds among the Baptists. Health concerns dogged the Judsons as well. Ann had become pregnant while on the voyage. After sailing from India, Ann went into labor, but sadly gave birth to a stillborn baby boy. The Judsons' journey ended on 13 July 1813, when they first gazed at the port city of Rangoon, Burma, where no other missionary lived. After finding a place to live, Judson quickly turned to the task of learning the Burmese language. There were no aids to help in the learning process, so Judson, thinking of those who he hoped would soon join the mission effort, began writing a Burmese grammar text. Both Ann and Adoniram acknowledged the importance of learning the language well enough to begin translating religious material into Burmese. Judson's goal was to translate the Bible into the people's language. Judson believed that fully adopting the culture was important to evangelizing the people, prompting both he and Ann to wear Burmese clothing and leading Judson to preach in the manner of the Buddhist teachers.[175]

Anticipation of new mission volunteers greatly increased when, in 1815, news arrived that the Baptists had formed the Baptist Board of Foreign Missions. In 1816, George and Phoebe Hough arrived. Hough proved to be a great boon for the Judsons' translation efforts, as he was a skilled printer. The printing press soon rolled out copies of a catechism and a tract in the Burmese language. Although Judson spent much of his time translating—his main goal was to translate the New Testament—he also spent many hours sharing the gospel with those who would listen. The first fruit of these efforts was reaped with the baptism of the first Burmese convert in 1819. Though numbers of believers remained low, the small group endured in faith in the face of great danger. These were people who had rejected their traditional beliefs for the teachings of unwelcomed foreigners.

The Judsons' work among the Burmese, in a tropical climate where diseases flourished, led to health problems for both Ann and Adoniram. Ann's health failed to the point that, in 1822, she had to return to America. Upon her return, she found, to her surprise, that she and Adoniram were now considered heroes in the field of foreign missions. While in America, Ann was able to write a history of the work in Burma. Health did return to Ann and she once again left family behind and sailed for Rangoon. It would be the last time she would see her family.

Conditions worsened for the Baptist mission as relations between Burma and Great Britain deteriorated. Brought on by Burmese attacks in territories along British India's eastern border, the first Anglo-Burmese War began in 1824. By this time, the Judsons had moved to Ava, the Burmese capital. Following the British capture of Rangoon, all Westerners, not just the English, were suspect and often imprisoned. In June 1824, Burmese officials arrested Adoniram. Ann worked hard to ease his time in prison, bringing him food even as she denied herself. Even more dear to Adoniram than food, Ann had his completed copy of the Burmese New Testament covered to resemble a pillow and smuggled into the prison. In a letter to her brother dated 26 May 1826, Ann described the conditions of the prisoners: "The situation of the prisoners was now distressing beyond description. It was at the commencement of the hot season. There were above a hundred prisoners shut up in one room, without a breath of air excepting from the cracks in the boards. ...The White prisoners, from incessant perspiration and loss of appetite, looked more like the dead than the living."[176]

Despite inhumane prison conditions that resulted in many deaths, Judson persevered. In the midst of these difficulties, Ann gave birth to a daughter, Maria. Caring for the infant, finding food for both herself and Judson, and arguing for Adoniram's release with officials filled Ann's days; eventually, the strain led to life-threatening illness. On 31 December 1825, officials finally released Judson.

Initially, the small family returned to Rangoon, but the atmosphere was poisonous to Westerners. They next moved to an area the British controlled, the new city of Amherst. Here, Judson could preach and the new Burmese believers could safely worship in public. However, no new city could heal the years of deprivation Ann had endured; her health failed and she died on 24 October 1826. Judson's loss grew when, six months later, little Maria joined her mother at the heavenly gates.

Grieving for these two loved ones, Judson continued his mission work and his translation efforts. The British decided their capital would not be Amherst, but rather the city of Moulmein. Judson and another missionary couple decided to locate there. Here, Judson built the first permanent church in Burma. Along with evangelizing, Judson took on the task of translating the Old Testament into Burmese. The numbers of both missionaries and believers continued to grow.

In 1831, the mission learned the sad news that missionary George Dana Boardman had died. He and his wife, Sarah, had been working among the Karen people, a minority group in the country. Following the loss of her husband, many of the Americans believed that Sarah should return to the states with her three-year-old son, George, Jr. However, Adoniram encouraged her to continue her work among the Karen. She stayed and continued to evangelize the people. Judson's admiration grew into something deeper, and on 10 April 1834, the two were married. Sarah was as gifted a language learner as Judson. She, too, was involved in translating religious material into the Karen language. She and Adoniram decided that, given the mortality rate among missionary children in Burma, they would send young George to live in America. Sarah taught Bible classes and wrote hymns in the vernacular. She also threw herself into the role of mother as young Judsons were born, beginning with Abigail (Abby) Judson, born in 1835. In all, Sarah gave birth to eight Judson children; five lived into adulthood. During these years, Judson began having throat and lung ailments, but still took on writing both English-Burmese and Burmese-English dictionaries. Sarah had multiple health problems as well. Her doctor insisted that she must return to America if she were to grow strong again. The couple decided they would make the trip together and take the three older children with them, leaving the younger children in the care of missionary friends. Sarah failed to see the shores of her homeland. Her health worsened on the journey, and she died on 26 August 1845 as the ship was moored off the coast of St. Helena in the southeast Atlantic. Judson and the children watched as she was buried on the island.

Thus, a grieving Judson family arrived in Boston harbor. Adoniram was not prepared for the large crowd that waited on the docks to greet him. American Baptists hailed Judson as a hero for his efforts to bring the gospel to the Burmese. As a young man, Judson had dreamed of reaching great acclaim in his career, but now the mature man shunned the praise Baptists heaped on him. He was not allowed to hide away and work on his dictionaries as he had hoped. Churches across America wanted to hear him tell of his life and work in Burma. The story of the Judsons' suffering for Christ in a faraway land had united Baptists, who believed in the autonomy of the local church, to join together to support the mission work, creating the Triennial Convention. Over all the uproar his presence caused, Judson gave his attention to one specific project; he wanted to find an author who could write Sarah's biography. One evening, his host handed him a book by Fanny Forester, the pen name of popular author Emily Chubbuck. Fascinated, Judson asked if he could meet her. They met on Christmas Day in 1845. A romance developed, and on 2 June 1846, Adoniram and Emily were married; she was 29, he was 57. The next month the couple sailed for Burma, leaving the three older children to live in America.

Emily arrived in Burma and found herself the mother of two children. The family settled into their home in Moulmein. Soon the family grew, as Emily gave birth to Emily Frances Judson. Adoniram only had a few years to enjoy his daughter. His health was failing and doctors insisted that a sea voyage would help, but the voyage proved too much for Judson. He died at sea on 12 April 1850. Emily did not learn of his death until August. With great sadness, she and the three children soon departed for America. Upon arrival, Emily worked toward two goals: to gather all six Judson children under one roof and to find a scholar to write Adoniram's biography. She successfully assembled the children for parts of two summers. She chose Dr. Francis Wayland, president of Brown University, as the author of her husband's book. Emily died on 1 June 1854.

Adoniram Judson was a trailblazer in Baptist missions. He was the first international missionary from the US and demonstrated a passion for evangelizing the Burmese people. He realized the importance of people having the Bible available in their own language and paved the way for future missionaries with his Burmese grammar and dictionaries. For his commitment to the gospel, Judson suffered hardships, deprivation, imprisonment, and illness. Working side by side with him were three amazing women, each as committed to missions as Adoniram. This great man was heralded in his time. He is honored today.

Suggested Reading

Duesing, Jason, editor. *Adoniram Judson: A Bicentennial Appreciation of the Pioneer American Missionary.* Nashville TN: B&H Publishing Group, 2012.

Hunt, Rosalie Hall. *Bless God and Take Courage: The Judson History and Legacy.* Valley Forge: Judson Press, 2005.

Pleasants, Phyllis Rodgerson. "Beyond Translation: The Work of the Judsons in Burma." *Baptist History and Heritage* 42 (Spring 2007):19–35.

Raymond, David B. "The Controversy over Adoniram Judson's Famous 'Change of Sentiments,' 1813–1820." *Baptist History and Heritage* 45 (Spring 2010): 59-71.

Wayland, Francis. *Memoir of the Life and Labors of the Rev. Adoniram Judson, D.D.* Boston: Phillips, Sampson, and Company, 1853.

Johann Gerhard Oncken
(1800–1884)

Catalyst of European Church Planting Movements

Missions

Gregory Nichols

> Without doubt, the greatest pioneer of the Baptist faith in Europe was J. G. Oncken. He stands head and shoulders above all others; some have suggested that Oncken's life and ministry could form the framework for the history of Baptists in Europe. —H. Leon McBeth[177]

H. LEON MCBETH, one of the leading Baptist historians of our time, has provided this powerful statement on the witness of one man in regards to a turning point in Baptist history. Johann Gerhard Oncken (1800–1884) has been called the "Father of the German Baptists," "Apostle of the European Baptists," and the "Father of the Continental Baptists." These three designations can be seen as radiating ripples across the surface of Europe. He was a man of tremendous energy who was brought into the Baptist story at a time when Europeans were prepared to accept the Baptist message and Germans were poised to transmit it across the continent. A visionary leader, Oncken instilled the seminal idea that every Baptist is by definition a missionary through his often repeated motto "Every Baptist a Missionary."[178] This seed took hold in the thousands of believers whom he touched, sparking a church-planting movement that swept Europe for decades.

Johann G. Oncken was born in Varel, Germany on 26 January 1800. At the age of twenty, he surrendered his life completely to Christ during a service in London at the Great Queen Street Methodist Chapel.[179] The revival movement that the Methodist Chapel exposed him to was part of a larger movement just beginning to take hold in England, which eventually shaped the broader Evangelical movement. His revivalistic enthusiasm led him to the "Continental Society,"[180] a

London-based missionary organization focused on propagation of the evangelical faith into the European continent. In 1823, the Continental Society commissioned Oncken for service to Hamburg, Germany. This city served as a strategic communications hub for Central Europe, especially for its main port for passenger and freight service on the Atlantic Ocean. Oncken quickly picked up on this unique opportunity and purposefully associated with the seamen who were docked in port, sharing the gospel and passing out literature. The Continental Society had placed him under the care of the Hamburg congregation of the English-Reformed Church. In 1825, in cooperation with the Lutheran Church, Oncken started the first German-speaking Sunday school program on continental Europe. Thirty-one years later, German Baptist Sunday schools had enrolled 1,322 children instructed by 145 teachers. By 1880, the number of children had increased to over 10,000.[181]

A gifted communicator, Oncken soon began to preach in Hamburg. By 1824, these meetings drew approximately 280 people. Oncken and his "new English Religion" attracted the attention of the city officials who arrested and fined him for preaching without a license.[182] This imprisonment did not dissuade Oncken. He began to preach in homes at the invitation of local citizens. As the house church movement grew, he became more distant from the English-Reformed congregation. Beginning in 1826, he openly expressed his reservations of infant baptism. By 1829, he became convinced that baptism "was a blessed privilege and sacred duty of all those who have been regenerated by the Holy Spirit" and began to seek a "Philip" who would baptize them.[183] He never left his Calvinistic moorings, but by 1829 he was openly convinced of the need for believer's baptism and the resulting conviction that church membership was to be only for the regenerated.

These new convictions carried Oncken into a dilemma. As with the start of the Anabaptist Movement in the early sixteenth century, the solution to the dilemma came in two steps. The first step was to withhold one's own children from baptism into the state church; in 1829 Oncken declined the baptism of his infant child. The second step was to seek a believer's baptism. Oncken was in a quandary, for he was too busy leading the movement to go to England to be baptized and he could not find a biblical example of self-baptism. He remained in this state for nearly five years until Barnas Sears, a Baptist professor from Hamilton College,[184] came to study in Halle, Germany. At the invitation of Oncken, Sears travelled to Hamburg. On 22 April 1834, under the cover of darkness, Sears baptized Oncken, his wife, and five others of the house church movement in the Elbe River.

The arrival of the Baptist message in Hamburg concerned citizens and city officials who perceived it to be an echo of the radical Anabaptist rebellion in Munster during the 1530s. Authorities soon arrested and imprisoned Oncken and other leaders of the Baptist congregation for illegal religious activity. Meeting places became difficult to obtain, members were threatened, fined, and imprisoned, and the chief of police was vocal on his intent to squelch the Baptist work. This persecution did not deter the young Baptist congregation, for within two years, Oncken had baptized and commissioned a new congregation in Berlin, installing Gottfried W. Lehmann as its pastor. Within fourteen years of his baptism, Oncken started twenty-six reproducing congregations among German-speakers. It has been stated that in 1815, there were no Baptist churches on the continent of Europe,[185] despite nearly two centuries of Baptist expansion in England and the American colonies.[186] Oncken's efforts sparked a church-planting movement: in thirty years there were 11,275 Baptists in Germany; in eighty years there were 45,583 Baptists in Germany.[187] Before the first Baptist congregation on the continent of Europe celebrated its centennial, there were approximately 250,000 registered Baptist members across Europe.[188] The first unique feature about Oncken was his foundational belief: "Every Baptist a Missionary." Oncken passed this on to his spiritual protégés with a passion that caused them to likewise pass it on to those whom they discipled.

A second unique feature about Oncken's ministry was timing; Germany was ripe for the Baptist message. There was a general dissatisfaction among the members of European state churches over the interpretation of the gospel through an Enlightenment grid. Beginning in the 1830s, Pietistic revivals brought a fresh approach to spirituality for many Europeans, which produced an openness to new thoughts, including believer's baptism.[189] Additionally, the early nineteenth century experienced a season of economic unrest, causing many Germans to seek a fresh start abroad. As Germans emigrated, Baptists were among them, carrying Oncken's mandate "Every Baptist a Missionary." Related to the movement of people in Europe at the time was the Great Hamburg Fire of 1842. Tradesmen from across Germany and Europe rebuilt the city after the fire. During the three years following the fire, Oncken and his congregations baptized 975 people,[190] with more than half being tradesmen who returned to their home carrying the commission of "Every Baptist a Missionary." Today, a Baptist movement in Austria, Bulgaria, Denmark, Estonia, France, Holland, Hungary, Latvia, Lithuania, Poland, Romania, Sweden, Switzerland, and the current countries of the old Russian Empire can each trace their beginnings to Oncken and the Hamburg congregation.[191] The Baptist message was carried through many different conduits from Oncken's ministry center in Hamburg—literature, sailors, tradesmen, itinerant preachers, and German emigrants—all transmitting the message of the gospel with the deep understanding that all Baptists are commissioned to preach the gospel.

The third unique feature of Oncken was that he demonstrated the remarkable ability to gather catalytic leaders around him. Oncken baptized Julius Köbner, a Danish son of a rabbi, in 1836. Köbner often traveled with Oncken on missionary treks, helped to establish the Hamburg training center, wrote hymns, and played a key role in the Baptist expansion into Denmark and the Scandinavian area. Another was Gottfried W. Lehmann, mentioned earlier as the founding pastor of the second Baptist church in Germany. Before his baptism, Lehmann grew dissatisfied with the state church and gathered a core group around him in his home for prayer and the study of scripture. After his baptism, in addition to leading the Berlin congregation, he travelled extensively across Europe preaching the gospel, commissioning all he baptized as missionaries. Together, they were known as the "Cloverleaf" of the German Baptist movement.

A fourth feature of Oncken's ministry was his unique skill set. A quintessential catalytic leader, Oncken exhibited unending energy, strong persuasive powers, administrative skill, and a God-sized vision. Beginning in 1848, he started to organize the German-speaking Baptist churches into a union using an American Baptist pattern of triennial conferences.[192] His passion to reach the lost drove Oncken's decision to organize the congregations. The first two decisions made by the organization were to establish a mission fund and appoint a church planter. In addition to the organization of the union, Oncken was involved in the founding and operations of a mission school in Hamburg. As the Baptist expression rapidly reproduced, Oncken clearly understood that the laity had to be empowered rather than producing a clerical elite. In 1849, he guided the formation of the Hamburg Mission School. Despite the fact that he had a modest education, Oncken, along with Lehmann and others, taught in this six-month program, ordaining their graduates as missionaries to unreached regions or developing preaching stations. Four years before his death, the school became a three-year program, renaming itself the Hamburg Baptist Seminary. The mission school was the heart of the early Baptist movement in Europe, training Baptist leaders from across Germany and Central and Eastern Europe. At the center of its curriculum was Oncken's Statement of Faith, adopted by the union in the same year as the school opened. It is thoroughly baptistic with a strong slant toward the reformed and Calvinistic heritage of Oncken, placing itself among the Particular Baptist creeds. The confession was soon translated into other languages and used to instruct the rapidly expanding movement on doctrine and scripture as many of the theological statements carried biblical references.[193]

Oncken encountered more than his fair share of troubles. Aside from the already mentioned persecution targeted personally against Oncken, in 1853, while traveling in the U.S. by rail, he was injured as the train plunged into the Norwalk Harbor.[194] He was married three times, widowed twice, and experienced the deaths of four of his seven children.[195] In 1871, he experienced a painful rift as pastor of the Hamburg congregation when he sought to limit the influence of its deacons. This produced a split that resulted in the formation of the Hamburg Altona Baptist Church. The struggle lasted for five years, sharply curtailing the momentum of the movement. The conflict was finally healed through the persistent efforts of Köbner, one of Oncken's closest associates. All three members of the "Cloverleaf" died within two years of each other. At the end of their lives, Oncken and Köbner, along with their congregations, were fully reconciled.

The baptism of Johann Gerhard Oncken served as the monumental turning point for the Continental Baptists. During the fifty years between his baptism and death, he baptized over 2,200 and assisted in nearly 100 German new church starts. He mentored and sent out catalytic leaders who sparked similar movements in over fifteen countries on three continents. Before his baptism, there were only a handful of Baptists in Europe; at his death, there were over 18,000 members in the German Union alone. He took time to identify and develop effective leaders, building a strong team around him in Germany as well as empowering others outside Germany. He was an exceptionally capable and visionary leader, overseeing the operations of a publishing house, the organization of a new denomination, and the start of European Baptist theological training. Yet, at the core of all this was the unquestioned, unreserved conviction that every follower of Christ was by definition one sent out into the harvest as a missionary. His spiritual DNA was effectively transmitted to others, who discipled others, who discipled others... "Every Baptist a Missionary."

Suggested Reading

Cooke, John Hunt. *Johann Gerhard Oncken: His Life and Work*. London: S.W. Partridge & Co., 1908.

McBeth, Leon H. *The Baptist Heritage: Four Centuries of Baptist Witness*. Nashville TN: Broadman Press, 1987.

Parker, G. Keith. *Baptists in Europe: History and Confessions of Faith*. Nashville TN: Broadman Press, 1982.

Randall, Ian. *Communities of Conviction: Baptist Beginnings in Europe*. Schwarzenfield, Germany / Prague: Neufeld Verlag / European Baptist Federation, 2009.

Rushbrooke, J. H. *The Baptist Movement on the Continent of Europe*. London: The Carey Press, 1923.

Wagner, William L. *New Move Forward in Europe: Growth Patterns of German-Speaking Baptists in Europe*. South Pasadena CA: William Carey Library, 1978.

Isaac Taylor Tichenor[196]
(1825–1902)

Father of Cooperative Baptist Missions

Missions

Michael E. (Mike) Williams, Sr.

Almost from the very beginning of English Baptist and American Baptist life, Baptists organized themselves into cooperative organizations called associations. As Walter Shurden demonstrates, these associations voiced Baptist concerns about religious liberty, promoted theological education, advised Baptist churches, and, after the formation of the Baptist Missionary Society in 1792, promoted the missions movement. Following the lead of British Baptists, Baptists in America formed the Triennial Convention (later called the American Baptist Missionary Union and then the American Baptist Foreign Mission Society) in 1814 to provide support for Baptist foreign missions. In 1817, the Triennial Convention appointed John Mason Peck to serve as a home missionary, and in 1832, created the Home Mission Society to furnish assistance for reaching and ministering to the growing population of the American frontier. Unfortunately, the growing crisis of the Union and disputes about sectionalism and slavery, as well as disagreements about the correct approach to fund and administer missions, divided Baptists into northern and southern entities in 1845, leading to the formation of the Southern Baptist Convention. To support its missions endeavors, the new SBC created the Foreign Mission Board and the Domestic Mission Board that year. The division of the denomination heralded the division of the nation, and Southern Baptists suffered greatly both during the Civil War and during the Reconstruction Era that followed.[197]

By 1882, Baptists seriously questioned if the Southern Baptist Convention would or should survive. While support for foreign missions had rebounded somewhat in the aftermath of the Civil War and

Reconstruction, Southern Baptists failed to sustain any sort of publishing board and the Southern Baptist Domestic Mission Board languished in the aftermath of the devastation wrought by the war. Some state mission boards and associations sought to strengthen those ties with the North and continued to receive funding that had begun in the Reconstruction era from the Northern Baptist Home Mission Society. Indeed, some believed that Southern Baptists should reunite with Northern Baptists. With sectional tensions still strong a decade and a half after the cataclysm, other Southern Baptists rejected any thought of reuniting with the North. On the fringes of the South, particularly in Texas, Missouri, and the Indian Territory, Baptist work was severely divided between those linked with the Home Mission Society, those tied to the Domestic Mission Board, and those with connections to both entities. Southern Baptist Theological Seminary had relocated to Louisville, Kentucky in an effort to survive, and Baptist colleges across the South struggled to attract students and operating funds. Agents from all of these institutions fanned out across the South, visiting churches regularly and pleading for support for their respective enterprises.

Within ten years, many of these circumstances and situations had changed. Much of the revival of Southern Baptist work centered around the work of the newly-named and relocated Home Mission Board, a combination of the old Domestic and Indian Mission Board, and despite setbacks and disagreements, the future for Southern Baptists looked far brighter. While there were many factors in this Southern Baptist resurgence, the leadership of Isaac Taylor Tichenor emerged as one of the most important factors.

Born in Kentucky in 1825, reared in the Baptist church, and educated in frontier schools, Isaac Taylor Tichenor committed his life to vocational Christian ministry as a young man, serving as a collecting agent for the Indian Mission Association, an evangelist leading revivals in Texas, and as pastor of churches in Mississippi and Kentucky. Late in 1851, the First Baptist Church of Montgomery called Tichenor to serve as their pastor. Tichenor served as the congregation's pastor until late 1860, a critical time in the life of the congregation, the nascent Southern Baptist Convention, the deep-South state of Alabama, and the United States. After serving briefly as a collecting agent for the newly created

Southern Baptist Theological Seminary, an institution he had supported at its inception a few years earlier, Tichenor volunteered to serve the Seventeenth Alabama regiment in the Confederate Army. He distinguished himself in the Battle of Shiloh, and then served briefly as a Southern Baptist missionary to the army in the Kentucky campaign of 1862 prior to accepting a call to return to FBC of Montgomery as its pastor in January 1863.[198]

The situation to which he returned in 1863 dramatically differed from that he had left. The turmoil of the war had not only reached Montgomery but also continued to worsen as the Confederacy's fortunes declined. The end of the war, collapse of slavery, and onset of the Reconstruction era in the South hammered the southern economy. Eventually, forced to leave the pastorate of First Baptist in 1868 due to financial reasons, and also drawn by business opportunities, Tichenor spent the next three years as the president of the Montevallo Coal Mining Company, an enterprise Tichenor had helped begin during the Civil War. During this time, Tichenor became intimately involved with the "New South" movement just then beginning in the former Confederacy. Tichenor also continued to be involved in ministerial and denominational work. The business techniques that he developed and the philosophical adjustments he made during this time proved critical in later years. While his business enterprises never provided the return on his investment that he anticipated, the few years that he spent there convinced Tichenor of the vast economic potential of the South. In subsequent years, he drew frequently upon this experience to promote his work.[199]

After a brief sojourn as a pastor in Tennessee, Tichenor returned to Alabama in 1872 as the president of Alabama A & M College [now Auburn University], the newly chartered land-grant college in Auburn, Alabama. Building on a fragile foundation inherited from the East Alabama Male College, for ten years Tichenor strove to graft a land-grant college with a focus on mechanical and agricultural sciences onto the formerly small liberal-arts denominational school and its classical approach to education. He sought to integrate New South business techniques in the administration of the institution. While he did not completely succeed in his endeavors, he acquired knowledge that aided him as he came to his life work, that of serving as the corresponding secretary of the Southern Baptist Home Mission Board.[200]

In 1882 the Southern Baptist Convention made two momentous decisions. The first was to rename the Domestic Mission Board as the Home Mission Board and relocate it from tiny Marion, Alabama, a tiny, prototypical "Old South"-style town in the heart of the Black Belt, to bustling Atlanta, Georgia, symbol of the emerging "New South." They also chose to replace the board's current chief executive, W. H. McIntosh, with an energetic new corresponding secretary, I. T. Tichenor, well known for his denominational service, magnificent speaking skills, and his innovations at Alabama A & M. While they never mentioned Tichenor's developing vision for the South, it may have figured into their selection as well.[201]

Tichenor began his tenure with a whirlwind of activity. After resigning his presidency at Alabama A & M and moving his family to Atlanta, Tichenor journeyed across the South, meeting with influential Southern Baptists. Tichenor subsequently attended the state conventions or associations of ten southern states plus the Indian Territory. He generated more than twenty thousand dollars of commitments from those conventions and associations that he visited.[202]

Tichenor initiated or enhanced several practices that radically reoriented the Home Mission Board and, therefore, the SBC. He prioritized those works that he considered essential for the survival of the board. For example, he recognized the vast potential that Texas held for the future of the SBC. He encouraged Texas Baptist leaders to unify the five separate associations and conventions in Texas into a single entity. He insisted that home missionaries in the South come under the umbrella of the Home Mission Board and that state conventions choose between the Home Mission Board and the Home Mission Society. While this direction did not occur without conflict and his sectionalism exacerbated the divisions between Northern and Southern Baptists, it did rally Southern Baptists behind the banner of home missions. With inspirational preaching, vigorous correspondence, and improved business techniques and planning, Tichenor established the Home Mission Board as the primary domestic missions entity in the South. In ten years the receipts of the HMB almost tripled. The number of churches planted by the board increased almost between 1887 and 1892 as compared with those planted between 1882 and 1887, and the number of missionaries supported by the HMB almost quadrupled in that same ten years.[203]

Tichenor devoted the remaining years of his tenure as corresponding secretary of the HMB to consolidating control over the home missions endeavors of Southern Baptists, expanding the vision of Southern Baptist possibilities, and casting a vision for other agencies and techniques that would increase Southern Baptist influence, such as the re-establishment of the Sunday School Board, which became the publishing arm of the SBC. He especially linked his work with that of the emerging Women's Missionary Union, especially that of Annie Armstrong. One of the most critical tasks that he performed came as he worked with others to define Southern Baptist territory. When he died in 1902, Southern Baptist leadership widely lauded him as one of the greatest leaders in Southern Baptist history.[204]

Having briefly served as agent of the Indian Missions Association and a collecting agent for Southern Seminary, Tichenor recognized the inefficient, haphazard manner of supporting missions and education enterprises practiced by Southern Baptists. His tenure as corresponding secretary of the Home Mission Board convinced Tichenor that if Southern Baptists ever hoped to fulfill their potential, they must adopt a more systematic and effective fashion of supporting their collaborative enterprises. He also demonstrated that if Southern Baptists were to survive into the twentieth century, they must define their identity and embrace at least some of the changes sweeping the nation's business circles.

Tichenor contributed much to Baptist life, both positive and negative. He cast a vision that blended the deep southern pride of the Old South with the progressive business techniques and aspirations of the New South. He established priorities for the Home Mission Board and shifted the focus of Southern Baptist work toward developing southern urban areas as well as the emerging Baptist stronghold in Texas. He retired the board's debt and exercised fiscal responsibility. As one historian has noted, he "defined what was 'southern' about the SBC."[205]

Tichenor exuded confidence. He recognized how Baptists could be swayed by powerful oratory and utilized his considerable speaking skills to his advantage. As one of the South's most visible religious leaders, he utilized these abilities to their fullest extent. He restored Southern Baptists their regional and religious pride.

More than these things, perhaps, he called repeatedly for a more systematic method of supporting mission endeavors. Continuing throughout his tenure as correspondence but beginning with his address before the SBC in 1883, he stated, "The grandest duty of the hour, the noblest work of this Convention is to devise and make effective some plan that will elicit and combine the benevolence of our people." Due to his consistent advocacy for a more organized approach to financial support of SBC work, Tichenor might correctly be identified as the Grandfather of the SBC Cooperative Program, one of the most effective missions support systems in American evangelicalism's history.[206]

Not all Tichenor's contributions were positive. He did little to alleviate the spirit of competition that existed with Northern Baptists. In fact, he cultivated the sectionalism that enhanced it and utilized that spirit to rally Southern Baptist support. He continued and furthered the racial paternalism that existed among southern Whites. The materialism of the Gilded Age captivated and captured him and carried over into his work.

Despite these negative influences, Tichenor remains the quintessential Southern Baptist of the late nineteenth century, the period in which major elements of Southern Baptist life for the twentieth century developed. Indeed, as his biography states, "In the life and work of Isaac Taylor Tichenor, one may see a microcosm of the Southern Baptist Convention. …As the convention has a left a legacy to this nation's and the world's religious heritage, so too has Isaac Taylor Tichenor left a legacy of cooperation, optimism, and mission to the Southern Baptist Convention and to the world."[207]

Suggested Reading

Fletcher, Jesse C. *The Southern Baptist Convention: A Sesquicentennial History*. Nashville TN: Broadman & Holman, 1994.

Flynt, J. Wayne. *Alabama Baptists: Southern Baptists in the Heart of Dixie*. Tuscaloosa: University of Alabama Press, 1998.

Harvey, Paul. *Redeeming the South: Religious Cultures and Racial Identities Among Southern Baptists, 1865–1925*. Chapel Hill NC: University of North Carolina Press, 1997.

Williams, Michael E., Sr. *Isaac Taylor Tichenor: The Creation of the Baptist New South*. Tuscaloosa: University of Alabama Press, 2005.

Williams, Michael E., Sr., and Walter B. Shurden. *Turning Points in Baptist History: A Festschrift in Honor of Harry Leon McBeth*. Macon GA: Mercer University Press, 2008.

Robert Cooke Buckner
(1833–1919)

Father of Social Christianity

Social Justice

Karen O'Dell Bullock

FOR SOME MEN, existence on earth leaves no record, no echo of passing. This cannot be said of Robert Cooke Buckner, who was a remarkable man among many outstanding American "Builders" between the years 1850 to 1920. His contemporaries included Andrew Carnegie (1835–1919), steel industry tycoon; J. P. Morgan (1837–1913), of banking and Wall Street fame; John D. Rockefeller (1839–1937), creator of Standard Oil; and Henry Ford (1863–1947), who built "an affordable car for every home."

If Walter Rauschenbusch (1861–1918), Baptist pastor, was the Father of the Social Gospel movement in the North, Robert Cooke Buckner, also a Baptist pastor, was the Father of Social Christianity in the South. A Tennessean by birth, Buckner came early to Texas and stayed to plant his life in its churches, its children, and its Baptist denomination. The pages of history mirror his eighty-seven-year investment. What Buckner so uniquely pioneered in Baptist life was *organized social reform* based upon a strong, biblical conviction that individual regeneration is a key to societal change. Buckner combined praxis with theory, and applied Christianity's teachings to his search for the holistic transformation of both individuals and society.

This chapter examines the contributions of R. C. Buckner to Baptist life. As a pastor, philanthropist, denominational leader, newspaper editor, businessman, and "Father" to thousands of orphans, Bucker was a peacemaker in a time when Baptists were far more fractured than whole. It was the work of this man, to a large degree, that propelled Baptists in the South toward alleviating social injustices, and gave to the Texas body a vision of missions and service to others. It is in recognition of this noble and selfless character that Texas Baptists gave to R. C. Buckner the name "Sir Great-Heart."[208]

Shortly after the Second Great Awakening, Robert Cooke was born in a log cabin in Madisonville, Tennessee, on 3 January 1833, to Daniel and Mary Buckner.[209] His Baptist church-planting father was well known as favoring missions, Sunday schools, and an educated clergy.[210] The family moved to Kentucky to undertake a new pastorate and, in Somerset, Buckner grew to young manhood, was converted at age eleven, and was educated at the "Old Brick Seminary." Like his father, Robert began preaching at age seventeen. In 1850, he enrolled in Georgetown College, where he studied Greek, Latin, the law of Blackstone, and theology.[211] What he had learned at his father's knee and from the African-American preachers of his youth laid a strong foundation for his later life and ministry.[212]

Robert's first church was in Albany, Kentucky, where he met and married Vienna Long in 1854.[213] He then pastored churches in Owensboro and Salvisa and became the first agent for the Kentucky Domestic Mission Board. When he contracted typhoid-pneumonia in summer 1859, however, he determined to move west to a dryer, healthier climate. He resigned his church, packed his family, and trundled the 900 wagon-miles to the Lone Star State. In 1860, Texas Baptists numbered nearly 30,000 members in eighty churches. With about 600,000 citizens occupying the state's vast expanse, the increase was slow and the labor difficult, even though twenty-six fledgling Baptist associations were already in place.[214]

On the brink of the Civil War, in 1860, young Robert Cooke was called to pastor the Baptist church in Paris, Texas, and proved to be an innovative missionary pastor for the next fourteen years. He organized a Ladies' Aid Society for missions, operated a year-round Sunday school, started an academy, and served as general agent for the Baptist General Association in the northern part of the state from 1877 to 1882. In that span, he planted churches and organized associations across much of north Texas.[215]

In order to connect and unify the work among Baptists, and because the railroads had not yet crossed the region, communication by newspaper was of vital importance. In 1874, while continuing his role as general agent, Buckner resigned his pastorate and moved to Dallas to become the editor of a new Baptist paper, *The Religious Messenger*, launched that year. This was to be his final move, allowing him the focus to fulfill his dream—to establish an orphanage for children. Even Buckner could not have imagined all that would emerge in the decades to follow.

Children's Work—Buckner called for the formation of a deacon's convention in July 1877, specifically directed towards caring for destitute orphans and elder persons in the state. The deacons eagerly responded, gathering under an oak tree in Paris, Texas, during a break between sessions of the General Association Meeting that year. R.C. Buckner contributed the first dollar "just to get the thing started," he said, and his friend, B. H. Carroll, followed suit.[216] The new group resolved to establish the Orphans' Home and tasked Buckner with soliciting funds for and organizing the project. In anticipation, Buckner rented a three-room cottage at the corner of Junius Street and Haskell Avenue in Dallas.

Eight months later, on 2 December 1879, the home opened its doors to three children. The Executive Board of the Deacon's Convention, meanwhile, met to name the enterprise "Buckner Orphans' Home" and appointed Robert as General Manager, the position he shouldered until his death in 1919. According to its State of Texas Charter of April 1879, the home was constituted on the broad platform of receiving and caring for all dependent orphan children, regardless of "partiality, section, or sectarian grounds."[217]

In 1880, J. T. Pinson sold forty-four acres of land ten miles east of downtown Dallas to Buckner for $500. On 27 September, a small group drove out to the site to gather and kneel inside the small sharecropper's cabin on the property to dedicate the land for God's purposes.[218] By spring 1881, the first frame house, suitable to house twenty-five children, was erected on the new site at a total cost of $841.19.[219]

Within two years, fifty children lived at the home, the Buckner Home Baptist Church was constituted with Robert Cooke as pastor, and a school was established. In 1905 a half-orphanage opened for children of single parents unable to provide adequately for their little ones. In

1914, just as World War I began, Buckner transferred the home to Texas Baptists, the institution they had enthusiastically supported for many years. At that time, more than 700 children resided in three-story brick dorms, and another 100 in the Sunbeam Nursery.[220] Worth $700,412 and debt-free, Buckner Home was a City of Children and stable.

Elder Care—Buckner had urged deacons as early as 1877 to make some provision for retiring and destitute Baptist ministers. His editorials in the *Texas Baptist* and *Religious Messenger* agitated the question. In response, Texas Baptists formed the Ministers' Relief Board of the Baptist General Convention of Texas [BGCT] in 1886.

Buckner built an entire row of "Cottages for the Aged" at Buckner Home in 1905, where retired preachers or their widows could come to live their final years. Children visited their older friends daily, helped them to button shoes and plant flowers. In turn, the elder ones became "grandparents" to the orphans who had no family of their own. Buckner's was a visionary arrangement of fostering mutually beneficial intergenerational relationships that championed the dignity of both elders and the children.

Better Race Relations—Buckner had been reared in Kentucky with Black preachers as mentors and he valued these close relationships his entire life. His African-American friend in Paris during the Civil War, A. R. Griggs, was a strong partner in church growth work. Buckner and Griggs started the first Black Baptist association, Zion, in Bowie County in 1869, with Buckner organizing the session as moderator. They and other Black Baptists also opened the "Ministers' Institute" in 1874, where Buckner was invited to train Black pastors in ministry and theology. They published the first Black Baptist paper in Texas, called *Baptist Journal*, in 1878.

Perhaps their largest enterprise of all, Buckner and Griggs partnered in founding the Dickson Negro Orphanage, chartered at a convention held at New Hope Baptist Church, Dallas, in July 1900. Buckner agreed to serve as President for the first five years as long as Griggs would serve as Vice President. They settled the orphanage in Gilmer on seventy-five acres, and by 1905, more than 1,120 children had been received and the campus boasted 162 acres.[221]

Educational Ventures—Buckner founded more schools than orphanages. In a day when boys were educated apart from girls, Buckner found good reasons to include both boys and girls of all ages in classrooms and to teach the same subjects to both. He also combined academic learning experiences with vocational and technical training, or "life skills," so that the children could grow to become independent and contributing members of society.

Buckner founded three high schools. He also called for and raised money toward organizing the first Black high school in North Texas, which was opened in 1877 at Antioch Church, Grayson County, by the Sister Grove Association.[222] Moreover, he was so concerned about the needs of young boys growing up on the streets of Dallas that, in 1881, he also started a "Newsboys'" or a "Twilight" school for newspaper carriers and bootblacks.

Meanwhile, Buckner Home School had one teacher from 1880–1892. Half of the children attended in the morning and the other half in the afternoon. A second teacher opened a kindergarten class in 1893. The industrial training program began in 1896, by which students could specialize in photography, stenography, pharmacology, and piano and organ instruction.

Buckner Home School from 1900–1917 had a principal and six teachers and became an independent school district in 1917. By 1918, the home had a library of 12,000 volumes and natural history and science museums.[223]

Women's Theological Education—Buckner was convinced that women contributed valuable gifts both to society and ministry. He introduced a motion to welcome women into denominational work at the 1895 Dallas Association Pastors' Conference. This motion that "seated" women delegates gave them the right to vote and affirmed their placement on working committees in the BGCT. His articles in Baptist newspapers also urged Texas Baptist women to organize the Baptist Women Mission Workers in 1886 for the purpose of building schools, orphanages, and mission centers, and for appointing Bible Women as agents.

Concerned about the home's "daughters" who were being called to ministry but lacked theological training, Buckner announced the opening of the Baptist Women's Missionary Training School at the Dallas Association Pastor's Conference on 1 September 1903. It passed unanimously and opened on 2 October 1904 at the Buckner Home Annex in Dallas with seven women students, the first of its kind in the South.[224] Graduates from this school were sent as international missionaries in 1906. Four years later, this school became part of Southwestern Baptist Theological Seminary when it was relocated from Waco to Fort Worth in 1910. That year, thirty-eight women enrolled in courses and, by 1913, eighty-five women were students. The Texas Baptist Women Mission Workers paid for and furnished the building.[225]

Health Care Innovations—Buckner demonstrated a prescient view of healthcare as he aimed for holistic healing: spiritual, emotional, psychological, and physical. He built a hospital to care for children on the campus in 1891, called "Bethshan." Six years later, his newspaper articles called for the establishment of a public children's hospital, which opened in 1897 as the Children's Hospital in Dallas. This was the year he opened the "Annex," so that newly arriving children could first be observed for the presence of communicable diseases as a precautionary measure before being moved into the resident halls with other children on campus.

He opened a center for the treatment of epilepsy in 1903, the Texas Baptist Memorial Sanitarium in 1904; founded the American Baptist Hospital Association in 1906 and served as its first president; established the "Pasteur Institute" to train nurses in 1909; and built an open-air "Tuberculosis Sanatorium" in 1910 to treat the home children who had contracted this disease.[226]

Prison Reform—Noting the inhumane treatment of human beings in the penal systems across the south, Buckner boldly challenged prevailing practices of his day. Work camp deaths abounded. The Texas prison system had allowed private contractors full control over inmates since 1870 and, when the horrific abuse became public in 1880, Buckner demanded reform. He was appointed to the National Conference of Charities and Corrections [NCCC], which he served from 1885–1915. He called for the placement of Bibles and other good reading material in prisons and recommended the removal of minors from adult penitentiaries to juvenile reformatories. He published invitations for released convicts to find gainful employment in 1885. In the next year, he publicized the opening of women's shelters and homes for transitional living, and called for the formation of a Texas Prison Board chapter of NCCC.[227]

Buckner articulated the difference between criminals and persons with mental disabilities and pled for the creation of special-needs asylums in 1887, the same year he formed the Texas Prisoner's Aid Association. In 1888 he urged the State of Texas to implement a system of police matron-ship, which was adopted in Dallas, so that female officers, rather than men, would oversee women incarcerated in prisons.

Legislation and Baptist Leadership—In the political arena, Buckner was instrumental in the articulation and passage of the Texas Child Labor Law of 1902 and 1903, and was a leading spokesman in the national Home-Finding vs. Orphanage debates of 1897–1910. He called for laws to protect mothers and children who had been abandoned by husbands and fathers, and in 1908, was invited by President Roosevelt to the White House Conference on Dependent Children. He helped to pass the Children's Bureau Bill that year and gave the Home-Finding State Conference Address in 1909.

In Baptist life, he was also known as the peacemaker, healing rifts between newspapers, individuals, and Baptist bodies. In Texas, Buckner was instrumental in the reconciliation of competing Baptist denominations, newspapers, and colleges in 1886, forming the BGCT. He served this body as president for two decades, from 1894–1914, helped to establish the Civic Righteousness and Social Services Committees in the year 1915, and served on the Executive Committee until his death in January 1919 at the age of eighty-six. Upon his home-going, Texas Baptists published the following paean of tribute: "No purer soul led a braver band, Nor braver served a brighter land, Nor brighter land had a cause so grand, Nor cause a chief like he."[228]

Of the institutions and organizations that sprang from Buckner's initiatives, most of them still thrive today, more than a century later.[229] Buckner's six decades of work to alleviate the suffering of humanity, to champion justice and dignity for all persons, and to engage succeeding generations in this work remains his legacy. Twenty-first-century advances in social reform still travel the roadbed he built. Baptists do well to remember and imitate the unique contributions of Robert Cooke Buckner who, for sixty years, showed men and women how to *be* the hands and feet and face of Christ as they responded to the needs of society's most vulnerable.

Suggested Reading

Bullock, Karen O'Dell. *Homeward Bound: The Heart and Heritage of Buckner*. Dallas TX: Buckner Children's Home, 1993.

———. "Life and Contributions of Robert Cooke Buckner: Progenitor of Social Christianity Among Texas Baptists 1860–1919." Ph.D. dissertation, Southwestern Baptist Theological Seminary, 1991.

McBeth, Harry Leon. *Texas Baptists: A Sesquicentennial History*. Waco [now Fort Worth] TX: Eakin [now Wild Horse] Press, 1999.

Charles H. Spurgeon
(1834–1892)

Baptist Prince of Preachers

Preaching

Todd von Helms

CHARLES HADDON SPURGEON was born on 19 June 1834 in a small cottage in Essex County. His father worked part-time as the clerk of a coalminer, and also served as a Congregational preacher. Because of financial reasons, just after his first birthday, Charles went to live with his grandparents in the small village of Stambourne, where his grandfather, the Reverend James Spurgeon, led the local Congregational church. Before learning how to read, Charles marveled at the pictures in Bunyan's *Pilgrim's Progress,* a classic that he first read at age six and would go on to read more than 100 times during his lifetime. Young Charles enjoyed a photographic memory, took full advantage of his grandfather's Puritan library, would often memorize scripture and hymns, and quote the works of Bunyan, Baxter, Owen, and Edwards. Despite his growing knowledge of scripture and Puritan literature, Charles wrestled with his spiritual condition until the day that he experienced salvation while taking shelter from a snowstorm in a Primitive Methodist Church in Colchester, forty miles north of London. On this particular Sunday in 1850, when the snow prevented the minister from making it to the meetinghouse, an ill-prepared layman, after fumbling through a text, said directly to Spurgeon, *"Young man, look to Jesus Christ. Look! Look! Look! You have nothing to do but to look and live."*[230] From that day forward, Christ, as revealed in scripture, became central to everything Spurgeon believed, preached, taught, and lived.

Spurgeon believed preaching to be God's primary means of drawing sinners, and that every sermon should contain the gospel and aim at conversion. Regardless of tradition or popular opinion, every decision

Spurgeon made had to be informed and supported by the Word of God. The first major decision came just months after his conversion, when Spurgeon chose to break with his family's Independent religious tradition when he became convinced that scripture did not support the ritual of infant baptism. Though he did not agree that a second baptism was necessary, Spurgeon's father allowed his son to be baptized by immersion as an adult in the Lark River, the same river in which Andrew Fuller had baptized believers a half-century earlier.

During the months following his baptism, Spurgeon delivered homilies as a lay preacher before becoming the minister to a small village Baptist church in Waterbeach, located a few miles from Cambridge University. Though Spurgeon was small in stature and appeared younger than he was, his powerful, eloquent voice and compelling sermons, delivered extemporaneously from a one-page outline, attracted listeners from many miles away. Though the church had only forty members when Spurgeon arrived, within two years, nearly half of the 1,300 residents came to hear the preaching sensation each week. Before long, the rural pastor's reputation reached the big city.

In 1854, the Particular Baptist Church meeting at New Park Street in London, which had an honorable history of preachers, including Benjamin Keach, John Gill, and John Rippon, called the nineteen-year-old "boy preacher" to be its pastor. In 1856, Charles married Susannah Thompson, the daughter of a prosperous ribbon manufacturer, whom he had baptized the previous year. In 1857, Susannah gave birth to twin sons, Charles and Thomas, both of whom would eventually be baptized by their father and go on to become ministers. At a time when London was experiencing considerable economic and social distress, thousands came to hear Spurgeon offer hope and Good News. Much of his success stemmed from his ability to convey the doctrines of grace in the language of the people.

On many occasions, Spurgeon preached to audiences in excess of ten thousand. Not since the days of Whitefield had England experienced one who attracted so many to hear a sermon. Despite enlarging the meetinghouse twice, making plans for a larger space became inevitable. In order to accommodate the burgeoning crowds while the larger church was being built, services were held at concert venues, such as Exeter Hall and Royal Surrey Gardens Music Hall. Nearly twenty-four thousand came to hear Spurgeon preach at the Crystal Palace in London. During the three-year construction period of the new building, church membership grew to more than five thousand. In addition to his listeners, even more people read Spurgeon's published sermons. In his heyday, twenty-five thousand copies of his sermons were sold each week. When the fully paid-for Metropolitan Tabernacle Church opened in south London in 1861, twenty-seven-year-old Spurgeon served the largest Protestant congregation in the world. He would preach from the large platform, often walking back and forth as he delivered graphic stories and thoroughly biblical sermons. Every Sunday for the next thirty-one years, six thousand congregants seated inside, as well as those standing shoulder-to-shoulder outside listening through the windows, would marvel at Spurgeon's persuasive oration.

Spurgeon built his extraordinary life and ministry upon the foundation of prayer and humility. Spurgeon claimed that "the minister who does not earnestly pray over his work must be vain and conceited, and careless about his ministry."[231] He constantly sought an outpouring of power, and fervently prayed for revival. He spoke the language of the common people, and even critics appreciated his oratory skills. Always motivated by pleasing the Lord, Spurgeon seldom responded to the negative press, which in turn caused his fame to spread even more. Despite the continual increase in parishioners and popularity, Spurgeon remained humble, never sought ordination, and preferred the title "Pastor" instead of "Reverend." The only time he wore clerical garb was when he preached in Calvin's pulpit in Geneva. His compelling sermons were filled with stories and occasional humor that resonated with everyone—rich and poor, educated and uneducated, young and old. When asked why God granted him so much success in ministry, Spurgeon replied, "My people pray for me."

Spurgeon viewed London as a mission field, and the tabernacle as the epicenter for launching ministries in order to shower God's grace on the entire city. Schools, orphanages, and nursing homes were founded, as well as a pastors' college to train ministers. In an age of social reform, Spurgeon never believed that social reforms were enough. Though he was willing to cooperate on matters of social concern with those holding differing theological views, he always made sure people knew that social reform was meaningless without sound theology and a personal relationship with Christ. Though Spurgeon saw himself as a Particular Baptist as defined by the Second London Confession of 1689, in the effort to win souls, he often crossed denominational lines. He frequently met with well-known Christians of influence, such as orphanage founder George Muller, missionary David Livingstone, and William Booth, cofounder of the Salvation Army.

Spurgeon often worked long hours, which is not surprising considering that each week was filled with personal interviews with every person desiring church membership or admission to the pastors' college. He was a voracious reader who was seldom seen without a book in hand. Each week Spurgeon conducted personal visits, distributed witnessing tracts, responded to hundreds of letters, taught at the college, edited weekly sermons for publication, worked on the monthly *Sword and the Trowel* magazine, and preached on numerous occasions.

Considering the hardships faced throughout much of his adult life, Spurgeon's achievements are even more remarkable. He often suffered from depression and periodic illness, including rheumatic gout and invalidism. His wife, Susannah, became an invalid at age thirty-three in 1868, and was seldom able to accompany her husband in public. From age thirty-five onward, Spurgeon dealt with insomnia because of physical pain, and typically needed several weeks every year in order to overcome exhaustion. Instead of desiring pity, Spurgeon embraced hardship as God's way of strengthening his faith and ability to help those entrusted to his care. Spurgeon claimed that his firsthand experience enabled him to "speak a word in season to one that is weary," and that "the way to stronger faith usually lies along the rough pathway of sorrow."[232]

The final five years of Spurgeon's life were filled with controversy, particularly what came to be known as the "Down Grade Controversy." Spurgeon was seldom hospitable to those with whom he disagreed, especially when he believed that theological truth was being compromised. Spurgeon tried to warn fellow ministers about the rise of liberalism within many churches that comprised the Baptist Union. Spurgeon charged that some ministers were abandoning traditional doctrines such as biblical infallibility and Christ's substitutionary atonement, and were thus, "on a slippery slope, or Down Grade" from the essential doctrines. Members of the Baptist Union, rather than addressing the central theological issues in dispute, chose to censor Spurgeon, which led to his grudging resignation in 1887. The majority in the denomination agreed with Spurgeon's unwavering stance on doctrinal purity, but for the sake of unity remained silent. Many resented Spurgeon's uncompromising actions during the denominational dispute, and neither the Baptist Union nor Spurgeon would fully recover from the damage caused by the controversy.

Spurgeon claimed that, "the way to be very great is to be very little," and that "we must see to it that God's glory is the one sole object of all that we do."[233] Spurgeon died on 31 January 1892. An estimated sixty thousand people visited the tabernacle to see where his body lay during a three-day period. All businesses, including pubs, were closed on the day that one hundred thousand people stood along his two-mile funeral procession. Spurgeon never sought great things for himself, yet few could resist the magnetic influence that clearly resulted from his dependence on the sovereign Lord. He had no university or seminary degree, yet is the most widely published English-speaking preacher in history. He always preached the Bible, and did so whenever and wherever he could. By the time of his death, Spurgeon had preached nearly thirty-six thousand sermons, many of which have been published in a sixty-three volume set. Additionally, Spurgeon published 140 works during his lifetime, including his seven-volume *Treasury of David*, considered to be one of the best commentaries on the Psalms ever written. His personal library of twelve thousand volumes contained one thousand works published before 1700, including all of the writings of his favorite Puritan heroes that often appeared in his sermons. Spurgeon baptized more than ten thousand converts during his thirty-five years of faithful soul-winning. The aforementioned glimpse of Spurgeon's life and ministry should give every reader a sense of why this Baptist minister was the greatest preacher of the nineteenth century and has been fittingly labeled the "Prince of Preachers."

Suggested Reading

Dallimore, Arnold. *Spurgeon: A New Biography*. Carlisle PA: Banner of Truth, 2005.
Drummond, Lewis A. *Spurgeon: Prince of Preachers*. Grand Rapids: Kregel, 1992.
Spurgeon, Charles. *C.H. Spurgeon Autobiography*. 2 volumes. Carlisle PA: Banner of Truth, 2011.
———. *Lectures to My Students: Complete and Unabridged*. Grand Rapids: Zondervan, 1954.
———. *The Treasury of David*. 3 volumes. Grand Rapids: Kregel, 2004.

Lottie Moon
(1840–1912)

Pioneer Missionary and Southern Baptist "Saint"

Missions

Melody Maxwell

COSTUMED INTERPRETERS ACROSS several states regularly reenact her life, although more than one hundred years have passed since her death. She is the subject of a forthcoming full-length feature film. Hundreds of Southern Baptists have traveled more than six thousand miles each way to visit locations associated with her life, while others continue to make shorter pilgrimages to sites scattered across central Virginia. The Episcopal Church observes an annual feast day in her honor. More than two billion dollars have been raised through an offering named in her memory. Mission board leaders and other fans have carried a paper doll and a life-sized cutout of her on their travels around the world. Hers is a household name among millions of current and former Southern Baptists. Publishers have produced scores of books, articles, pamphlets, plays, children's books, a cookbook, and even a musical about her. And although she lived before the days of the computer, she currently has more than 4,500 friends on Facebook.

Who is this renowned woman? She is none other than Lottie Moon, of course. Has any other Southern Baptist, past or present, male or female, ever garnered such acclaim? With little exaggeration, Moon has been called "an acknowledged saint to a church that suspects saints"; "the quintessential symbol of foreign missions"; and "perhaps the most familiar of all Southern Baptists."[234] Her service as a Foreign Mission Board missionary to China from 1873 to 1912 has captured the hearts and imaginations of Southern Baptists as has none other, influencing countless individuals to pray, give, and even serve as missionaries themselves. Even women and men who no longer consider themselves

Southern Baptists often recall how they were inspired by hearing stories about Moon in their childhood churches every December. She was one of the first single women sent by FMB, one of the board's most prodigious letter writers, a catalyst for the SBC's most significant missions offering, and a figure whose story was considered even more meaningful upon her death. Through her life of mission service, as well as her ongoing legacy, Lottie Moon has proved an enduring witness to the Baptist heritage.

Charlotte Digges Moon was born into a position of privilege on 12 December 1840, in Albemarle County, Virginia. Her parents, Edward and Anna Moon, owned the expansive Viewmont plantation and, with it, more than fifty slaves. Along with the six of her siblings who survived infancy, Lottie Moon benefitted from private tutoring as well as attendance at Scottsville Baptist Church, which her father helped found. Despite his death in 1853, the family's wealth allowed Moon—like her siblings—to continue her studies, first at Hollins Institute and then at Albemarle Female Institute, where she became one of the first Southern women to complete coursework for a master's degree. During this period, she also professed faith in Christ, joining Charlottesville's First Baptist Church. However, the fortunes of the Moon family, like those of many across the South, suffered as a result of the Civil War. Unable to fulfill her desire to serve as a missionary during these turbulent years, Lottie Moon returned to Viewmont, watching her family's wealth decline precipitously as a result of wartime circumstances. After at least one stint as a private tutor, she moved to Danville, Kentucky by 1868, where she taught at Danville Female Seminary and Caldwell Female Institute. In 1871 Moon and her friend Anna Safford moved to Cartersville, Georgia and opened a school for girls, which prospered under their leadership.

Meanwhile, Lottie Moon's youngest sister, Edmonia, learned in 1872 that FMB had recently reversed its policy against sending single women to serve as missionaries, due in part to the rise of female missions supporters among Southern Baptists. Edmonia quickly applied for missionary service, was appointed, and arrived in China later that year alongside Lula Whilden, the other single woman sent by the board at that time. These events caused Lottie Moon to reconsider her previous interest in missions work, soon leading her to seek appointment with

FMB as well. On 1 September 1873, Moon (along with Safford, a new Presbyterian missionary) set sail for China, one of the first single women to do so under the auspices of the SBC.

Once in China, Moon began her ministry in the city of Tengchow in Shantung Province (now Penglai in Shandong Province), which would remain her home for most of the next forty years. As was typical of the contemporary woman's missionary movement, she began her work largely among women and children. In addition to leading various girls' schools—which she later disparaged as "petty work"[235]—Moon and her female colleagues also participated in itinerant ministry in rural villages, teaching the women and children they encountered about God. But as she once explained to FMB leader Henry Tupper, "That the men chose to listen, too, was no fault of mine."[236] During these years, Moon also weathered the chronic illness and departure of her sister Edmonia, an ongoing controversy between North China mission leaders T. P. Crawford and J. B. Hartwell, and a broken engagement with religion professor Crawford Toy, possibly because of his unorthodox beliefs. She threatened to resign, however, when FMB considered prohibiting single female missionaries from voting at mission meetings, partially in response to her impassioned writings on the subject. Perhaps due to her influence, this ban did not occur.

Energized by her evangelistic work, in 1885 Moon moved around one hundred miles inland to the city of Pingtu (now Pingdu), becoming the first Southern Baptist woman to pioneer a mission station in China's interior. Here she began a productive ministry of several years, which included frequent evangelistic visits to nearby villages such as Shaling. In order to better identify with those around her, she adopted Chinese dress, an action that was controversial among Western missionaries at the time. And as in previous years, she maintained voluminous correspondence with Southern Baptists in the United States, with her letters frequently printed in the *Foreign Mission Journal*. Recognizing the need for additional workers—and for furloughs for those already on the field—Moon encouraged Southern Baptist women to give generously and to consider organizing for greater support of missions. In what became her most famous letter, written in 1887, she urged the women to observe a week of prayer and self-denial for missions in December: "Is not 'the festive season,' when families and friends exchange gifts in memory of The Gift laid on the altar of the world…the most appropriate time to consecrate a portion from abounding riches and scant poverty to send forth the good tidings of great joy into all the earth?"[237] Detailing the advances that had resulted when Southern Methodist women formed a national board of missions, she also asserted that for Southern Baptist women, "organization in subordination to the [Foreign Mission] Board is the imperative need of the hour."[238]

With these words, Moon cast her support behind the emerging efforts of Southern Baptist women to establish a national missions organization, as women of many other denominations had done in previous years. A few months later, the organization that became known as Woman's Missionary Union, Auxiliary to the Southern Baptist Convention, was formed. The women also heeded her recommendation to pray and give, in December 1888 and early 1889 contributing enough funds to send three new single women to China to assist "our dear Miss Moon."[239] This Christmas offering became a longstanding and respected tradition among Southern Baptists. Moon's suggestions thus helped lead Southern Baptist women to a position of greater influence within a denomination in which they were often marginalized. Soon the women's determined missions efforts and fundraising were not easily ignored.

As WMU grew in number and influence, its members—along with other Southern Baptists—were thrilled to hear stories of Moon's continuing work in China. Now a respected veteran in the North China mission, Moon mentored younger missionaries, some of whom had felt led to mission service after hearing about her ministry. As these new recruits took up the work at Pingtu, Moon hosted dozens of Chinese visitors in her home in Tengchow, undertook schoolwork once again, and nursed several ill missionaries back to health. While at times delayed from her work because of war, whenever possible she continued her duties even after other missionaries had fled. By fall 1912, however, other missionaries noticed a sharp decline in Moon's health. With deep concern over local famine victims and the growing debt of FMB, along with what she described as "troubles in my mind,"[240] Moon became convinced that she had exhausted her bank account when, in fact, she still had sufficient funds. A missionary nurse noted her depression and mental decline, as well as the large growth behind her ear and her greatly decreased appetite. After being moved from place to place for care, Moon was eventually carried aboard a ship bound for the United States, accompanied by a missionary nurse. On 24 December 1912, at age seventy-two, she passed away at the port of Kobe, Japan. The ship's captain attributed her death to "melancholia and senility";[241] her remains were soon cremated and transported to Virginia.

The circumstances surrounding Lottie Moon's death are a matter of debate. Current and former Southern Baptists will likely recall hearing that Moon starved herself to death in order to feed the Chinese people. The first—and highly influential—book-length biography of Moon put it this way: "If her Pingtu Christians were starving, then she would eat no more! If the debt on the Board could not be lifted, then she would live no more on borrowed money."[242] Years later, another prominent biography explained that "Miss Moon had ceased to eat so that her impoverished Chinese might be fed."[243] However, a scholarly biography of Moon published in 2011 compellingly challenged this claim, carefully detailing the circumstances surrounding Moon's death and explaining how the legend of her starvation arose to glorify her legacy and encourage Southern Baptists to greater financial sacrifice.[244] According to this account, the missionary who had checked Moon's bank account in 1912 later protested, "I never heard a missionary [at the time] say that she starved to death to help with relief."[245] Perhaps dementia, rather than self-sacrifice, was the primary factor in Moon's death. Nearly all interpreters agree that Moon's mental capacities declined in her last days; whether this was a cause or an effect of her intense concern for the needy and her lack of nourishment continues to be contested.

Even if Moon did not actually die as a Christ-like martyr[246] for the people of North China, inspirational stories of her self-sacrifice have helped motivate Southern Baptists' missions giving for more than one hundred years. The Christmas offering that Moon began among Southern Baptist women in 1888 was renamed the Lottie Moon Christmas Offering in 1918, and has remained a fixture on the denominational calendar to this day. Indeed, a visitor to a present-day Southern Baptist church during the month of December would likely hear more about Lottie Moon than about Advent, demonstrating both the denomination's historic emphasis on missions and its aversion to the liturgical calendar. Through LMCO, the SBC has raised more than two billion dollars for international missions; giving increased dramatically the first year Moon's story was included in offering materials. "Because so much emotion went with the money,"[247] as one interpreter put it, LMCO (along with its counterpart, the Annie Armstrong Offering for home missions) was not subsumed into the SBC's coordinated giving plan in the 1920s, as were other special offerings.

However, LMCO did become entangled in the conflict surrounding the SBC during the latter years of the twentieth century, demonstrating the offering's significance within the denomination. WMU, whose founding Moon had supported a century earlier, continued to promote LMCO, although the women no longer dictated its allocations and now encouraged all church members to give to the offering to support FMB. However, FMB suspected WMU leaders of sympathizing with SBC moderates instead of conservatives. In 1995 WMU discovered that FMB had secretly attempted to trademark LMCO, presumably so that WMU would not use the offering to support moderate causes. Conflict ensued, although the two parties eventually came to an agreement on the matter. Evidently, Lottie Moon's name carried so much weight among Southern Baptists by this time that denominational leaders fought to control it.

Indeed, Southern Baptists have appropriated Moon's name and her legacy for a variety of emphases throughout the years, including both conservative and moderate ideals. During a period of significant denominational debt, her action and sacrifice were emphasized to encourage larger financial gifts; but by the 1950s, Lottie Moon was identified as a Southern belle, a figure admirable to middle-class Southern Baptist homemakers during a period of increased racial turmoil.[248] By the 1970s, Moon became revered by some as a radical; as one writer put it, she had been "a 'women's libber' who threatened to resign unless FMB allowed her to participate in policy-making."[249] Even today, Moon's life is explained in divergent ways—and ones often mirroring the convictions of her interpreters. Moderate Baptists emphasize that she was "an early Southern Baptist women's rights advocate" who "argu[ed] with the SBC's male patriarchy";[250] conservatives praise (among other things) her "deep affirmation of biblical authority, inerrancy and infallibility…[and]

urgent focus on conversion."[251] Everyone, it seems, is eager to claim the heritage of the woman who has become a legend in Baptist life. Continued discussions about Moon's views and strategies demonstrate her abiding influence in the twenty-first century.

"To be a Southern Baptist is to understand Lottie Moon," one seminary president recently asserted.[252] Few current or former Southern Baptists would likely disagree. It is remarkable that in a tradition that opposes the veneration of saints and promotes almost exclusively male leadership, one woman has been extolled far and wide for over a century. Moon's life was certainly outstanding: she served as a pioneer female missionary, helped begin a significant women's organization and offering, and contributed to mission policies on single women and on furloughs, among other accomplishments. But Moon's enduring legacy is also noteworthy. Her widespread acclaim demonstrates the varied ways that Southern Baptists have thought about missions and women's roles over the course of more than a century. Even today, pastors invoke Moon's name from the pulpit to support the denomination's missions emphases, while children's teachers shape stories about "Miss Lottie" for a new generation. Perhaps it is not an exaggeration to say that anyone who wants to better understand Baptists, missions history, or Christian women's roles would do well to examine the life and legacy of Lottie Moon.

Suggested Reading

Allen, Catherine. *The New Lottie Moon Story*. 2nd edition. Birmingham AL: Woman's Missionary Union, 1997.

Flowers, Elizabeth. "The Contested Legacy of Lottie Moon: Southern Baptists, Women, and Partisan Protestantism." In *Through a Glass Darkly: Contested Notions of Baptist Identity*, edited by Keith Harper, 112–44. Tuscaloosa: University of Alabama Press, 2012.

Harper, Keith, ed. *Send the Light: Lottie Moon's Letters and Other Writings*. Macon GA: Mercer University Press, 2002.

Hyatt, Irwin T., Jr. *Our Ordered Lives Confess: Three Nineteenth-Century American Missionaries in East Shantung*. Cambridge MA: Harvard University Press, 1976.

Sullivan, Regina. *Lottie Moon: A Southern Baptist Missionary to China in History and Legend*. Baton Rouge: Louisiana State University Press, 2011.

E. C. Morris
(1855–1922)

Trailblazer for Racial Equality

Social Justice

Pamela R. Durso

ELECTED IN 1895 as president of the National Baptist Convention (NBC), Elias Camp Morris served faithfully in the role for twenty-seven years. While today his name is not well known, even among African-American Baptists, his influence continues to this day. Morris used his denominational leadership position, his community involvement, and his pulpit as a means to work for religious autonomy and full freedom for African Americans. His strong calls for and work toward racial equality in the churches and in American society pre-dated the Civil Rights Movement by nearly fifty years, making him a trailblazer, one who helped pave the way for other Baptist ministers who took up this cause in the 1950s.

Born a slave on 7 May 1855 in Murray County, Georgia, Morris moved with his family after the end of the Civil War to Tennessee and then to Alabama. He attended school only sporadically during his childhood and was mostly self-educated. Both his parents died by the time he was fourteen years old, and formal education ceased to be even a possibility. To support himself, Morris became an apprentice to a shoemaker.[253]

In 1874, Morris began his faith journey, converting to Christianity that year and answering a call to ministry the next. He soon began preaching whenever and wherever he had opportunity. Two years later, he moved to Helena, Arkansas, where he worked as a shoemaker during the week and preached in churches on Sundays. Five years later, Morris accepted the pastorate of Centennial Baptist Church in Helena, a church with only twenty-three members. He served the congregation for forty-three years, and at the time of his death, the church had 1,000 members.

During his early years as pastor of Centennial Baptist Church, Morris quickly rose to prominence as a denominational leader among Arkansas Baptists. He assisted in the organization of Black Baptist associations in Phillips, Lee, and Monroe Counties. He served from 1880 to 1881 as the secretary of the African-American Arkansas Baptist State Convention, and in 1882, he became that convention's president, an office he held for the next thirty-five years. In that role, Morris supervised the development of a state denominational newspaper, the *Arkansas Times*, which was later renamed the *Baptist Vanguard*.[254]

As a denominational leader in the state, Morris served as a catalyst in 1884 for the founding of an African-American Baptist seminary and then served as the chair of its trustee board for many years. Originally known as the Minister's Institute, the school took the name Arkansas Baptist College in 1886. In 2014, the school continues to live into the vision set forth by Morris. Now a private, four-year liberal arts college located in downtown Little Rock, Arkansas Baptist College "is dedicated to the development of graduates who are exceptionally educated, spiritually and culturally aware, and able to meet the demands of our rapidly advancing society."[255]

In the same year that he helped found the school, Morris married Fannie Ella Austin, of whom he later wrote, "[N]othing has added so much to" my success "as the faithfulness and devotion of her who has willingly shared all my griefs and sorrows and…been so very self-denying that the cause of God and the Baptists might go on, so far was we had to do with it."[256] The couple had eight children, five who lived past childhood and three of whom became Baptist.

In 1895, Morris's prominence on the denominational scene grew as he took on a national leadership role. That year the newly established National Baptist Convention elected him to his first term as president. He served in that role for the next twenty-seven years. As president of this African-American Baptist convention, Morris began working alongside White Baptists. He was a speaker at the November 1911 meeting of Arkansas's White state Baptist convention and served on the predominantly White executive committees of the General Convention of Baptists of North America and the Baptist World Alliance (BWA). His leadership soon expanded outside Baptist circles, and he became a member of the executive committee of the Congress of English Speaking Peoples of the World and served as a vice president of the interracial Federal Council of Churches of Christ.[257]

Morris's skill at connecting and partnering with other organizations was especially evident in his relationship to the global Baptist organization, the BWA, which first convened in 1905. At its first congress held in London, European Baptist leaders, unaware of the existence of more than two million African-American Baptists and their denominational organizations, did not invite any African Americans to participate in the program. Fortunately, Morris was aware of this new movement, and he gathered a group of over thirty National Baptists and together they traveled to the congress, where they submitted their credentials. BWA leaders then invited several National Baptists, including Morris, to speak, and they made a "splendid impression."[258] For the next congress, held in 1911 in Philadelphia, over one hundred National Baptists participated in its planning and programing.

As a longtime pastor and denominational statesman, Morris left many legacies in Baptist life, and he accomplished much despite his own limited educational background. In recognition of his work, the State University in Louisville, Kentucky bestowed on Morris an honorary Doctor of Divinity degree, and in 1902, the Agricultural and Mechanical College in Normal, Alabama awarded him an honorary Doctor of Philosophy degree.[259]

Over the course of his ministry career, Morris preached and spoke regularly at denominational meetings. In 1901, the National Baptist Publication Board gathered many of Morris's addresses and published them in *Sermons, Addresses and Reminiscences, and Important Correspondence, with a Picture Gallery of Eminent Ministers and Scholars.* In the preface to this book, Morris, like many nineteenth-century people of faith, expressed in it his desire to be useful. He also humbly apologized for even printing his writings. He did note that he hoped to "leave to the denomination a written record of what was accomplished by the Negro Baptists in the United States in the first years of their separate effort at Christian work." Morris also stated that he firmly believed "in the possibilities of the race," and that it was "the imperative duty of Negro Baptists leaders to develop this mighty force for the glory of God and the further redemption of the race."[260] Morris's words, while exaggerated in their expression of humility, reflect his driving need to contribute to the betterment of the world and to racial equality in churches and in American society.

In his 1898 and 1900 NBC addresses, Morris spoke of his understanding of Baptist origins, making reference to the founding of the Baptist tradition and revealing his Landmark leanings. Convinced that Baptists could trace their beginnings back to John the Baptist, "the greatest of Baptist preachers," Morris proclaimed in 1898, "I do not fear the criticism that may follow after I tell you that the history of the Baptists covers all the time from the days of John the Baptist until now, with the possible exception of that 'time and half a time' spoken of in the prophecy of this book, where the Church appears to be in obscurity, but by no means is it extinct." Two years later, Morris noted, "Baptists believe that John the Baptist was a man sent from God, but that Heaven only gave him the honor of introducing the Son of God, who is the embodiment of the Church—the Alpha and Omega. The figures and shadows of the Church set forth in prophecy all go to show that the Baptists represent the true intent and purpose which God had in mind before the incarnation of his Son." He then stated, "Was Christ a Baptist? is a question which can be answered by asking, *Was he baptized?* If he was baptized, he was a Baptist or else baptism will not make one a Baptist. If he was a Baptist, then the Baptists originated in him, for he is the first and the last, the beginning and the ending of all things."[261]

While Morris may not have been on the right track with regard to Baptist beginnings, he certainly was a prophetic preacher. His sermons revealed his willingness to speak words of truth, no matter how painful they might be to his audience. In his 1898 convention sermon, Morris retold the story of Joseph, focusing on Joseph's involuntary separation from his family. Morris then moved to denounce slavery, professing that enslavement must be seen as the involuntary separation of a man or woman from their family: "It has separated husband and wife, parents and children, brother and sister, and broken the cords of affection which nature and nature's God have entwined around the hearts of a happy family."²⁶²

In this same sermon, Morris proclaimed that the church "has apparently gone to sleep" and allowed politicians and other leaders to silence what should have been the church's message, which was "the heaven-appointed doctrine" of "the social equality of the races and classes." Surely, this doctrine was what Jesus taught, Morris concluded, and this doctrine was how Jesus lived. "'Christ Jesus came into the world to save sinners,' not White sinners, nor Black sinners, nor red sinners, but sinners!" All people of all races who enlist under the banner of the Cross, Morris asserted, "will form one mighty army to go mightily against the power of darkness…and break down the strong towers of Satan."²⁶³

Morris's sermons revealed his commitment to racial equality, but a sermon he delivered on 15 September 1897, "Negro Baptists—Retrospective and Prospective," demonstrated his willingness to fight for racial equality. In the sermon, the Baptist leader alluded to a problem that brought about the NBC's organization. The American Baptist Publication Society, an entity of the White Northern Baptist Convention, realized by the late nineteenth century that African Americans made up a large portion of that society's patronage. Thus, the society's administrators thought it practical to encourage this constituency by inviting African-American writers to contribute articles, and many well-qualified leaders accepted the invitation. Unfortunately, White Baptists protested so intensely that the publishers discontinued the employment of the African-American writers.

After this rejection, African-American Baptists decided to begin a publishing effort of their own, and Morris used his influence as a pastor and as NBC president to further this new venture. He denounced the decision of the Northern Baptists, speaking forceful words in favor of the African-American Baptists, declaring that they had the skills and knowledge to operate their own educational printing business. National Baptists lived up to his expectations, and in January 1897, they began publishing and distributing their own curriculum.

Nine months later, Morris preached the sermon "Negro Baptists—Retrospective and Prospective" to the "Brethren of the Convention,

Ladies and Gentlemen" who had gathered in Boston for the NBC meeting. In his sermon, Morris clearly established the rights of African Americans. He stated, "Permit me to say in this connection, that when these chosen men of God, carved in ebony, shall be permitted to publish the gospel of God's dear son to every creature, and not forced to preach it to creatures of their own race, there will be a wonderful change of belief among the White Christians of this country."[264]

Morris, in this sermon and all his writings, indicted the White Christians who remained silent about racial injustices. He took a strong stand in advocating the right of African Americans to establish independent religious associations, believing that they must be free from White leadership and become self-sufficient. Such freedom, Morris contended, was needed not only of publishing but also in all other efforts, including education. He concluded the sermon by calling those gathered to work harder:

> We have done fairly well in establishing and maintaining Christian schools and have made some progress in the professions. But these are not enough. Our people are to be led to the business of commercial affairs of the country and into the industrial and agricultural pursuits, and in this, as in other matters, they must be taught by their ministers. Encourage the people to go into business and become noteworthy in commerce as well as in religion, thereby commanding the respect of all mankind.[265]

While Morris's audiences applauded his strong commitment to racial equality, his belief that equality should extend beyond race and class to gender may have surprised them. In his "Brotherhood of Man" sermon, Morris stated that the "Syro-Phenician woman had no legal, social, or racial rights which would warrant her in approaching the Son of God, but she had a religious right, and she contended for that right." The Baptist leader then proclaimed, "Christ is not the Saviour of any particular race or class, but 'whosoever will may take the water of life freely.'" In a later writing, "The National Baptist Catechism," Morris noted that the NBC meetings would receive women as delegates at NBC meetings and "no discrimination" should exist because of gender.

Women were to be "given the same privileges as the men" and should be named to committees and be put on the program.[266]

Baptists today need to be reminded of Morris's great legacy, his long tenure as pastor of a great church, his participation in the founding and support of a college for African-American Baptists, his faithful leadership of state and national denominational organizations, his charismatic preaching and writing, and his willingness to speak truth to people of all races on the important issues of his day. Phyllis Hammonds, who grew up in Centennial Baptist Church and, in 2004, established the E. C. Morris Foundation, said of Morris, "I see him as the precursor to Martin Luther King".... Not only was he an organizer, he was a humanitarian, an entrepreneur. He was an author. He took care of the poor. He spoke for the disenfranchised. He was the person who was recognized and well-respected in both African-American and the White communities."[267] Morris was certainly a trailblazer for the cause of racial equality, and his leadership among Baptists, both African American and White, helped lay the foundation for the work done by other Baptist preachers in the late twentieth century.

Suggested Reading

Lewis, Todd. *Encyclopedia of Arkansas History and Culture*, "Elias Camp Morris (1855–1922)," http://encyclopediaofarkansas.net/encyclopedia/entry-detail.aspx?entryID=433.

Morris, E. C. *Sermons, Addresses and Reminiscences, and Important Correspondence, with a Picture Gallery of Eminent Ministers and Scholars*. Nashville TN: National Baptist Publication Board, 1901, http://docsouth.unc.edu/church/morris/morris.html.

Simmons, Martha, and Frank A. Thomas, editors. *Preaching with Sacred Fire: An Anthology of African American Sermons, 1750 to the Present*. New York: W. W. Norton and Company, 2010.

Washington, James Melvin. *Frustrated Fellowship: The Black Baptist Quest for Social Power*. Macon GA: Mercer University Press, 2004.

E. Y. Mullins
(1860–1928)

Guardian of Voluntary Faith

Freedom of Conscience

Douglas Weaver

EDGAR YOUNG MULLINS was born in Franklin County, Mississippi on 5 January 1860. One of nine siblings, Mullins's family moved to Corsicana, Texas, when he was eight years old. After high school, Mullins graduated as part of the first class of what is now Texas A&M University (1876–1879).

Mullins's background was deeply religious—both his father and grandfather were Baptist ministers—but he only became a Christian the year after college, when he had a conversion experience while attending a revival at First Baptist Church, Dallas. Consequently, he abandoned plans for law school in order to attend seminary and enter the ministry. He graduated from Southern Baptists' only seminary at that time, Southern Baptist Theological Seminary, Louisville, Kentucky, in 1885.

After seminary, Mullins wanted to be a missionary to Brazil, but funds were not available through the Foreign Mission Board of the Southern Baptist Convention. He then became pastor of Harrodsburg Baptist Church (Kentucky). A year later (2 June 1886), Mullins married Isla May Hawley (who became a writer of novels). She gave birth to two sons but both died at an early age. In spring 1888, Mullins declined an opportunity to move to San Antonio in his home state of Texas when his wife's health would not permit relocation.

In July 1888, Mullins began a seven-year pastorate at Lee Street Baptist Church, Baltimore, Maryland. In many ways, Mullins was a typical southern evangelical; he made evangelism the priority of his ministry. However, he combined the focus on personal faith with a moderate type of social gospel. During Baltimore's encounters of labor strife in 1894–1895, for example, Mullins normally supported the grievances of laborers on strike. Mullins also maintained an interest in scholarly pursuits. He took a course in logic at John Hopkins University and contributed a weekly column called "The Signal Station" while serving as one of the editors of the *Maryland Baptist*. His first book, a series of sermons titled *Christ's Coming and His Kingdom*, was also published (1894).

Mullins left the pastorate to become an associate secretary at the Foreign Mission Board of the SBC in 1895, but stayed only six months (September 1895–March 1896). Evidently, his popularity as a lecturer across the South created tension with the agency's leader, R. H. Willingham. Mullins returned to the pastorate at Newton Centre Baptist Church, Newton, Massachusetts, a highly educated congregation that included numerous faculty members of Newton Theological Institution, including the school's president, Alvah Hovey. Mullins did not trumpet social themes as he had in Baltimore, though he encouraged American Baptists to be involved in the education of African Americans in the South. The call of southern ministers to Northern Baptist churches was not a rarity in the late nineteenth century, but with the tightening of denominational identities in the early decades of the twentieth century, Mullins's extensive work North and South would soon be a relic.

Mullins became the fourth president of his alma mater, Southern Baptist Theological Seminary, in 1899. The seminary was engulfed in a life-threatening conflict now called the "Whitsitt Controversy." President William H. Whitsitt had created a firestorm in his work as a church historian. From his primary source research, Whitsitt concluded that Baptist origins dated to 1644 in England and the recovery of believer's baptism by immersion. The existing popular belief in church secessionism—identified with the influential nineteenth-century Baptist movement called Landmarks, but with precedents throughout Baptist history—was that Baptists could trace their lineage directly back to the New Testament and, thus, were the only apostolic New Testament Church. When Southern Baptists threatened to withhold financial support and, thus, endanger the life of the seminary on account of Whitsitt's views, he resigned.

During the Whitsitt Controversy, Mullins wrote articles for the *Religious Herald* of Virginia that voiced strong support for Whitsitt and portrayed his opponents as pitiless and reckless. Yet, when Mullins was mentioned as a candidate for the seminary presidency, he was considered an outsider to the Whitsitt conflict. While surprised he had been nominated, Mullins accepted the presidency and began a twenty-eight-year tenure (1899–1928). Beyond presidential duties, Mullins was a professor of theology.

The Louisville Seminary accomplished several "firsts" during Mullins's initial decade. In 1902, the seminary opened classes to women, although they were not registered as students. In 1907, with the strong support of Professor W. O. Carver, the Woman's Missionary Union Training School was opened. Mullins also established "Founders Day" and ventured to invite former President Whitsitt to return to speak at the anniversary of the seminary's origins. A year earlier, a new chair in Sunday school pedagogy was initiated that was financially underwritten by both the seminary and the Sunday School Board of the SBC.

Mullins provided a forum for seminary scholarship with the creation of the *Review and Expositor* (1904). In his position as editor-in-chief, he wanted the journal to help unify Baptists by providing a safe setting for scholarly Baptist voices among Baptists across the globe. The journal allowed for diverse opinions, and its existence in the post-Whitsitt era was a sign of academic freedom. Mullins's involvement in the *Review and Expositor* also revealed his participation—at least for the first half of his presidency—in the emerging emphasis on social reform in Southern Progressivism in the early twentieth century. He never advocated social programs in the vein of American Baptist Walter Rauschenbusch, however; in evangelical fashion, he supported social ministry as an outgrowth of redeemed individuals.

Mullins was the dominant scholarly voice among Southern Baptists in the first half of the twentieth century. He wrote prolifically in popular and scholarly journals and was at heart an apologist for the Christian faith. He penned seven books while seminary president: *Why Is Christianity True?* (1905), *The Axioms of Religion* (1908), *Baptist Beliefs* (1912), *Freedom and Authority in Religion* (1913), *Commentary on Ephesians and Colossians* (1913), *The Christian Religion in Its Doctrinal*

Expression (1917), and *Christianity at the Crossroads* (1924). Besides *The Axioms of Religion*, the book that received the widest attention was *The Christian Religion in Its Doctrinal Expression*. Southern Seminary used the book as its standard textbook in theology until 1947.

Mullins modeled robust denominational identity. He was involved in the Baptist World Alliance from its inception in 1905; he served as its president from 1923 to 1928 and gave a significant speech affirming the Baptist support of religious liberty in 1923. He served as president of the Southern Baptist Convention from 1921 to 1924. Mullins was also active at the state and associational levels in Kentucky. He preached and even served on ordination councils while a member of Broadway Baptist Church, Louisville.

In the 1920s, Mullins was involved in the Southern Baptist version of the Fundamentalist/ Modernist conflict that wreaked havoc in northern denominations. The dominant issues were biblical authority and evolution; teachers at denominational schools were accused of liberalism/heresy. Mullins contributed to a series of pamphlets, *The Fundamentals* (1910–1915), but his contribution was part of the more "moderate" phase of the developing fundamentalist movement. His article on the "testimony of Christian experience" touted personal experience as the cornerstone of theological method.

Mullins was no fundamentalist and clashed with those who insisted that the Southern Baptist Convention adopt a creed with an explicit anti-evolution statement. He called fundamentalists "Radicals and Extremists" and "hyper-orthodox" leaders "who want to put the thumb screws on everybody who does not agree in every detail with their statements of doctrine." They desired to control the SBC, Mullins warned, and in so doing "harass and muzzle teachers in our schools."[268] Mullins attempted to mediate the discontent of anti-evolutionists. He told the 1922 annual meeting of the SBC that denominational schools should teach the historic beliefs of the Christian faith. However, the Bible was a book of religion, not a scientific text. Evolution should not be taught as fact, yet firm faith and free research in the realm of science were both needed. The real issue was the affirmation of supernaturalism in the face of naturalistic claims.

In an attempt to keep the convention united, Mullins and other denominational loyalists led in the adoption of a new confession of faith, the *Baptist Faith and Message* (1925). The confession, largely written by Mullins, was based on the New Hampshire Confession of Faith, and included a preface emphasizing that confessions were not creeds but, rather, voluntary formulations of faith. The confession affirmed the sole authority of the Bible for "all religious opinions," but Mullins resisted the fundamentalist call to impose a specific scientific stance upon teachers in Baptist schools.

Mullins touted the compatibility of political democracy and Baptist principles, though he criticized the blind allegiance of "love it or leave it" nationalism. He normally refrained from political activity, but during the 1928 presidential election campaign, he openly opposed Al Smith, a Roman Catholic and soft on Prohibition in the minds of Southern Baptists. Unlike fundamentalists, however, Mullins focused only on Smith's views of Prohibition and he insisted that his opposition had nothing to do with religion.

In 1928, Mullins became ill and died. Baptists everywhere acknowledged his accomplishments. Some scholars believe that Mullins became more conservative in his last years. Others added that the conflicting requirements of being a diplomatic seminary president responsible for fundraising eventually made Mullins generally more cautious.

As his biography reveals, Mullins was an influential spokesperson for Baptists in his day. His enduring legacy, however, is often attributed to his publication of *The Axioms of Religion* (1908), which is usually regarded as the most significant work in defining Baptist identity in the twentieth century. Mullins himself desired a "fresh statement" on Baptist identity that said Baptist principles were the best hope to restore New Testament Christianity, but at the same time distanced Baptists from the intolerance and inferior history/tradition of church secessionism upon which Landmarkism (and some other denominations) was based.

Mullins outlined six axioms that shared much in common with earlier Baptist thought:

1. The theological axiom: The holy and loving God has a right to be sovereign.
2. The religious axiom: All souls have an equal right to direct access to God.
3. The ecclesiastical axiom: All believers have a right to equal privileges in the church (which thus affirmed longstanding Baptist ideas of local church autonomy, congregational polity, and the priesthood of believers).
4. The moral axiom: To be responsible, man must be free.
5. The religio-civic axiom: A free Church in a free State (i.e., separation of Church and State and religious freedom for all).
6. The social axiom: Love your neighbor as yourself.

At the base of the axioms, Mullins said, was soul competency, the concept most associated with his legacy. Mullins defined soul competency as the right of each individual (soul) to relate directly to God—that religion was a personal matter between the soul and God.[269] Baptists, of course, had highlighted the idea of soul liberty, the sacredness of the unfettered individual conscience, and the focus on individual voluntary faith since their origins in the seventeenth century. Mullins intensified this freedom tradition. He declared that soul competency was the "peculiar teaching" and the "historical significance" of Baptists.[270]

Mullins thus highlighted a trilogy: voluntary personal spiritual experience that answered to the sole authority of the Bible and the Lordship of Christ. Soul competency undergirded, then, the Baptist (and biblical, Mullins affirmed) practices of opposing infant baptism, affirming the necessity of personal conversion/believer's baptism/regenerate church membership and religious freedom for all, since every person was accountable to God individually at the Last Judgment. Soul competency further led, according to Mullins, to the right to private judgment in the reading of scripture ("The right of private judgment is a dangerous word, but it is a winged and emancipating word"[271]), which frowned upon creeds that could lead to a barren orthodoxy. Soul competency was not excessive individualism, for it was answerable to the spiritual egalitarianism of democratic congregationalism under the authority of the Bible and the Lordship of Christ.

Mullins believed soul competency and the axioms were foundational for the creation of authentic ecclesiology. The New Testament church was a spiritual community of "competent" believers who had a common individual experience of grace and a common loyalty to Jesus Christ. These believers were impelled by the Holy Spirit to be a part of the church. A biblical church was thus rooted in freedom and had no room for decision-making restricted to ecclesiastical oligarchies (i.e., sacerdotalism) or anything that hindered the voluntary faith and free conscience.

Not unexpectedly, given the influence of E. Y. Mullins, his legacy in the twentieth century has attracted attention. He has been viewed as the major denominational loyalist/centrist of the "Grand Compromise," which kept diverse constituencies of Southern Baptists united around the goals of missions, evangelism, local church independence, and personal freedom rather than a union based on doctrinal conformity.[272] Some detractors have accused him of introducing in Baptist life an excessive individualism (however his views are evaluated today, Mullins was not introducing, but continuing and popularizing, a deeply rooted Baptist focus on personal faith). He has also been attacked by some for facilitating a lack of focus upon doctrinal orthodoxy with his anti-creedalism. At the same time, Mullins's focus on voluntarism, personal religious experience, and religious liberty/free conscience has been praised for its continued relevance. For many Baptists, Mullins's focus on freedom for individual conscience captures both the best and the essence of 400-year-old Baptist DNA.

Suggested Reading

Ellis, William E. *A Man of Books and a Man of the People.* Macon GA: Mercer University Press, 1985.

Mullins, E. Y. *The Axioms of Religion* (1908). Edited by C. Douglas Weaver. Macon GA: Mercer University Press, 2010. Includes biographical material and a survey of the literature about Mullins.

———. "Why I Am a Baptist (1926)." *The Whitsitt Journal* 15/1 (Spring 2007): 3–6.

Weaver, C. Douglas. "The Baptist Ecclesiology of E. Y. Mullins: Individualism and the New Testament Church." *Baptist History and Heritage* 43/1 (Winter 2008): 18–34.

———. "E. Y. Mullins: Soul Competency and Social Ministry." *Perspectives in Religious Studies* 36/4 (Winter 2010): 447–62.

Walter Rauschenbusch
(1861–1918)

Pioneer of the Social Gospel

Social Justice

Glenn Jonas

WALTER RAUSCHENBUSCH HAD the unique ability to appeal to a variety of people on different levels. His greatness and popular appeal might best be illustrated in a story told by his first biographer, Dores Sharpe. Through much of his career, he struggled with deafness and, consequently, had difficulty communicating with strangers. Once, a friend met Rauschenbusch at Ellis Island to help him through U.S. Customs after a trip to Europe. The friend explained the situation to the Customs agent and asked him to be sympathetic. "Who did you say he was?" the agent asked. "Professor Walter Rauschenbusch," the friend replied. "Is he the duck that writes them prayers?" "Yes, that's the man." "Well, they're damn good prayers. I'll pass him as quickly as possible."[273]

Rauschenbusch was born in Rochester, New York, the son of German immigrants. His father came to the United States to be a Lutheran missionary, but became a Baptist and finally a professor in the German Department at Rochester Theological Seminary. Walter completed his early education in both the United States and Germany. He returned to the University of Rochester where he completed the B.A. degree in 1884 and a seminary degree from Rochester Theological Seminary in 1886.

Upon seminary graduation, he accepted a call as pastor to the Second German Baptist Church in New York City, located on the city's West Side on the edge of a section known as "Hell's Kitchen." This area of the city, notorious for gang activity, prostitution, crime, and general human misery, gave Rauschenbusch a perfect opportunity to express some of his developing ideas about how Christianity could impact society's problems. The city, filled with immigrants, held about 400,000 German immigrants, with only five German Baptist churches to minister to this large ethnic population. Therefore, he considered this move to be both challenging and exhilarating.[274]

Rauschenbusch assumed his pastoral duties with diligence and enthusiasm. The congregation of Second German Baptist Church had been through years of turmoil and bad ministers before he arrived. There were only about 125 members, mostly poor factory workers. The salary was a meager $600 per year. Many seminary graduates would have passed on this situation. Rauschenbusch, however, surprised the congregation when he accepted their invitation—a "miracle before our eyes," as one member wrote. They quickly grew to love their new pastor.[275]

Not everything, however, was positive for Rauschenbusch during this initial year as a pastor. In the previous year, while still in Rochester, he noticed a gradual decline in his hearing and, after beginning his pastorate, he discovered that he was rapidly losing his hearing. Numerous visits to the doctor and minor surgery failed to correct the problem. Eventually, his doctor informed him that he had a "neurological defect" and that the prospects for improved hearing were dim. Within a few short years, Rauschenbusch was totally deaf, forcing him to rely for the rest of his life on reading lips to communicate. The deafness affected both his personality and his pastoral ministry as the typically gregarious Rauschenbusch slowly retreated into more of a shy demeanor.[276] Despite the handicap, Rauschenbusch continued to fulfill his pastoral responsibilities largely due to the willingness of the congregation to accommodate him. They patiently allowed him approximately two months' leave while he underwent treatment in an attempt to conquer the problem. Eventually, Rauschenbusch's hearing became so problematic that he believed he needed to resign. In his diary, he wrote: "My hearing which had steadily decreased since I first discovered its failing in 1885 took a sudden drop downward, so that I could hear only what was spoken directly to me and very near to me. I saw then that I should have to resign my position."[277]

In 1891, Rauschenbusch offered his resignation so that he might spend a year of study in Germany. To his surprise and pleasure, the church refused to accept his resignation and offered to hire an interim minister in his place. They treated his absence as a sabbatical with pay. He wrote: "Their affection surprised me and held me. I also realized that the church gave me a position for effective work such as I could scarcely find elsewhere."[278] After his return, he remained their pastor until resigning in 1897 to become successor to his father in the German Department of Rochester Theological Seminary.

Though Walter Rauschenbusch was a beloved pastor, he is best remembered as the prophet of the Social Gospel movement. He first began to develop a consciousness of the social problem in America while he was a student at Rochester Theological Seminary. Even so, his experience as a pastor in Hell's Kitchen accelerated his development of a philosophy of social Christianity and as a strong prophetic voice on its behalf.

Within Protestant circles at the end of the nineteenth century, the traditional strategy for the betterment of society was revivalism. Rauschenbusch was reared on this concept. His father, and most of his fellow German Baptists, believed that if they preached the Gospel and people experienced salvation, revivalism would inaugurate the Kingdom of God. However, Rauschenbusch's encounter with the misery of tenement living, the horrible working conditions in the factories, the unchecked crime on the streets, the corruption of city officials, and the generally oppressed lives of his church members caused an awakening within himself, leading to a new concept of how to better society. While he never lost his commitment to personal evangelism, he shifted his emphasis to ways to change the structure of society. His ideas became the heart of the Social Gospel Movement, with Rauschenbusch its most recognized spokesman.[279]

In 1907 Rauschenbusch published *Christianity and the Social Crisis*. Paul Minus indicates that the book's ideas had germinated in Rauschenbusch's mind for sixteen years before he finally produced the book. Throughout the writing process, Rauschenbusch was anxious about its content because it was so radical for its day. Now serving as a professor of church history at Rochester Theological Seminary, he believed the book would be so controversial that his job would be jeopardized. The book was released in April 1907, just as Rauschenbusch and his family prepared to leave for a sabbatical in Germany. It was several weeks before he received word that the book had become extremely popular. Within three years, Macmillan Publishers informed him that the book had sold more copies than any other religious book they had published. It went through several reprints and became popular both in America and Europe.[280]

The impact that the pastoral years had on Rauschenbusch and the development of his thought is apparent in *Christianity and the Social Crisis*. He wrote the book "to discharge a debt" to his parishioners whom he never forgot, "the working people on the West Side of New York City." He hoped the book would serve "to ease the pressure that bears them down and increases the forces that bear them up."[281] Rauschenbusch had a passionate concern for change within the economic system and society in general, and this flowed from his compassion for less-fortunate people like his earlier parishioners.

Rauschenbusch began *Christianity and the Social Crisis* with two assumptions. First, he believed that a wide gulf existed between the very wealthy and the very poor, a result of the industrial revolution. Second, he believed that capitalism was in direct opposition and contradiction to Christianity. Drawing an illustration from agriculture, he said, "[w]ealth...is to a nation what manure is to a farm. If the farmer spreads it evenly over the soil, it will enrich the whole. If he should leave it in heaps, the land would be impoverished and under the rich heaps the vegetation would be killed."[282]

The book easily divides into three sections. In the first section, he described how, beginning with the Hebrew prophets and moving through the ministry of Jesus and the early Church, Christianity was a "great revolutionary movement, pledged to change the world-as-it-is into the world-as-it-ought-to-be." Its original ideal was to establish the Kingdom of God on earth by transforming human society through "regenerating all human relations and reconstituting them in accordance with the will of God."[283]

Rauschenbusch provided his interpretation of why Christianity's original vision was not realized in the second section of the book. He blamed the failure on the developments within Christianity from the fourth century on through the Middle Ages. As the Church became institutionalized and united with the State, the social consciousness of the religion was relegated to the background.[284]

The solution to the problem comprised the final section of *Christianity and the Social Crisis*. Rauschenbusch discussed the American context for Christianity and the problems that existed as a result of an economic system he considered to be anti-Christian. He argued that, because of the separation of Church and State, American Christianity is uniquely situated to restore the original intention of early Christianity, namely the transformation of society. Rauschenbusch prophetically called for Christians to act: "If the Church tries to confine itself to theology and the Bible, and refuses its larger mission to humanity, its theology will gradually become mythology and its Bible a closed book." He argued that evangelism and its emphasis on individual salvation will not make a difference in changing the structures of society: "Individualistic Christianity has almost lost sight of the great idea of the kingdom of God, which was the inspiration and center of the thought of Jesus. Social Christianity would once more enable us to understand the purpose and thought of Jesus and take the veil from our eyes when we read the synoptic gospels." Rauschenbusch's central thought was that a Christianized form of socialism should replace the American system of capitalism. Rauschenbusch believed that there had to be an economically level playing field before the social problems created by industrialism would ever disappear, and that the redistribution of wealth was the means to achieve lasting social change.[285]

As popular as *Christianity and the Social Crisis* was, it also had its critics. His departure from traditional ideas concerning society's betterment outraged many conservative Christians. Also, Rauschenbusch's favorable position toward socialism and opposition to capitalism added fuel to the fire. Minus indicates that the chairman of the trustees of the Rochester Theological Seminary objected to the book's claims, and that the seminary had received a number of other complaints, though the administration and the faculty supported Rauschenbusch. The *Journal and Messenger*, a conservative Baptist periodical published in Cincinnati, published a review calling Rauschenbusch "a Socialist of the German school." I. M. Haldeman, pastor of the First Baptist Church of New York, wrote an entire pamphlet titled, "Rauschenbusch's Christianity and the Social Crisis," which called for true believers to ignore false teachers like Rauschenbusch.[286]

Christianity and the Social Crisis propelled Rauschenbusch onto the national scene. He began to receive requests to lecture from universities, church groups, civic organizations, and other such opportunities from all over the country. He also continued writing and produced several additional works, including *Christianizing the Social Order* (1912) and *A Theology for the Social Gospel* (1917).[287]

Unfortunately, his popularity was relatively short-lived. When war broke out in Europe in 1914, Rauschenbusch's close ties to Germany and his strong attempts on behalf of peace were not received well in the United States. For some time, Rauschenbusch had feared that a climate was developing in Europe that might lead to conflict. When war finally began, he was torn by a conflict of loyalty. He had extended family in Germany who fought for Germany. His own sister, living in Germany, became a strong voice in support of the Kaiser. He also feared that if America entered the war, his own sons might also become involved.[288]

Early in the war, Rauschenbusch encouraged peace between England and Germany. However, British propaganda heavily influenced American opposition to Germany, so much that many Americans began to view the war as a righteous crusade against an evil Germany. This led Rauschenbusch to speak in defense of Germany. In 1914, he published an article titled, "Be Fair to Germany," in which he encouraged Americans to look less myopically at the war. At first, he heard positive responses about the article. Nevertheless, when it was republished later that year in *Literary Digest,* a firestorm of protest, particularly in Canada, arose. Rauschenbusch had always had his critics, but this reaction was different. He heard rumors that farmers near his Ontario vacation home might attempt to harm him when the family came for summer vacation the next year. He also began to receive anonymous threatening letters. Newspapers editorialized against him, questioning his patriotism. These events burdened him tremendously and caused him great pain. He said, "Unfortunately, I am not thick-skinned.... I love [others] and have tried to live without having enemies. It is physical misery...to get mail [filled] with scornful and hateful letters, and I cannot do my work."[289]

The fall from public popularity to scorn during the war years took its toll on Rauschenbusch physically. Tragically, he began to experience some serious health problems. In March 1918, he was diagnosed with "pernicious anemia" and was forced to give up his teaching responsibilities at the seminary. On 14 June 1918, doctors performed surgery to remove a malignant tumor in his abdominal area, along with a section of his large intestine. On 25 July 1918, the great prophet of the Social Gospel died.[290] The life, ministry, and teachings of Jesus were always central to Rauschenbusch's thought. Perhaps, in the last years of his life, it could be said that he experienced what Jesus himself experienced and commented about: "Prophets are not without honor except in their own country."[291]

Suggested Reading

Evans, Christopher H. *The Kingdom Is Always but Coming: A Life of Walter Rauschenbusch.* Grand Rapids: Eerdmans, 2004.
Minus, Paul M. *Walter Rauschenbusch: American Reformer.* New York: MacMillan, 1988.
Rauschenbusch, Walter. *Christianity and the Social Crisis.* New York: Macmillan, 1907.
———. *Christianizing the Social Order.* New York: MacMillan, 1912.
———. *A Theology for the Social Gospel.* New York: MacMillan, 1918.
Sharpe, Dores R. *Walter Rauschenbusch.* New York: Macmillan, 1942.

Helen Barrett Montgomery (1861–1934)

Apostle of "Woman's Work for Woman" Missions

Kendal Mobley

HELEN BARRETT MONTGOMERY was one of the most remarkable Baptists of the late nineteenth and early twentieth centuries. The daughter of a Baptist minister, she was a lifelong, faithful churchwoman and Sunday school teacher, a licensed preacher, and a pioneering civic leader, politician, and social reformer. Her deep personal commitment to Christ and substantial intellectual gifts propelled her to leadership in Baptist missions and in the ecumenical woman's missionary movement. In recognition of her significant contributions, the Northern Baptist Convention elected her president in 1921. If these accomplishments were not enough, the American Baptist Publication Society published her *Centenary Translation* of the New Testament in 1924. Montgomery was a powerful advocate for women and children, for "Woman's Work for Woman,"[292] and for liberty and equality in Christ, whom she called "the great Emancipator of woman."[293]

Helen Barrett was born to Amos Judson Barrett and Emily B. Barrows Barrett on 31 July 1861 in Kingsville, Ohio. Her father was called to the pastorate of Lake Avenue Baptist Church upon his graduation from the Rochester Theological Seminary in 1876, and he baptized fifteen-year-old Helen into church membership that winter.

For young "Nellie," as Helen was called, church membership at Lake Avenue meant a commitment to evangelism and discipleship. In addition to attending morning worship, she taught a boy's Sunday school class on Sunday mornings, and on Sunday afternoons she walked two miles to the Lyell Avenue Mission Sunday school, where she taught another class of boys. Sunday also included the young people's meeting and evening worship.

Helen received much of her basic education at home—primarily from her father. Later, she studied at Livingston Park Seminary, a private school for girls. She entered Wellesley in 1880, where she was initiated into the tiny elite of college-educated women in the United States, many of whom provided leadership for the burgeoning women's movements in religion, politics, and social reform in the late nineteenth and early twentieth centuries. Her Wellesley experience challenged what she described as her "stiff little Baptist"[294] worldview, although she remained committed to the Baptist movement throughout her life. One of her most important influences from Wellesley was Alice Freeman, who became president in 1881. She left Wellesley as an activist and intellectual who believed that women had a major role to play in public life.

After graduating from Wellesley, Helen Barrett spent a year teaching high school at the Rochester Free Academy in Rochester, New York, and two more years as co-principal of the Wellesley Preparatory School in Philadelphia, Pennsylvania. She married William A. Montgomery, a Rochester businessman, on 6 September 1887. He was a widower, seven years her senior, who had joined the Lake Avenue Baptist Church around 1873. A faithful churchman, he took over the boy's Sunday school class when Helen went off to college, and that became the subject of their earliest correspondence.

After her marriage to William Montgomery, Helen gave up her position in the Wellesley Preparatory School and the couple settled in Rochester. Helen earned a modest income as a private tutor for young women preparing for college, and as a public lecturer. In 1895, Helen and William adopted a five-year-old daughter named Edith.

When Helen returned to Rochester as Mrs. William A. Montgomery, she became involved once again in the life of Lake Avenue Baptist Church and the Monroe Baptist Association, and it was at the 1887 meeting of the Monroe Baptist Association where she first met Lucy (Mrs. N.M.) Waterbury (later Lucy Waterbury Peabody), who later became her partner in so many endeavors on behalf of the ecumenical woman's missionary movement. Caroline Atwater Mason, another future leader of the ecumenical woman's missionary movement, also joined them on the platform at that meeting.

After her father's death in 1889, Montgomery organized the Barrett Memorial Sunday school class in Lake Avenue Baptist Church, the enrollment of which grew to 250 women. It became an important base of power for Montgomery in the church and in the city. For forty-four years, she taught the class whenever she was in town. Her lessons covered a wide range of topics, from the Bible to social issues to politics, and the weekly meetings gave her a regular and influential platform for her views. In 1898, the Lake Avenue Baptist Church licensed her to preach.[295]

Montgomery was active in several of the leading women's civic clubs in Rochester, including the Political Equality Club (whose members dubbed her "Helen Barrett Montgomery," rather than "Mrs. William A. Montgomery"), the Wednesday Morning Club, the Woman's Ethical Club, and the College Women's Club. She took an active role in the statewide attempt to pass a women's suffrage amendment to the New York State Constitution in 1894.

At the recommendation of Susan B. Anthony, Montgomery became the first president of Rochester's Women's Educational and Industrial Union (WEIU) in 1893. It was the first women's club in Rochester to move beyond culture study and self-improvement into municipal reform. Its reform agenda included citizenship training for women, legal protection for women in the workplace, self-improvement programs for poor and working women, civic art projects, and educational reform in the public schools, such as free kindergartens, vocational training and domestic science, free summer educational programs for poor children, and the improvement and beautification of school property. Because of her WEIU leadership, Montgomery's status as a leader of the women in the city grew rapidly. She remained president of the WEIU until 1911.

Montgomery was elected president of the New York State Federation of Women's Clubs in 1896, but a sudden illness prevented her from serving the full term. In 1898, the trustees of the University of Rochester voted to accept women as students if the women of the city could raise $100,000 for the university. With Susan B. Anthony's encouragement, Montgomery chaired the fundraising committee.

Montgomery became the first woman elected to public office in Rochester, when in 1899, with the support of the women's clubs and the city's "Good Government" movement, she won a seat on the schoolboard. For ten years, she consistently pressed for progressive educational reform and the latest advances in pedagogy and curriculum. She was an advocate for the women in the school system, who filled the vast majority of the teaching posts but held few administrative positions. Likewise, she believed she had been elected to serve the interests of the mothers and children in Rochester, and she saw herself as their voice on the schoolboard. She viewed public education as essential to democracy, and she worked to extend educational resources to the entire community, especially through the development of after-hours community programs in school buildings.

Ironically, Montgomery's service on the schoolboard brought her into conflict with fellow Baptist social reformer Walter Rauschenbusch, whose educational views were decidedly more conservative and traditional. Indeed, Rauschenbusch led a popular movement against the board's progressive reforms that ultimately contributed to Montgomery's departure from the schoolboard.

As Montgomery's role on the Rochester schoolboard came to an end, her leadership role in the ecumenical woman's missionary movement accelerated. She served as a representative of the Woman's Baptist Foreign Missionary Society to the Ecumenical Missionary Conference in New York City in 1900, during which she gave two addresses on themes related to the ecumenical woman's missionary movement. The deliberations of the women's missionary organizations at the Ecumenical Missionary Conference led to the formation of the Central Committee on the United Study of Foreign Missions, which published shared mission-study books and materials for the women's missionary organizations of the mainline Protestant denominations in the United States. Montgomery wrote six books and many other publications for the Central Committee. Her most successful book, *Western Women in Eastern Lands* (1910), celebrated the fifty-year history of American women's organized mission work. It sold about 100,000 copies and inspired the Golden Jubilee celebrations of 1910–1911, a coast-to-coast traveling mission conference that toured thirty-four cities and raised more than $1,000,000 for women's missionary work. Montgomery spoke 209 times on the tour.

In 1912, Montgomery was instrumental in organizing the World Day of Prayer and what became the Committee on Christian Literature for Women and Children in Mission Fields. In 1920, she was a key force behind the organization of the Joint Committee for Women's Union Christian Colleges in Foreign Fields.

Montgomery is remembered among Baptists primarily because of her service to the Northern Baptist Convention. The American Baptist Foreign Mission Society recruited her in 1913 to write a centennial history of Baptist missions, *Following the Sunrise*. She served as president of the Woman's American Baptist Foreign Mission Society from 1914–1924, with the exception of 1921–1922, when she served one term as president of the Northern Baptist Convention and became the first woman to serve as president of a major American denomination. In 1915, she, Lucy W. Peabody, and Martha Hillard MacLeish organized the World Wide Guild, a mission education organization for young women in Northern Baptist churches, known today as AB GIRLS, a program of American Baptist Women's Ministries.[296] In 1921, as president of the Woman's American Baptist Foreign Mission Society, Montgomery led the women of the Northern Baptist Convention to raise more than $450,000 as a gift to missions in celebration of their jubilee.

In consequence of the jubilee gift, the 1921 meeting of the Northern Baptist Convention elected Montgomery as its next president. In anticipation of the 1922 Northern Baptist Convention meeting, Montgomery helped to organize the moderate and liberal forces that stopped the fundamentalists' attempt to establish a creedal statement, and she presided over the session in which the debate over the statement occurred.

It would be a mistake to interpret Montgomery's opposition to a statement of faith as theological liberalism. She was a self-described "Middle-of-the-Road Baptist." Although she ultimately opposed the adoption of a creedal statement, she initially favored the idea because she believed that it might help to unify the deeply divided Northern Baptist Convention, and because she remained unconvinced that the conservative critics of the convention were entirely wrong. She tried to work inclusively with the fundamentalists, and their refusal to abandon militant tactics finally convinced Montgomery to oppose them at the 1922 annual meeting. In her president's address, she confronted the issue directly. She told the delegates that if they did authorize a committee to write a new confession of faith, they should see to it that the committee never reported back to the convention. They should provide the committee with adequate funds to publicize its statement to the churches and let the churches decide individually what to do with it. By that time, she had come to believe that Baptists could not adopt a confession of faith without threatening liberty of conscience. In the end, she opposed the fundamentalists who wanted a confession, but she did it in defense of Baptist liberty, not liberal theology.[297]

Following her year of service as president of the Northern Baptist Convention, Montgomery attended the 1923 meeting of the Baptist World Alliance in Stockholm as a delegate from the United States. She was one of only two women to address the meeting, and her topic was "New Opportunities for Baptist Women." As she spoke to the thousands assembled from thirty-five different countries, she reiterated the theme to which she had dedicated her life—Jesus, "the great Emancipator of woman," who

> alone among the founders of the great religions of the world looked upon men and women with level eyes, seeing not their differences but their oneness, their humanity.... In the mind of the Founder of Christianity there is no area of religious privilege fenced off for the exclusive use of men. In this attitude Jesus Christ stands absolutely alone among religious teachers.[298]

The American Baptist Publication Society published Montgomery's original translation of the Greek New Testament in 1924 to celebrate its centenary. The *Centenary Translation* was not reviewed outside the denominational press, and apparently was little used outside the women's organizations in which Montgomery was so prominent, but it was one of the most creative and progressive translations of its day, in both style and content. Even today, it maintains a small but loyal readership. Montgomery wanted it to be simple and clear, and she anticipated many interpretive debates in her translations of passages such as Romans 16:1–2; 1 Corinthians 11:1–16, 14:33–36; and 1 Timothy 2:15, 3:11. In its clarity and sensibilities, the *Centenary Translation* reflects the theological value Montgomery placed on liberty. She believed the gospel ought to be liberated from the dead hand of tradition and made accessible because the gospel was itself liberating.

In recognition of her lifetime of service to the cause of Christ, Montgomery received an honorary master's degree from Brown University in 1917. She received honorary doctorates from Franklin College and Denison University in 1922 and from Wellesley College in 1925. She delivered the John M. English lectures on preaching at the Newton Theological Institution in 1929, which were published as *The Preaching Value of Missions*. Helen Barrett Montgomery died on 19 October 1934 at the age of seventy-three. There is a stained-glass window memorializing her in First Baptist Church, Washington, D.C.

Suggested Reading

Cattan, Louise A. *Lamps Are for Lighting: The Story of Helen Barrett Montgomery and Lucy Waterbury Peabody*. Grand Rapids: Eerdmans, 1972.

Mobley, Kendal P. *Helen Barrett Montgomery: The Global Mission of Domestic Feminism*. Waco: Baylor University Press, 2009.

Montgomery, Helen Barrett. *Following the Sunrise: A Century of Baptist Missions, 1813–1913*. Philadelphia: American Baptist Publication Society, 1913.

———. *Western Women in Eastern Lands*. New York: MacMillan, 1910.

———, translator. *Centenary Translation of the New Testament*. Philadelphia: American Baptist Publication Society, 1924. Reprint, *Montgomery New Testament*. Nashville TN: Holman Bible Publishers, 1988.

George W. Truett
(1867–1944)

Preacher to Preachers

Preaching

Keith Durso

GEORGE WASHINGTON TRUETT was born on 6 May 1867, on a farm near Hayesville, North Carolina. During a revival meeting at Hayesville's Baptist church on 3 October 1886, he gave his life to Christ. In 1889, Truett moved to Whitewright, Texas to join other members of his family who had moved previously, and there he joined Whitewright Baptist Church.

From childhood, Truett had his heart set on becoming a lawyer, but his administrative skills as his church's Sunday school superintendent, his teaching abilities as a Sunday school teacher, and his preaching during the pastor's absence led him to a different path. While attending his church's monthly conference one Saturday evening in 1890, those in attendance voted to ordain him to the gospel ministry, a vote that greatly shocked Truett. This meeting eventually derailed Truett's vocation plans, for in 1893 he matriculated at Baylor University and began pastoring East Waco Baptist Church. Four years later, Truett graduated from Baylor and accepted the call of First Baptist Church, Dallas, to become its pastor.

Many readers of *Witnesses to the Baptist Heritage* might have expected an essay on Truett's position on religious liberty, a topic that he addressed most powerfully on 16 May 1920 to approximately 15,000 people gathered at the steps of the United States Capitol.[299] But Truett's influence on Baptist life was much broader than one powerful, eloquent speech. He was a master pulpiteer and was perhaps the most famous Baptist preacher in America during the first half of the twentieth century. Pastors, in his opinion, had the highest calling of anyone on earth, for they were the heralds of the gospel of Jesus Christ, and with that calling came awesome responsibilities. In Truett's mind, preachers were not only men who *do* certain things; they were people called to *be* certain kind of men, men whose lives were to be a perfect sermon. "Character is far more important" than knowledge, which is power, he told a gathering of ministers, but character is far more powerful:

> What a man is in himself counts for far more than anything he will ever say with this tongue or work with his hands. This great business of the preacher needs to have the background and the reinforcement of men of the highest, deepest, and worthiest type of character. The world will forgive our mistakes quickly if the world is apprised of the fact that we are fundamental in our sincerity, in our integrity, in our inner life.[300]

Often in his sermons to his congregation and his addresses to ministerial students and fellow preachers, Truett presented *advice to preachers* on several characteristics and qualities that defined *what a preacher ought to be.*

A man (and Truett always meant a male) who stands before any congregation must always *be biblical.* Truett had no patience with those who preached silly sermons with even sillier titles designed to draw crowds. In his notes for a lecture on preaching, he listed some such sermons: "Bycycle [*sic*]—Shakespeare—Courting—The Ugly Husband—The Ugly Wife—Reform in Dress—The 2 headed Woman—Jack & the Bean Stalk." Though Truett often had much to say about such sermons, a one-sentence comment in his notes says volumes: "*God* save us fr[om] such truckling!"[301]

For Truett, being biblical meant that preachers must preach about sin and salvation. People must be told that sin separates them from God, and to be separated from God means to be damned. Such a message is difficult to preach and to hear, but it must not be downplayed. Along with this awful truth, however, preachers must proclaim salvation through Christ. No matter how despicable a person might be, no matter what dastardly deed a person might have done, no one is beyond the reach and love of Christ.

According to Truett, every "preacher should be possessed with the living, unhesitating conviction that the aim and object of his ministry is to win people to God,"[302] which meant that every preacher must *be a soul-winner*. The preaching event should be aimed at saving people's souls, not at addressing economic, political, sanitation, housing, or alcohol problems. Such evils "should receive serious consideration," Truett maintained, but they should never supplant the preaching aimed at the regeneration and transformation of the individual soul.[303]

Throughout his ministry, Truett preached thousands of sermons and hundreds of people came to salvation in Christ as a result. Yet he also worked tirelessly to raise money for hospitals and outlaw gambling and alcohol. He would have agreed with most of Reinhold Neibuhr's dictum, "The whip of the law cannot change the heart, but…it can restrain the heartless until they change their mind and heart."[304] Only the gospel, according to Truett, could change hearts, but, apparently, the law could only restrain the heartless on certain social issues. For example, Truett remained silent on the issue of racism. Personally, he loved African Americans and praised them in letters and in public, and they in turn loved him. But a prophetic word on such a heinous social blight is lacking in Truett's preaching.

All Christians must know what they believe, but pastors, especially, must *be confident* that what they preach is true. "The *pulpit is no place for a religious stammerer…*," Truett maintained. "It is *conviction* that convinces everywhere."[305] Because God had called preachers to speak with authority, they must preach positive words of hope, not their doubts, guesses, or speculations.

Although Truett exhorted preachers to have strong convictions and be confident in the pulpit, he had the nauseating habit of starting messages to seminary students or fellow pastors with comments emphasizing his "painful sense of unworthiness" to speak to such a crowd, or noting that he was unfit or unprepared to stand before them to speak his poor words. Such self-deprecation hardly exudes confidence. One wonders, however, if he really believed such self-denigrations. Certainly no one in the audience believed that he was unfit or unprepared. They knew that he was worthy and fit to speak, that he was always prepared, and that he always preached with confidence. If he truly was unworthy and unfit, he would not have been in constant demand to speak all over the country. Truett might have lacked many qualities, but confidence was not one of them.

Despite his feeble pretentions otherwise, Truett was always prepared, whether he preached to thousands or to a single person, like a newspaper boy. Truett believed that the Bible was a pastor's most important text to study, but no subject was off limits. Preachers must *be prepared* and should constantly study history, current events, books, newspapers, and people's lives.

Truett spent many hours each week preparing his sermons. When he spoke to an audience, he never took his eyes off them. For example, when Truett preached for nearly an hour to over 60,000 people in Atlanta at the 1939 Baptist World Alliance Congress, he used no notes. Journalists who had received a copy of the sermon before the session were amazed at how close the manuscript was to Truett's actual words that day.[306]

Not only must pastors be prepared to preach at gatherings, they also had to be ready to preach during their "wayside ministries" as they moved among the people during the week. Pastors were shepherds of souls, not just preachers of sermons, Truett contended. They had to meet face-to-face with people in their homes, at their jobs, and in their offices. Things like "a letter here, and a whispered word there, and a visit yonder, and a prayer for some burdened battling soul"[307] during such ministries were tokens of love that helped spread the gospel, because people needed individual attention. There was no substitute for such an intimate ministry, for pastors must hear the people's cries and feel the battles they were fighting.

The "wayside ministries" called for a personal touch and the sacrifice of time. Although Truett was the pastor of a large, urban church, he did not feel that such things like preaching the funeral of a mother whose child was a visitor to the church's Sunday school, or hand-addressing approximately 10,000 envelopes containing his annual Christmas greeting and marking each one "Personal," was beneath him. James W. Vardaman, who was a member of First Baptist, Dallas, noted as a boy that such expressions of pastoral love flowed from Truett because of his love for people: "But you knew, I knew, that George Truett loved me. I suspect that most everyone who ever encountered him, in a close relationship, no matter how brief, would probably assume the same thing."[308]

Another of Truett's convictions was that preachers must *be active*. Only preachers with well-disciplined minds and bodies do much for the kingdom of God. However, too many preachers, according to Truett, were idlers wasting their time on "little nothings" rather than on their ministries. They looked for any excuse not to prepare their sermons, hunted for any activity to keep from praying, and followed any road that led them away from personal encounters with other people. God did not need dawdlers, but "indefatigable toilers." Preachers should be the busiest people in every city.

Truett practiced what he preached to other ministers, for he was an "indefatigable toiler." In 1942, for example, Truett, at the age of seventy-five, was away from Dallas 153 days, ministering in other cities. Also during that year, he preached 251 sermons, gave fifty speeches, and officiated at twenty-eight funerals and forty-seven weddings.

Being an optimist, Truett counseled other preachers to *be optimistic*, too. No Christian should "be a whining blubberer" or "a wailing pessimist," Truett urged his colleagues. Christians are on the winning side of history; therefore, never preach doubts, for people have enough of them already. Moreover, true gospel preachers must believe what they preach. The hopeful message that they preach must become part of each "preacher's own soul, and turned over and thought out and prayed over and experimentally digested until it becomes a burning, living message from the preacher's heart."[309] Unlike many wearisome politicians, preachers should not be a bunch of "pessimistic croakers" and "calamity howlers" who see disasters coming wherever they look.[310] Preachers should be people who see the bright side of every dark cloud, for the gospel they preach is a victorious message despite the calamities that their congregations experience.

Truett warned his brother preachers to guard against being ensnared by "professionalism," and by the itch to always be looking for a larger church and a larger salary. Preachers should worry more about how much money is placed in the offering plates for missions than in how much goes into their pockets. Preachers must put down roots and then, with gladness, thanksgiving, and enthusiastic devotion, give their lives to the ministry and to the place to which God had called them.

Advising preachers to *be content* might have sounded a bit condescending coming from someone who pastored a large church like First Baptist, Dallas, and who earned what today would amount to a six-figure salary, but Truett spoke from conviction. During his fifty-one years as a pastor, he pastored only two churches, East Waco Baptist Church (1893–1897) and First Baptist, Dallas (1897–1944). He received several offers from other churches to double or triple his salary, but he remained in Dallas. And the comfortable salary he made was spent on life's necessities. In fact, despite his admonition to pastors not to be in debt, Truett was constantly borrowing money because he gave money to needy people who came to his home, bought unneeded items from traveling salesmen, returned honorariums to churches that paid him for speaking, paid the rent for an unemployed man, or borrowed money to pay the funeral expenses for a poor family. Truett was a content man, for he believed that money was to be used to help others and for nothing else.

According to Truett, preachers do many things, but most importantly, they should be biblical, soul-winners, confident in what they preach, prepared to minister at every moment, optimistic to a fault, and content with their income and with where God had placed them. Such were the qualities that should define the character of every preacher.

Truett strove to embody the qualities listed above, but he also hoped that he would have another quality, a personal one that could not be required of every preacher. In a sermon to his congregation, Truett told his church that he hoped he would die preaching to the end of his life. He also confessed that pastoring was a weighty calling and that he had often begged God to find something else for him to do, but each time that prayer was uttered, he quickly said, "Nay, Lord, nay, only give me the grace to be the preacher I ought to be!"[311] He then quoted one of Charles Wesley's hymns, words, Truett said, that he sang every hour: "Happy if with my latest breath, I may but speak His name; Preach Him to all, and gasp in death, Behold, behold the lamb!"

Truett's earthly journey came to an end, probably from bone cancer, at 11:50 P.M. on Friday, 7 July 1944, at his home in Dallas. Near the end, doctors had to medicate him heavily, which often caused him to lose consciousness, but not his passion to preach, for even in his delirium, Truett exhorted men and women to surrender their lives to God. Eventually the preaching ceased and Truett slipped into eternity. But as long as he could preach, Truett was a *preacher to the very end* because, in his mind, that is *what a preacher ought to be.*

Suggested Reading

Durso, Keith E. "George W. Truett: Making a Life Versus Making a Living." *Texas Baptist Journal* 29 (2009): 77–87.

———. *Thy Will Be Done: A Biography of George W. Truett*. Macon GA: Mercer University Press, 2009.

McBeth, H. Leon. *The First Baptist Church of Dallas: Centennial History (1868–1968)*. Grand Rapids MI: Zondervan Publishing House, 1968.

Truett, George W. *The Baptist Message and Mission for the World Today*. Nashville TN: Sunday School Board, 1939.

———. *God's Call to America*. Edited by J. B. Cranfill. Philadelphia: Judson Press, 1923.

William Owen Carver (1868–1954)

Theologian for a New Era

Theology

Mark Wilson

WILLIAM OWEN CARVER (1868–1954) lived between the two Reconstructions of the American South. He was born in Wilson County, Tennessee on 10 April 1868, three years after the Confederacy's surrender at the Appomattox Courthouse, and he died 24 May 1954, one week after the U.S. Supreme Court ruled in *Brown v. Board of Education* that racially segregated educational facilities were unconstitutional. Culturally and socially, he was an ordinary son of Southern Baptists who became, in the denomination's eyes, the intellectual architect of the SBC's foreign missions and one of the brightest minds at the flagship seminary in Louisville. A graduate of two Southern Baptist institutions—Richmond College and Southern Baptist Theological Seminary—he served the denomination as the seminary's professor of missions and comparative religions for over four decades and remained an active participant in the denomination until his death. A prolific author of books and articles, he served as the managing editor of the seminary's theological journal, *Review and Expositor*, and as frequent editorialist for convention periodicals. A seminary building, denominational library, and Baptist school of social work carry his name today.[312]

Theologically speaking, he was no ordinary Southern Baptist, and he represented a level of leadership in the SBC during the first half of the twentieth century that was neither liberal nor fundamentalist. He was a free-thinking Baptist, deeply committed to his denomination, anxious to pass along the best of modern thought, yet unwilling to blindly subscribe to every new fad. He did not suffer professional martyrdom for any progressive ideal, but gently prodded Southern Baptists to see beyond the narrow confines of conservatism and join the dangerous, modern theological world. He spent a significant amount of time corresponding with critics, Southern Baptists who felt that seminary professors ought to educate young ministers and missionaries in ways that reflected the dominant theological attitudes of the denomination's membership.

Carver's mediating position on the controversial topic of creationism and scientific evolution is a good example. In 1921 the Baptist Pastors' Conference in Louisville invited Carver to address the relationship of the biblical account of creation and science. Anti-evolutionist crusader William Jennings Bryan had recently delivered a spirited address in Louisville, so many pastors likely listened with great interest to see how an esteemed seminary professor who taught courses on theology and modern thought would deal with the controversial subject. Carver suggested that the Genesis account of creation should be read as a theological text, not a scientific text. The story was a work of art, he said, that had as its purpose an explanation for the beginning of humankind rather than a detailed look at the entire universe. "Let the geologist bring his study to the strata, the formations, the variations, and set forth as many ages as he will," he dared.[313] No theory of origins could overturn the fact that God created the world and its inhabitants. Carver sought a middle way that displayed confidence in God's creative power but still respected the inquisitiveness of humankind.

Caver's speech and subsequent newspaper article did not draw major criticism, but as the tempestuous 1920s unfolded, many Southern Baptists saw more at stake for Christianity in the science vs. religion debate. In 1926, he published in the *Review and Expositor* a six-page review of three books that sought to "introduce the theory of Evolution…into the fellowship of the Christian faith." In a diary entry, he described the review as his "moderating and mediating" view of the issue. He began the essay, titled "Christianizing Evolution," with a strong disclaimer: "Please let no one be alarmed or angered by the heading for this review article." Carver used the term "Fundamentalist" to describe those persons who would certainly consider the authors of the three books more dangerous than "open infidels," and juxtaposed Fundamentalists with "Modernists" who ridiculed the faith claims of

Christianity. Both groups hindered the intellectual journey of leaders, such as himself, who believed that "Christianity can recognize no truth as foreign to its interest and no sphere outside its realm." Carver critiqued one author for his lack of emphasis on sin, praised the second author for his "maturity, breadth of vision, [and] security of faith," and appreciated the third author's bold statement that the modern world needed to consider the positive aspects of Christianity.[314] John W. Porter and T. T. Martin, editors of the conservative *American Baptist* based in Memphis, Tennessee, were "disappointed and grieved" at some of Carver's statements and considered "Christianizing Evolution" a contradiction in terms. Believing that "every known theory of evolution inevitably leads to the land of free love," the editors chastened Carver for his unwillingness to plainly state his views on the controversial subject. For Porter and Martin, evolution challenged the very heart of Christian faith: the inspiration of scripture. Carver argued that the natural world acted as a revelation from God, a role that only scripture could fill, according to the editors. They commended Carver for some of his statements but deemed his review "a plea for a middle ground" between Christians and "Theistic evolutionists," one that was an "iridescent dream, an impossible objective, and an automatic contradiction."[315] Carver found the middle of the road a difficult place to stand.

That same year, Carver went on the offensive in a review of a prominent Southern Baptist pastor's anti-evolution book. Joseph Judson Taylor wrote *The Evolution Theory: Plain Words for Plain Folks* as a part of his campaign to rid schools of the evolution menace, and Carver considered it shallow and unconvincing. He called it "highly satisfactory to the eager Fundamentalists, irritating to the evolutionists, and of little value to troubled souls." Taylor and Carver began a cordial correspondence related to the review, but the discussion quickly turned into a heated controversy. Taylor turned a private debate public in the Missouri Baptist newspaper, and he insinuated that Carver must be a closet theistic evolutionist. Carver never allowed private and public disputes to get out of hand, and he exhibited the kind of restraint that would allow him to continue to serve the denomination.

In response to those Southern Baptists who demanded clarity and not confusion concerning denominational loyalty to the Bible, Southern

Seminary President E. Y. Mullins, a quintessential theological moderate, chaired a committee to write a "Statement of Baptist Faith and Message," a concession to conservatives, one that Carver considered a big mistake. When Mullins called the faculty together to discuss a draft of the statement, Carver recorded in his diary, "I am wholly opposed to their making such (or any) creed." When the convention met in 1925 to adopt the faith statement, Carver was disgusted and called the meeting "the worst I ever attended from the standpoint of things it should be and seek." He issued a public word against the faith statement in a newspaper editorial, arguing that Baptists, like first-century Christians, had no creed because they scrutinized each individual's profession of faith. "We seek to preserve the individuality, the vitality, and the fervor of experience," he said, "by thus allowing each man to have his own experience and his own statement of it." Likely, local Baptist churches should deal with heresy; any other solution violated Southern Baptist history, principles, and practice. Carver suspected that creed advocates sought to invade the rights of individuals and churches in an effort that expressed distrust rather than faith.[316]

Just as he sought reconciliation between science and faith, Carver demonstrated a similar strategy regarding the relationship between Southern Baptists and other Christian denominations. When the SBC declined an invitation to join the World Council of Churches in 1940, Carver stood in the middle of dissent, although a former seminary trustee talked him out of signing his name to the minority opinion delivered at the annual convention. In one editorial, Carver interpreted the refusal to join the World Council of Churches as "a sad blunder." Southern Baptists missed their greatest opportunity to voice their faith and chose, instead, to say to the world, "We have the truth and we propose to keep it." He argued that the question was not one of orthodoxy. The only thing Southern Baptists would be expected to give up would be "our selfishness, our complacency, and our unholy ambition and conceit that makes us feel we can save the word by ourselves alone."[317]

Carver referred to his theology as "progressive orthodoxy," and he reconciled the tension between historic Christian faith and modern ideas by emphasizing spiritual experience and individual autonomy, two contributions he claimed were central to the Baptist understanding of

Christianity. The "fundamental" Baptist principle, he argued throughout his career, was regenerate individualism. Since God relates to individuals and not groups, denominations, or nations, Christians need not consider themselves under attack from ideas such as ecumenism, liberalism, the Social Gospel, evolution, or any other challenge. Carver emphasized spiritual experience over doctrine and applied Christianity over what he considered mundane and lifeless theological correctness.

In 1954, at the age of eighty-five and a few months before his death, Carver delivered the prestigious Founder's Day address at Southern Seminary. His topic was William H. Whitsitt, the infamous SBTS seminary president forced to resign in 1899 for challenging the Landmark belief of Baptist origins. He described Whitsitt as the "seminary's first martyr" for academic freedom and theological education, and he used the address to vindicate Whitsitt. "No man in the history of the [seminary] ever received so little recognition for so great service," he began his address. Carver suggested that Whitsitt's resignation ultimately resulted in greater freedom for seminary faculty to research, write, and teach.[318]

In preparation for the address, Carver reflected on Whitsitt's life in his diary and concluded that the professor was "at home, though not happy" in the denomination, a statement that could very well apply to himself. Despite his disappointments, controversies, and frustrations, Carver remained committed to Southern Baptists who had baptized, educated, and employed him for his entire career. He represents a minority theological tradition in Southern Baptist history, one that provides insight into the complex nature of a denomination orienting itself to the modern world.

Suggested Reading

Carver, William Owen. *The Glory of God in the Christian Calling: A Study of the Ephesian Epistle*. Nashville TN: Broadman Press, 1949.

———. *Missions and Modern Thought*. New York: Macmillan, 1910.

———. *Out of His Treasure: Unfinished Memoirs*. Nashville TN: Broadman Press, 1951.

Wilson, Mark R. *William Owen Carver's Controversies in the Baptist South*. Macon GA: Mercer University Press, 2010.

James Henry Rushbrooke
(1870–1947)

Baptist Peacemaker

Religious Freedom

Karen O'Dell Bullock

LONDON WAS A bustling metropolis in the year 1870, despite the fact that Queen Victoria had worn widow's weeds for nearly a decade. The Liberal party's William Ewing Gladstone served as Prime Minister during her long periods of absence and, under his watch, Britain flourished. That year, for the first time, Londoners purchased postcards and half-penny stamps from the General Post Office. The Tower Subway beneath the River Thames opened successfully, the first underground passenger tube railway in existence. The Married Women's Property Act confirmed upon women the right of ownership, and the British Red Cross was established. Charles Dickens died in June, the same month that Keble College in Oxford opened to train ministers for the High Church Movement in the Anglican Church.[319]

Two famous Baptist pastors were also making headlines as they preached in London that year: Charles Haddon Spurgeon (1834–1892), pastor of Metropolitan Tabernacle, and his contemporary John Clifford (1836–1923), pastor of Praed Street Chapel in Paddington. This dynamic pair packed their preaching hall pews with eager parishioners and earned great favor with rich and poor alike. Underneath the surface, however, the Down Grade Controversy was beginning to fester, as modernism and liberal views pervaded the culture.[320]

During these years of rising tension between General and Particular Baptists, Dr. John Clifford's irenic spirit modeled the qualities of brokering peace and offering reconciliation, of crafting within his own being a neutral space wherein people with opposing ideas could safely meet, dialogue, and come to an understanding based upon shared values.³²¹ One of Clifford's most able students and spiritual sons was James Henry Rushbrooke, who, because of the global extent of his influence, may perhaps be called one of the Baptists' greatest peacemakers of the modern period. This is the story of a most remarkable man.

"Peace" seemed to be the middle name of the babe born that sunny day in Bethnal Green, on the eastern outskirts of London, on 29 July 1870. He was the son of devout Anglican parents James and Sarah Rushbrooke, who were known for their fine Christian example at home and strength of industry and commitment in the community. Tiny James Henry, called Harry, was a precocious and thoughtful child, earning the reputation as a careful reconciler of differences even in his boyhood. Growing up in a stable, working-class railway family with five sisters and one brother prepared him in many ways to become the responsible, energetic leader who was sensitive to the plight of the poor and oppressed.³²²

At age fifteen, Harry left home for London to live with his aunt and to become a clerk to the Willesden District Council. Here he served with distinction for the next seven years, rising to the rank of chief clerk to the District Engineer. His future looked promising as a civil engineer. One Sunday, Harry's aunt took him to the famous Westbourne Park Baptist Chapel to hear her famous preacher, John Clifford, and his life was changed. Within a short time, Harry had joined the Young Men's Bible Class and was regularly attending meetings there. He threw himself into the work of several ministries of that great church and came to respect the direct, evangelistic, and social justice emphases of its pastor.

Clifford took Harry under his wing, recognized his giftedness, answered his complex questions about faith and life, and modeled how Christians should address the social and political injustices of their day. When James Henry Rushbrooke surrendered to Christ's Lordship in 1887, John Clifford baptized him. Harry was one of twenty-eight young men who entered the ministry through Clifford's influence.³²³ Clifford formed the Preacher's Institute to train young men for the Gospel ministry, and Rushbrooke and his friends met eagerly each Thursday evening to study the Bible and to take classes in theology, logic, apologetics, sermon preparation, evangelism, and preaching.

In summer 1891, twenty-one-year-old Harry met and married Kate Partridge, a local music teacher. They married at St. Michael's Parish Church at Thorpe-le-Soken and purchased a little house in Kilburn. Three years later, they anticipated the birth of their first child. An unexpected double tragedy struck when Harry lost both his wife and infant son in childbirth. Inconsolable, Harry turned to Clifford for counseling and friendship and was not disappointed. Clifford ministered to Harry until he could see his way forward.

It was at this point that Harry, while still suffering deep grief, sensed a strong vocational call to the Baptist ministry and enrolled in the Midland Baptist College in Nottingham for further preparation. He proved himself, pastoring the Queensberry Street Baptist Church in Old Basford and becoming the most popular preacher at the college. He baptized dozens of converts, gathered people of all ages regularly to study the Bible and attend prayer meeting, led the church to become debt-free, and engaged the community both in addressing unjust conditions and meeting the needs of the poor.

He excelled in his classes and won the school's coveted Pegg Scholarship to study in Halle and Berlin from 1899 through 1901. The time he spent in Germany would prove to be pivotal for the rest of his life. Studying with Adolf von Harnack and the "Ritschlian School" taught him that Christianity was to be essentially practical, grounded in the historical Jesus as the divine revelation.[324] Harry learned much while retaining the evangelistic and evangelical aspects of the spiritual formation he had learned under his pastor, John Clifford. Aware of the dangers and limitations of biblical criticism and holding tightly to the authority of scripture and the centrality of a personal faith in Christ as Redeemer, Harry processed what he learned and grew theologically and intellectually. These confessional roots sustained Rushbrooke's work throughout the rest of his life, ministry, and global leadership.

Before returning to London, Rushbrooke became friends and fell in love with Dorothea Gertrud Weber, daughter of a distinguished German portrait painter. They married in 1902 after he returned to pastor St. Mary's Gate church in Derby. He subsequently pastored the Archway Road and Hampstead Garden Suburb Free Church churches in London.

His wise leadership and strong pastoral skills soon earned him a role in the British Baptist Union.[325]

Rushbrooke attended the first Congress of the Baptist World Alliance (BWA) in 1905 with its co-founder, John Clifford, and spoke at each of its subsequent gatherings for almost half a century. By the time another decade had passed, the BWA elected him as Commissioner for Europe. Fulfilling this role catapulted him into the ranks of the world's peacemakers. He resigned his church, became the BWA's European Secretary in 1925, and in 1928, shouldered the job of the first General Secretary of the Baptist World Alliance, which he faithfully executed until 1939, when he took up the mantle of President until his death eight years later. During this tenure, his stamp of reconciliation and peace upon global events was most profound.[326]

Bernard Green, Harry Rushbrooke, and others have recounted the heroic, courageous, and costly efforts of Baptists to work for peace after World War I and during and after the Nazi era in Europe. "Hitler's advance to conquest became a path to disaster," Green explains. "When the war ended, the occupied and the occupier faced the long and costly tasks of recovery, rebuilding, and rehabilitation. The victors, the liberated, and the vanquished had to find ways of creating a new Europe in which they could live together in peace. Baptists who had been on opposing sides faced excruciating challenges of forgiving one another in order to become reconciled in the one body of Christ."[327] This was unspeakably difficult.

For example, in England, 660 Baptist churches were bombed in the war, including fifty that were totally destroyed. Oldfield Park, in Bath, lost forty members in a single air raid. An incendiary bomb gutted the Baptist House, headquarters of the Baptist Union, in London. Claims to the government for damages to Baptist churches totaled more than £600,000 (an equivalent of more than £22,200,000 in 2014).[328] British Baptists raised more than £150,000 immediately, despite the privations of war rationing and economic instability, and dedicated a full one-third of this to helping Baptist brothers and sisters in Continental Europe, many of whose buildings, Bibles, and hymnals were lost, along with their ministers being conscripted and seminaries closed.[329] The brothers and sisters in Europe direly needed their help.

Germany faced a dismal situation as millions of people, uprooted from their homes, wandered aimlessly. The Displaced Persons (DPs), only a portion of whom had found shelter in camps, were mainly Eastern Europeans brought to Germany as forced laborers during the war buildup or who had fled ahead of the advancing Soviet armies in 1944. Although the Soviet Union and countries under Soviet control called for their return, for many DPs repatriation would have meant certain death or incarceration. Other refugees were ethnic Germans who had been expelled at war's end from the newly drawn borders of Eastern European countries. They thronged into a Germany gutted by Allied bombings, a land drowning in homeless people.[330]

James Rushbrooke established the BWA's World Emergency Relief Committee in 1943 to coordinate Baptist relief efforts in devastated countries. He made contact with Baptists in Scandinavia and as many other national groups as soon as possible. He surveyed their situations and, with their leaders, addressed the most pressing needs. BWA offered support and friendship and encouraged practical efforts to restore or establish peaceful relationships. This support included, among so much more, the formation of the Baptist Reconstruction of Europe Plan and the Baptist Reconstruction Committees that aided thousands of refugees where they were and provided travel expenses for the relocation of displaced persons to democratic countries. Rushbrooke became the face and hands of that aid.

He also used his influence to work for religious freedom. Rushbrooke served as mediator between government officials, rulers, and leaders of religious bodies to provide liberty of conscience for all persons, especially in Romania, Russia, and Spain, where persecution was severe. His ideal of Christian and Baptist unity was constant; yet, even within the Baptist family, this unity, for Rushbrooke, was conditional. He found it hard to associate with Baptists who continued to condone the persecution of others on religious grounds, or who remained silent in the face of such injustice.[331]

At the end of the war, correspondence and literature poured out of Europe and the British Isles from Baptist individuals and groups welcoming, with joyous relief, the possibilities of renewing correspondence and discussing future plans and proposals for reconciliation and restoration. Baptists in Sweden played a critical role by establishing a neutral site where reconciliation conversations were held, and Danish Baptists opened their country's doors for the 1947 Baptist Congress. Sadly, Rushbrooke did not live to attend.

When James Henry Rushbrooke died of a stroke on Saturday, 1 February 1947, the Baptist world mourned deeply. No single person of the twentieth century had influenced Baptist life as significantly as had Harry Rushbrooke. When the Council of the Baptist Union of Great Britain and Ireland met the next month, it passed a resolution recalling his monumental work. As a global Baptist leader, he had worked passionately for the following primary causes.

Rushbrooke, more than anyone else, unified Baptists of the world in establishing the Baptist World Alliance as an international and respected body based upon enduring Baptist principles. He contributed to this Baptist identity in both his writing and his person. He advocated religious freedom far beyond denominational lines to petition governments and global leaders on behalf of persecuted Christians. A peacemaker of rare ability, his reconciling work brought sworn enemies to the table of forgiveness and forged new friendships from the ashes of hatred and fear. Throughout the years, he remained passionate about the mission of the Church and the need to provide opportunities for the training of nationals to evangelize and plant churches within their own countries. As the council stated, he was "known to more of our people and by more of our people than any Baptist of his age."[332] He symbolized Baptist fellowship around the world.

In the decades since his death, Baptists have learned much from European and British Baptists of earlier generations in this matter of weaving peace. To stretch across external divides to aid in the reconciliation of political, economic, and social differences that separate humanity during wartime is noble work. Another is for Baptists to demonstrate peace-weaving within the Baptist family when power structures and theological concerns splinter the unity. In Baptist life, no single figure embodies reconciliation more than James Henry Rushbrooke, who, as a premier witness to Baptist heritage, left a legacy of unity and served nobly as a champion of peace.

Suggested Reading

Dekar, Paul R. *For the Healing of the Nations: Baptist Peacemakers.* Macon GA: Smyth and Helwys Publishers, 1993.

Green, Bernard. *European Baptists and the Third Reich.* Didcot, Oxford: The Baptist Historical Society, 2008.

———. *Tomorrow's Man: A Biography of James Henry Rushbrooke.* Didcot, Oxford: The Baptist Historical Society, 1997.

Rushbrooke, J. H. *The Baptist Movement in the Continent of Europe: A Contribution to Modern History.* London: Kingsgate Press, 1923.

Nannie Helen Burroughs
(1879–1962)

Voice for Gender Equality

Social Justice

Pamela R. Durso

IN THE EARLY twentieth century, American reformers seeking to bring an end to injustice and oppression worked tirelessly to eradicate urban poverty, the widespread lack of education, child labor, and gender and race discrimination. Included in those reformers was a Baptist woman, one whose name is largely unknown, even among Baptists. As a young adult, Nannie Helen Burroughs stepped into the role of prophet, speaking strong words about the right of women to be heard and the rights of women and girls to educational and vocational opportunities, and calling boldly for racial equality.

Nannie Helen Burroughs was born in Orange, Virginia, on 2 May 1879, two years after the end of Reconstruction and the withdrawal of federal military troops from the South. Her parents, John Burroughs and Jennie Poindexter Burroughs, had been born slaves but were still young children when the Emancipation Proclamation freed them. Following the Civil War, John attended Richmond Institute (now Virginia Union University) and served as an itinerant Baptist preacher. Apparently, he died a few years after the birth of Nannie, and in 1883, Jennie, who worked as a domestic laborer, moved to Washington, D.C. with hopes that her five-year-old child could have better access to educational opportunities.[333] Public schools for African-American children opened in Washington as early as 1864, and while they were segregated and most provided an inferior education, these schools offered the young Burroughs a higher quality of study and better-trained teachers than she would have ever encountered in rural Virginia.

As a teenager, Burroughs studied business and domestic science at the Washington Colored High School, commonly called M Street High School, the most successful African-American high school in the United States. While a student at M Street, she also took classes in the classical education program and organized the Harriet Beecher Stowe Literary Society, a club that allowed her to cultivate her gift for public speaking.[334] In 1896, Burroughs graduated as class valedictorian, having fulfilled her and her mother's dream that she receive an excellent education.

The same year that Burroughs graduated from high school, "segregation was legalized and sanctioned by the federal government,"[335] a roadblock that greatly hampered her job search. Looking for a teaching position, Burroughs applied at Tuskegee Institute in Alabama but was not hired. She then sought a position in the District of Columbia's "colored" public schools, but the schoolboard refused to hire her, apparently because of the darkness of her skin.[336] Of that experience, Burroughs noted, "It broke me up at first. I had my life all planned out to settle down in Washington with my mother, do that pleasant work, draw a good salary, and be comfortable the rest of my life." But her disappointment soon sparked within her a desire to build a school for African-American girls "that would give all sorts of girls a fair chance, without political pull, to help them overcome whatever handicaps they might have."[337]

Instead of teaching, Burroughs moved to Philadelphia to work as an associate editor of *The Christian Banner*, a Baptist newspaper. She returned to Washington a few years later and took the civil service examination in hopes of securing a government job, but Burroughs was told that there were no openings for "colored clerks."[338] To earn money, she took on work as a janitor.

In 1898, Burroughs accepted a position as bookkeeper and editorial secretary for L. G. Jordan, corresponding secretary of the National Baptist Convention's Foreign Mission Board. Since childhood, she had been an active member of the Nineteenth Street Baptist Church in Washington, and her new role at the convention offered her unexpected leadership opportunities, which she embraced eagerly.[339]

In 1900, the NBC moved its headquarters to Louisville, Kentucky, and Burroughs relocated there. She soon became a driving force for the organization of a women's convention. In the earliest years of this African-American convention, the women had taken on leadership positions and directed mission and education programs. Their ability to step into these roles was tied to their majority presence in local churches, regional organizations, and the national convention.

Given the high number of African-American women in the convention and their commitment to missions, their desire for a separate women's convention dedicated to support mission causes was not surprising. The journey toward that convention, however, had already begun in 1890. Representatives attending what was then named the Baptist Foreign Mission Convention (BFMC) voted to organize a national Women's Foreign Mission Convention, but in 1892, the ministerial-led BFMC reversed its position and blocked the formation of a women's auxiliary.[340] Instead, the leaders encouraged the women to participate in the already established male-led national convention, and they also promised that the women would be allowed to speak on important topics at every meeting.[341] Despite this promise and amid much protest, the women continued to move toward forming a national organization.

In 1895, the BFMC and two other existing conventions merged to form the National Baptist Convention. Five years later, the twenty-one-year-old Burroughs spoke to this male-dominated convention, delivering a prophetic speech, "How the Sisters Are Hindered from Helping." Boldly denouncing the limited opportunities for women in Baptist churches, she noted that "for a number of years there has been a discontent, a burning zeal to go forward in His [Christ's] name among the Baptist women of our churches."[342]

Following her speech, Jordan made a motion that the women be allowed to form their own convention. His support, along with Burroughs's speech, resulted in the formation of the Women's Auxiliary to the National Baptist Convention, and she was elected as the new organization's first corresponding secretary.

During her first year in office, Burroughs traveled 22,125 miles, delivered 215 speeches, organized 12 societies, and wrote 9,235 letters.[343] Of all the needs she addressed that first year, the one that seemed closest to her heart was the building of a training school for women and girls. In

1901, she appealed to the new women's convention to found such a school, stating "the preparation of our women for domestic and professional service, in the home and communities, ranks next in importance to preparing their souls for the world to come."[344] But Burroughs's cries went largely unheard. The women did not join in her vision, and the women's convention offered no money to support this dream.

In 1906, Burroughs found a site that was perfect for a training school, and almost single-handedly, she raised the down payment money to secure the land. The next year, she finally gained the support of the women's convention, which wrote a charter for the new school. Over the next few years, Burroughs continued raising money. By 1909, she had gathered enough funds to pay the full amount needed for the purchase of the property, and that year, a debt-free National Training School for Women and Girls opened its doors to seven students, five assistants, a matron, and teachers. By the end of the first school year, enrollment stood at thirty-one.[345]

The school adopted as its motto, "We specialize in the wholly impossible," which certainly reflected its reality. What began as an institution offering sixth-grade level classes in 1909 grew to one that offered junior high school, high school, and junior college classes in 1929, and within twenty-five years, Burroughs's school had provided education and training for over 2,000 girls and young women. The training school's curriculum centered on what Burroughs called the "Three Bs—The Bible, the Bath, and the Broom," or clean lives, clean bodies, and clean homes.[346]

Up until the time of her death in 1961, Burroughs remained as the school's president, raising the money needed, guarding the control of the school and preventing the male-led NBC from seizing its leadership, and educating thousands of women. After her death, the school's board of trustees voted to limit the programs offered to preschool and elementary levels and to change the school's name to the Nannie Helen Burroughs School.

In 2014, the school still stands as a testament to the fierceness of Burroughs's commitment to education. The school is now a co-educational "private educational institution dedicated to Christian principles, which embraces the African world experience and culture," and which provides a "holistic education" for children, instilling in them the "values, knowledge, and skills to ensure their role as productive world citizens and leaders in the global context of the 21st century."[347] The denominational alliance of the school has shifted, and in 2014, it affiliates with the Progressive National Baptist Convention.

All through her life and ministry, Burroughs offered prophetic words to Baptists and to all Americans. She directed her strong words about injustice and her passionate cries for freedom first to her fellow National Baptists. She willingly stood up and spoke out in conventions and meetings, criticizing cowardice, challenging gender oppression, and seeking to advance the cause of racial equality. Her prophetic role began early. She first spoke out at the age of twenty-one, calling male leaders to stop keeping the women from participating in the work of the convention. Twenty years later, she again stood up and rebuked the African-American male leaders of her denomination, telling them that they were preaching "too much heaven and too little practical Christian living." She challenged them to "make their religion a real, potent factor in race regeneration."[348] Burroughs also called on African Americans to stand up for their race, writing, "The Negro is opposed not because he is a Negro—but because he will take it. Negroes forget your color. Stop apologizing for not being White."[349]

In the 1950s especially, Burroughs extended her audience and challenged White churches, calling them to live out their commitment to Christ by welcoming people of all races to worship and fellowship with them. She wrote, "It is high time that the church were up to its business or [it should] stop preaching; stop building houses and calling those buildings 'churches of Christ' while excluding races that are not of the color that they like; stop teaching spurious doctrines and wearing the livery of heaven in which to masquerade and naming the name of Jesus and refuse to follow his teachings."[350]

Burroughs's strong words met with suspicion and criticism from African-American Baptist men, who sought to silence her voice by wrestling control of the training school from her. She also ran up against opposition from the White community, even government leaders, who believed she was a dangerous radical.[351]

Nannie Helen Burroughs died on 20 May 1961 at the age of eighty-two. More than 5,500 mourned her death at Nineteenth Street Baptist Church in Washington, a testimony to her influence on the people of her city and her world.[352] A strong advocate for equality, especially for the equality of African-American women and girls, Burroughs knew the power of education and the possibilities that it created. While she might be rightly criticized for emphasizing the domestic skills at her school and adhering to gender stereotypes, Burroughs believed that women had to first receive basic education and opportunity for employment before they could embrace roles as leaders and agents of change within their society. Because of this conviction and her passionate commitment to the causes of gender and racial equality, Burroughs devoted her time, resources, and energy into building a school that would help transform culture. She recognized the training school as her greatest legacy:

> I've put my whole life in this hill [school] but I have done it for God. He has chosen to use my life to build something for humanity, a place where women and girls of my race can come and learn some sense, about how to live to the glory of God. …I am going home [to heaven] one of these days but while my spirit serves in the divine realm I still will be helping some working woman or some growing girl here on this hill.[353]

In her roles as an educator, an activist, and a denominational leader, Burroughs offered to Baptists a prophetic voice, one that boldly and tirelessly called for gender and racial equality. Hers is a voice that is needed now in the early twenty-first century just as it was needed in the early twentieth century.

Suggested Reading

Hall, Prathia LauraAnn. "The Religious and Social Consciousness of African-American Baptist Women." Ph.D. dissertation, Princeton University, Princeton NJ, 1997.

Higginbotham, Evelyn Brooks. *Righteous Discontent: The Women's Movement in the Black Baptist Church, 1880–1920.* Cambridge MA: Harvard University Press, 1993.

Johnson, Karen A. *Uplifting the Women and the Race: The Educational Philosophies and Social Activism of Anna Julia Cooper and Nannie Helen Burroughs.* Garland Studies in African American History and Culture. New York: Routledge, 2000.

Smith, Karen E. "Nannie Helen Burroughs (1879–1961): A Voice for Social Justice and Reform." In *Twentieth-Century Shapers of Baptist Social Ethics*, edited by Larry L. McSwain and William Loyd Allen. Macon GA: Mercer University Press, 2008.

B. B. McKinney
(1886–1952)

The People's Musician

Ministry

Randall Bradley

Benjamin Baylus (B. B.) McKinney was the most well-known figure among Southern Baptist church musicians of the twentieth century. The hymns he wrote and led in camps, revivals, and denominational meetings formed an integral part of the core soundtrack of several generations of Baptists, and many of their important life decisions were made in response to his songs. His compiling and editing of the *Broadman Hymnal*, the most widely sold hymnal of the twentieth century—and perhaps of all time—made his songs and the name "B. B. McKinney" one of the most known and recognized Baptist names of his day.

Born in Heflin, Louisiana on 22 June 1886, the fifth of eleven children to James Calvin and Martha Heflin McKinney, B. B. McKinney, known to those who knew him well as "Ben" and in later years as "Uncle Mac," grew up on a 180-acre farm in Webster parish less than a dozen miles from Minden. He attended a crude one-room log schoolhouse in nearby Fryeburg about two miles from the farm.

McKinney, along with his father, attended local singing schools by such leaders as Aldine Kieffer and E. T. Hildebrand. While influenced by his father musically, Ben's mother influenced him spiritually by her unwavering faith and trusted prayer life. She readily shared her faith with others, and people from miles around came to receive her prayers.[354]

Ben McKinney played the harmonica, developed his baritone singing voice, and after his family purchased a pump organ around 1900 from a mail-order catalogue, the family was known for their lively singing. Martha McKinney often sang the song "Wayfaring Stranger."

The song later became McKinney's most requested solo and was the last song he sang at Ridgecrest Assembly just days before his death.

Having only completed school through the eighth grade at Fryeburg, McKinney enrolled in Mt. Lebanon Academy in 1906 at the age of twenty where he played football and sang in the school quartet. During these years, he accepted Christ, was baptized, and became a member of the Mt. Lebanon Baptist Church in 1909. He enrolled at Louisiana College at Pineville the following year where he was a student for two years. While at Mt. Lebanon and at Louisiana College, he was strongly influenced by C. J. Gilbert, who taught music at Mt. Lebanon and then at Louisiana College. Later in life, B. B. McKinney remarked that Gilbert "meant more to me in a musical way than any other musician I have ever met."[355] After leaving Louisiana College, McKinney clerked for two years at a store in Pineville and briefly attended a business school in Alexandria before entering Southwestern Baptist Theological Seminary in fall 1915.

During these final years in Louisiana, McKinney's commitment to pursue a life of music was solidified in large part due to the influence of Allen Pinckney Durham, who also happened to be the son-in-law of C. J. Gilbert. As Durham and McKinney led numerous revivals in North Louisiana, Durham recognized McKinney's musical and leadership skills and encouraged him to pursue a life of music and ministry.

In fall 1915, McKinney enrolled at Southwestern Seminary where he studied under the guidance of Southwestern's only music professor, I. E. Reynolds, who started teaching the same semester in which McKinney matriculated. At Southwestern, McKinney studied musical notation, sight-reading, voice, piano, history of music, history of hymns and tunes, evangelism, and church music practice—all with Reynolds.[356]

In November 1916 at a meeting in Waco, Texas, McKinney was introduced to Leila Routh, a Latin teacher at Mary-Hardin Baylor College in Belton, Texas. The meeting was "love at first sight," and Leila and Ben were married on 11 June 1918 at her mother's home in Giddings, Texas.[357] One month later, the U.S. Army inducted McKinney into the military at Camp Bowie, Texas, and sent him to Starkville, Mississippi for basic training. Before Christmas 1918, World War I ended and his military service was concluded. He returned to Fort

Worth where he rejoined Leila, who had continued teaching during his absence.[358]

I. E. Reynolds invited McKinney to join the seminary faculty in spring 1918. Shortly afterward, McKinney sensed the need for further education, and he enrolled at Siegel-Myers School of Music in Chicago, where he earned a Bachelor of Music degree through correspondence classes during the regular terms and through residency in Chicago in summer 1920 and 1921, both at Siegel-Myers and at the Bush Conservatory of Music.

No one knows exactly when McKinney began to notate his songs; however, in 1916 he privately published a small folder titled, "Six Gospel Songs, by B. B. McKinney. Evangelistic Singer, Box 995, Fort Worth, Texas."[359] Shortly afterward, McKinney began what was to be a longtime business relationship with Robert H. Coleman, a songbook publisher in Dallas, Texas.[360] McKinney contributed seven songs to Coleman's *Kingdom Songs* (1921). With Coleman's yearly publication, McKinney's songs reached a larger audience and became more popular.

Both McKinney and Coleman benefitted from the relationship, with McKinney getting his songs published and Coleman profiting from the many revival meetings and summer assemblies in which McKinney led the music. Starting in the early 1920s, McKinney served as Coleman's music editor. In this role, McKinney edited hundreds of songs in dozens of books; however, Coleman acknowledged McKinney's editorial contributions in only three collections.[361]

McKinney continued teaching at Southwestern for the next decade; however, in summer 1931 during the darkest days of the Great Depression, L. R. Scarborough, the president of Southwestern Seminary, notified I. E. Reynolds that, due to the seminary's dire financial condition, one of the School of Music's four faculty had to be released: Edwin McNeely, Ellis Garnett, McKinney, or Reynolds. Not being able to make such a difficult decision, Reynolds submitted his own resignation to the president.[362] When Dr. Scarborough summoned the music faculty to his office to announce Reynolds's resignation, however, the other faculty members also tendered their resignations, leaving Scarborough with the decision of whom to release. After consideration, Scarborough accepted McKinney's resignation because he knew that

McKinney was most capable of supporting his family as an evangelistic singer, through his work with Robert Coleman, and through his part-time ministry position at Travis Avenue Baptist Church in Fort Worth. McKinney remained in Fort Worth, where he became associate pastor and music director at Travis Avenue Baptist Church from 1931 to 1935 while also continuing his itinerant work. Many at the time, however, believed that a rift developed between McKinney and Reynolds that was partially responsible for McKinney's departure from Southwestern.[363] While this rift continued for many years, Reynolds and McKinney worked together on projects, serving alongside one another on conference programs and denominational projects.[364]

A discussion of B. B. McKinney would not be complete without chronicling his long and deep relationship with Oklahoma Baptists. McKinney began as the music director at Falls Creek Baptist Assembly in the Arbuckle Mountains near Davis, Oklahoma in 1925 and continued this relationship until 1947, except for 1943–1945 when World War II interrupted the annual assemblies. During those years, McKinney rehearsed the choir, which often numbered more than five hundred, and he taught a 7:15 A.M. music class during which McKinney stood on a hill while speaking to sometimes more than 1,000 people in attendance. Occasionally, in these early morning classes, McKinney introduced a new chorus or a refrain that he had written the night before in response to the sermon or a comment from a conversation.[365] During these years, McKinney became friends with Warren Angell, who had been recruited to Oklahoma Baptist University (OBU) in summer 1936 to build a music program there. The friendship between McKinney and OBU lasted throughout the rest of McKinney's life, and he visited OBU nearly every year. As a result, OBU bestowed an honorary doctorate on McKinney on 29 May 1942. After McKinney's death, OBU became home for McKinney's compositions and other papers, and in 1964–1965 Oklahoma Baptists pooled their resources and built the McKinney Chapel at Falls Creek, which still stands as a tribute to McKinney's significant contribution to the Baptists of Oklahoma.

In fall 1935, Thomas Luther Holcomb, newly appointed executive secretary-treasurer of the Baptist Sunday School Board, Nashville, Tennessee, visited McKinney unannounced in Fort Worth and invited him to join the Sunday School Board as music editor.[366] Shortly after Holcomb's visit to Fort Worth, McKinney resigned his position at Travis Avenue, severed his ties with Robert Coleman, and began his work in Nashville on 1 December 1935.

In the following years, McKinney traveled extensively, leading worship and teaching classes while also laying the groundwork for more extensive work to follow. On 30 December 1935, Holcomb's idea that the district association was the primary way in which the board's work would reach the churches was enthusiastically approved at a meeting in Birmingham, Alabama. A flurry of activity occurred in the following years as the Sunday School Board built relationships with local associations. McKinney's reports to the SBC recorded more than 25,000 miles and visited seventeen states in the first year. His activity grew in the next five years; for example, in 1937–1938 he led music and presented sessions for five summer encampments, five state conventions, and twenty-one associational conferences.[367] These active years led to the establishment of the church music department on 20 August 1941, with McKinney as its head.

All the while, McKinney was setting the stage for a major hymnal for Southern Baptists. In the meantime, however, he published *Songs of Victory* (1937).[368] Exactly when McKinney began to lay the groundwork for *The Broadman Hymnal* is not known. Although the *Minutes* of the Sunday School Board, 14 March 1940, mention that a "large number of music directors throughout the South have assisted in the selection of hymns and gospel songs for the book, and a committee here at the Board has worked earnestly to see that each number in the book is correct in doctrine expressed, the words used, and the music selected," there is no record of McKinney's having met with anyone concerning the hymnal's contents or organization.[369] All who have researched the *Broadman Hymnal's* formation surmise that it was solely the work of McKinney; at any rate, the completed hymnal was unveiled as scheduled on 25 May 1940.[370] In the years since its release, it has been used as widely as any hymnal ever published.[371]

Shortly after the release of the *Broadman Hymnal*, the Sunday School Board released *Let Us Sing*, the first book designed for training practitioners in the church. With McKinney's planning, the book was co-authored by Allen W. Graves with chapters contributed by Mattie C. Leatherwood and Robbie Trent.[372] The Sunday School Board widely distributed this book with thousands of individuals receiving study course credit.

In 1944, the Sunday School Board, through offering to pay one-third of the salary of a state worker, encouraged each state to enlist a person to lead his or her state's music program. Five states quickly got on board. Arkansas, Texas, Oklahoma, Mississippi, and Florida enlisted leaders, and McKinney met with this team in Nashville in January 1946 to launch what became one of the most successful and innovative programs ever introduced to disseminate music ministry. In the years that followed, dozens of other states followed the example of these original five. Shortly afterward, the expansion of the Church Music Department continued with the addition of W. Hines Sims, who went on to succeed McKinney after his death in 1952.

In 1945, at McKinney's encouragement, the Sunday School Board purchased the publishing interests of Robert H. Coleman, bringing all of McKinney's copyrights under the auspices of the Sunday School Board. Later in 1950, the church music department under McKinney's leadership started *The Church Musician* publication, containing both educational articles and choral anthems. This piece provided choral repertoire for churches, and these anthems were also published singly.

In 1952, the administration of the Sunday School Board, fully aware of McKinney's distaste for office work and administrative duties, were working to find a way to relieve him of these duties without appearing to demote him; they were designing an executive music editorial position. However, before this plan could be realized, McKinney was fatally injured in an auto accident while traveling from Ridgecrest, North Carolina, where he had participated in Church Music Week, to Gatlinburg, Tennessee for a brief vacation. The accident occurred on 2 September 1952, and he died on 7 September. Mrs. McKinney was also in the car but was unharmed.

B. B. McKinney is recognized for his thirty years of service to Baptists, from his teaching at Southwestern to his establishing the Music Department at the Baptist Sunday School Board and his guiding Southern Baptists during the early years of denominational leadership in music ministry. The music that he wrote continues to be used, and it is likely his greatest legacy. McKinney's total compositional output included 229 gospel songs (with stanza and refrain), twenty-seven hymns and hymn tunes (without refrain), fifty-one choruses, nine choral responses (prayer, etc.), six choir selections (in hymnals), eleven anthems (in *The Church Musician*), three music examples (in study course books), and 127 arrangements/adaptations. Of these compositions, many of his hymns remain in use today. The two most recent hymnals published by Baptists, *The Baptist Hymnal* (2008) and the *Celebrating Grace Hymnal* (2010) contain fifteen and five selections by McKinney, respectively. While picked up by a small number of evangelical hymnals, McKinney's hymns were never included in the hymnals of most major denominations but have been revered and beloved by several generations of Baptists.

Lastly, an analysis of McKinney reveals a humble man who deeply loved the church and its people. He wrote songs for the people of his time, and his songs touched common people in uncommon ways. From his rural upbringing in Louisiana, he had a heart for small churches with limited musical leadership. Perhaps as we look to the future, church music leaders today may do well to remember that most churches in the world are small, and their worship is led by people who are largely untrained. As a model for current worship leaders, much can be learned from B. B. McKinney's humble spirit, commitment to sing songs that touched the heart, and his untiring service.

Suggested Reading

Hastings, Robert J. *Glorious Is Thy Name: B. B. McKinney, the Man and His Music.* Nashville TN: Broadman, 1986.

McElrath, Hugh T. "Turning Points in the Story of Baptist Church Music." *Baptist History & Heritage* 19/1 (January 1984): 4–16.

Powell, Paul R. *Wherever He Leads I'll Go: The Story of B. B. McKinney.* New Orleans: Insight, 1974.

Reynolds, William J. "The Contributions of B. B. McKinney to Southern Baptist Church Music." *Baptist History & Heritage* 21/3 (1 July 1986): 41-49.

———, compiler. *The Songs of B. B. McKinney.* Edited by Alta C. Faircloth. Nashville TN: Broadman, 1974.

Thomas Buford Maston
(1897–1988)

Southern Baptist Pioneer in Race Relations

Social Justice

Michael E. (Mike) Williams, Sr.

IN 2006, THE COOPERATIVE Baptist Fellowship, an organization of Baptist churches formerly affiliated with the Southern Baptist Convention, chose its first African-American moderator, Emmanuel McCall, long-time seminary professor, pastor, theologian, and denominational servant. Seven years later, the Southern Baptist Convention chose veteran New Orleans pastor Fred Luter, Jr. as the denomination's first African-American president. Each choice was a far cry from earlier days in Southern Baptist life when, at best, African Americans were treated in paternalistic and prejudiced fashion and, at worst, were greeted with hostility and sometimes even violence by Southern Baptists or those who claimed to be Southern Baptists. While some might wonder why it had taken so long for Baptists in the South, both the SBC and the CBF, to choose Black Baptists for their top elective office,[373] all Baptists and Christians—from the South, especially—should acknowledge the immense contribution of T. B. Maston to making those days possible.

Born in 1897 in rural East Tennessee, Thomas Buford Maston rose from humble and impoverished beginnings to be one of Southern Baptists' greatest prophets. Educated first at Carson-Newman College, graduating in 1920, and then earning both a master's and doctorate in religious education from Southwestern Baptist Theological Seminary in the early 1920s, he also began his teaching part-time and then as part of the full-time faculty at Southwestern during that time. Maston went on to earn both an M. A. in sociology from Texas Christian University in 1927 and a Ph.D. at Yale University in 1939. He continued to teach at Southwestern Seminary until his retirement in the 1960s. Eventually, the administration at SWBTS agreed to shift the Christian ethics department from the school of religious education to the school of theology. Thus, Maston spent the bulk of his teaching career in the School of Theology, where he influenced more than a generation of pastors, missionaries, and other ministers in training.[374] Never isolating himself from his rural roots, Maston mastered translating the most difficult teachings in Christian theology and ethics into language that the average Christian could understand. He also spoke prophetically to Southern Baptists about the greatest ethical concerns of his era, especially that of race relations. Through his teaching and writing, he educated decades of students who passed through the doors of Southwestern as well as reaching countless Southern Baptists through his writing.

Maston invested his life at Southwestern Baptist Theological Seminary, but his influence expanded worldwide for two major reasons—his students and his writing. At one time, Dr. and Mrs. Maston had hoped to serve in foreign missions. Unable to serve on a full-time basis due to the disability of their son, Tom Mc, the Mastons did engage in lecture trips to speak abroad to both American military personnel and Southern Baptist missionaries. Additionally, Maston also served in visiting lectureships and as a guest professor in U.S. institutions. However, the Mastons also lived vicariously through the work of Maston's former students, as those students carried Maston's messages for social justice and racial equality around the world. As Bill Tillman writes, "Many of [Maston's former doctoral students] pursued mission endeavors, to a large extent because of the thoughtful authentic blending Maston did with ethics and evangelism."[375]

Maston wrote and taught during a critical period in Southern Baptist life. Increasingly in the 1940s, 1950s, and 1960s, Southern Baptist life focused upon supporting convention programs and strengthening institutional life. At a time when American and Southern culture changed dramatically and Southern Baptists grew rapidly, with his prophetic voice Maston called Southern Baptists to move from surface to substance. As Bill Tillman writes, Maston imbued "a prophetic demeanor and sense."[376]

Maston utilized two major types of writing—a popular style to reach the masses and a more academic type to reach students and scholars—

each having a strong scholarly base but written with each particular audience in mind.

While Maston's teaching and writing addressed many topics, the roots of his Christian ethical approach centered upon two main focuses. He was clearly and deeply both biblical and Christological in all that he did. Perhaps his most significant academic work was his *Biblical Ethics: A Guide to the Ethical Message of the Scriptures from Genesis through Revelation*. In this work, Maston drew eighteen specific conclusions about the ethical content of the Bible. The final two conclusions summarized not only this work but much about his entire ministry. He wrote that he grew ever more convinced that *"the Bible is authoritative"* and that "the Bible does not possess any authority independent of God. Its authority stems from the fact that it is a product of and contains God's word to man." Such a conclusion places Maston firmly within the Baptist heritage regarding biblical authority. In perhaps his most scholarly work, *Christianity and World Issues*, Maston began his discussion of "Christianity and World Transformation" with the Bible and its relevance. For Maston, the scripture became the starting place for any discussion of Christianity. But as his last conclusion in *Biblical Ethics* stated, *"There is a very real sense in which the authority is Christ's* (emphasis is Maston's) since He is the climax of the revelation of God. The Scriptures can lead us to Christ, but as sacred as they are, they cannot take the place of Christ." Furthermore, Maston added, "When properly understood, this does not detract from the authority of the Bible; it clarifies and deepens it." He also understood that Christ's cross should serve "Unifying Symbol" of the Christian life but "much more." As he explained in *Why Live the Christian Life?*, Maston meant that Christ's cross was not simply a symbol, but "a historic event" that "gives depth and meaning" to "the kind of life that [Christians] should live for Christ in the world."[377]

As William Pinson's *An Approach to Christian Ethics: The Life, Contribution, and Thought of T. B. Maston* demonstrates, Maston's "approach" to Christian ethics ran the full gamut of categories in contributions to various aspects of the Christian life. He contributed to many different areas of ethical thought, including topics and subjects such as "Citizenship," "War and Peace," and "Human Suffering." However, it was in the arena of the racial questions sweeping the South that Maston made his greatest contribution. As Tillman writes, "The hallmark issue of T. B. Maston's life and work was race relations."[378] Maston's efforts to address the issue of race followed a multi-fold pathway. The earliest books Maston published dealt with the issue of race relations. In 1946, his first book was *Of One: A Study of Christian Principles and Race Relations*. In 1957, he devoted one of his chapters in *Christianity and World Issues* to the problem of "Race and Racial Tension." The subtitle of his 1959 book, *The Bible and Race*, reflected his typical Biblicist approach. Subtitled *A Careful Examination of Biblical Teachings on Human Relations*, this book replaced *Of One* but, similar to his *Biblical Ethics*, demonstrates what scripture teaches about race relations. Furthermore, he wrote frequent articles in journals, state Baptist newspapers, and other Southern Baptist publications.[379]

He led the Baptist General Convention of Texas to form its Christian Life Commission of Texas and worked in committees and councils to address race issues. His involvement reached outside Southern Baptist life with his membership in the local Urban League and the NAACP, as well as other groups.[380]

Maston also spoke at every possible opportunity about the importance of race relations for believers. Once, after speaking about love at a conference, a young Black worker questioned Maston, critically asking if there was a real danger in substituting love for justice, making it a "mere sentimentality." Maston answered in typical fashion. "Not genuine love," he said. "It is inclusive of justice."[381]

In *Why Live the Christian Life?*, Maston expressed in greater detail the same concept. He wrote, "Love is basic and primary. Justice is a derivative of love, but is also an indispensable instrument or expression of love. Love demands justice; it is also the ground for the judgment of justice. Divorce justice from love and it becomes a 'soulless legalism.' Divorce love from justice and it becomes less than *agape*; it will become superficial sentimentality."[382]

In his chapter on Maston in *Twentieth-Century Shapers of Baptist Social Ethics*, Bill Tillman identifies a statement in Maston's *The Bible and Race* as being "typical of his comments regarding race."[383] After discussing the story in Acts of Peter and Cornelius and the following inquisition by "the circumcision party" in Jerusalem, Maston writes,

> The preceding may be disturbing to some Christians of the White race, but let all of us sincerely search for the fullest implications of the no-respecter-of-persons principle and of other great truths that are an integral part of the gospel we preach, teach, and profess to follow. If God is no respecter of persons, if he shows no partiality, our ultimate goal should be the elimination of all partiality, prejudice, and discrimination from our lives. All [people] should be considered as of infinite worth, created in the image of God, actual or potential children of God, and as members of the human race rather than of some division within that race. These attitudes may represent a long, long step for most of us, but is it not a direction that is plainly revealed by an examination of Peter's vision and of the results in his life of that vision?[384]

Maston lived race relations. He truly practiced what he preached. He befriended Black students at SWBTS before they were even allowed to live in the dorms. He invited African Americans to his church, Gambrell Street Baptist Church, met them outside, and walked with them inside.[385]

For his writing and speaking on race relations, Maston received both support and hatred. Despite the mixed reactions to his prophetic words, Maston always answered Southern Baptists who wrote and always responded in Christ-like fashion.[386]

T. B. Maston was a prophet at a time when Southern Baptists needed a prophet. While most of his writing, teaching, and speaking about Christian ethics fell inside conventional and traditional Southern Baptist values at that time, his challenge to his Southern Baptist contemporaries regarding race created the kind of tension that only true prophets generate. Additionally, as Tillman demonstrates, Maston mentored decades of Baptist prophets. Both these prophets and his writing reach beyond his immediate time and place and continue to influence Baptists directly and indirectly today. While in his efforts to reach the laity he may have neglected scholarship at the other end of the spectrum, he had the intellectual firepower and academic credentials to have been Southern Baptists' Richard or Reinhold Niebuhr or Stanley Hauerwas. Instead of being a nationally recognized ethicist, he focused his ministry where the overwhelming majority of Southern Baptists lived. He never forgot his East Tennessee roots. He never served as a marching activist, but with his quiet example and gentle yet strong voice, he provided a witness that sensitive Southern Baptists heard.

Near the end of his life, Maston wrote his last book, a handy little study, *To Walk As He Walked*. In it Maston stressed the need for Christians to imitate Jesus. Before it became cliché to ask the question, "What Would Jesus Do?," T. B. Maston implored his readers to "live as he lived."[387] But as multiple former students, colleagues, church members, and others testify, T. B. Maston walked like Jesus walked in his own life. Baptists and other Christians live better because he walked this way.

Suggested Reading

Maston, T. B. *Biblical Ethics: A Guide to the Ethical Message of the Scriptures from Genesis to Revelation*. Macon GA: Mercer University Press; reprint, 1988.

———. *To Walk As He Walked*. Nashville TN: Broadman Press, 1985.

———. *Why Live the Christian Life?* Nashville TN: Broadman Press, 1974.

Pinson, William M., Jr., editor. *An Approach to Christian Ethics*. Nashville TN: Broadman Press, 1979.

Tillman, William M., Jr. "T. B. Maston (1897–1988): Mentor to Southern Baptist Prophets." In *Twentieth-Century Shapers of Baptist Social Ethics*, edited by Larry L. McSwain and Wm. Loyd Allen. Macon GA: Mercer University Press, 2008.

Herschel H. Hobbs
(1907–1995)

Conservative Advocate for Denominational Unity

Theology

Jerry Faught

HERSCHEL H. HOBBS STANDS as one of Southern Baptists' foremost personalities and was likely the most significant leader in Southern Baptist life in the last half of the twentieth century. David Dockery noted that, due to Hobbs's work as church pastor, radio preacher, author, denominational leader, and theologian, Hobbs garnered the moniker "Mr. Southern Baptist."[388] Walter Shurden claimed that Hobbs served as Southern Baptists' theologian in the latter half of the twentieth century, as E.Y. Mullins had done in the first half of the century. According to Shurden, Southern Baptists must turn to the writings of Mullins and Hobbs if they want to become familiar with "historic" Southern Baptist distinctives.[389]

Leon McBeth listed Hobbs as one of several pastor-theologians who had greatly influenced Southern Baptists, and his colleague James Leo Garrett named Hobbs as one of the two most influential Southern Baptist pastor-theologians of the twentieth century. In December 1999, the editorial staff of the *Baptist Messenger*, the Oklahoma Baptist state paper, selected Hobbs as the Oklahoma Baptist of the Century.[390]

Above all his commitments, Hobbs was a pastor and believed God had called him to the pastorate. On more than one occasion, he turned down opportunities to assume other roles in the denomination. He stated in his autobiography that if he had ten thousand lives to live, he would "want to be a pastor in every one of them." During his days at Southern Seminary and after graduation, Hobbs pastored several churches, but by 1945, when he became pastor of the Dauphin Way Baptist Church in Mobile, Alabama, the second largest Baptist church east of the

Mississippi, Hobbs had established himself as an influential pastor. While at Dauphin Way, he achieved national prominence, preaching a revival at First Baptist, Dallas, and delivering a baccalaureate sermon at Southern Seminary. Hobbs's standing in the convention was such that the renowned R.G. Lee asked Hobbs to nominate him for the convention presidency in 1948.[391]

In 1949 Hobbs became pastor of the First Baptist Church of Oklahoma City, a position he would hold until 1972. Under Hobbs's leadership, First Baptist enjoyed substantial influence in the state and beyond and carried out vital ministries, never losing interest in the persons located in the surrounding area. His most difficult days as pastor occurred during the Civil Rights Movement. Although a self-identified gradualist in racial matters, in the early 1960s Hobbs led a divided congregation to remove barriers that would prevent Blacks from joining the church. Although the church never conducted a major outreach program into the Black community, a few Black members did join and, by 1969, First Baptist provided facilities for Black community action meetings.[392]

During the Oklahoma City years, Hobbs became one of the most recognized and respected figures in the Southern Baptist Convention (SBC). In 1958 Hobbs became the regular preacher for the popular "Baptist Hour" radio program. He preached over 700 messages during his eighteen-year tenure.[393] His sermons were broadcast over nearly four hundred stations around the world. According to some of his peers, he reached fifty million persons weekly.[394] Hobbs's expository sermons, which centered on salvation in Christ, earned him the label "Mr. Baptist Hour."[395]

Hobbs also distinguished himself as a writer, publishing approximately 160 books, all of which contained a grassroots theology. He wrote primarily for rank and file Southern Baptists, his theological ideas emerging from sermons he preached to his Oklahoma City congregation. In his books, he often cited and quoted from biblical commentaries and published sermons rather than academic theologians. Hobbs once chided Southern Baptist seminary professors for using academic terminology in their writings and sermons that the average Southern Baptist did not understand. He called on the professors to follow his example and use the "old cornbread and buttermilk" expressions.[396] Hobbs's theology rested upon biblical exposition. As James Leo Garrett has noted, Hobbs was an exegetical theologian who utilized the lexical-grammatical-historical hermeneutic he learned from A.T. Robertson and W. Hersey Davis at Southern Seminary.[397]

No professor at Southern Seminary shaped Hobbs, however, more than E.Y. Mullins. Hobbs never sat in a class taught by Mullins, arriving at Southern Seminary in 1932 four years after Mullins's death. Yet, Hobbs studied Mullins's books carefully and published a revision of Mullins's *The Axioms of Religion*. Above all, Hobbs appropriated Mullins's concept of soul competency and understood it as the foundational principle of Baptist belief.[398]

Over 100 of Hobbs's books were biblical commentaries for Sunday school teachers that he published quarterly from 1968–1993 for the Baptist Sunday School Board (now LifeWay). These Sunday school commentaries, called *Studying Adult Life and Work Lessons*, enjoyed a circulation of 100,000 copies per quarter.[399] Beginning in 1961, Hobbs wrote a weekly column on Baptist beliefs that appeared for many years in a number of Baptist state papers.[400]

From 1961–1963, Hobbs served as convention president during some of the stormiest years in the history of the SBC. Ralph Elliott, the first faculty member of Midwestern Seminary, established in 1958 in Kansas City, Missouri, published his first book with Broadman Press in July 1961. Elliott's book, *The Message of Genesis*,[401] received immediate criticism and, for the next year, Southern Baptists were bombarded with written materials from a variety of sources denouncing Elliott's book as a product of liberal scholarship.[402] At the annual convention in San Francisco in June 1962, Southern Baptists reaffirmed their faith in the Bible as the authoritative Word of God, encouraging trustees and administrators in Southern Baptist educational institutions to remedy at once those situations in which theological views were being disseminated that threatened the historical accuracy and doctrinal integrity of the Bible.[403] Hobbs feared that the controversy might result in schism in the SBC. As president of the convention, he felt obligated to involve himself in the conflict time and again in order to maintain unity. He held meetings with Elliott, Millard Berquist, president of Midwestern, the

Midwestern trustees, and other convention leaders and wrote many letters, primarily in response to critics.[404]

His most public action in dealing with the controversy occurred at the 1962 national convention meeting when he delivered the presidential sermon. Hobbs addressed the controversy directly and, although he never mentioned Elliott by name, his message did not appear to offer support for Elliott. While Hobbs affirmed the vast majority of seminary professors as people "worthy of our trust and understanding," he declared that a few Southern Baptist theologians had embraced neo-orthodoxy, a halfway point between liberalism and conservatism, and had made attempts to adjust the Southern Baptist faith to its position. He further declared that Southern Baptists' greatest contribution to the theological dilemma lay not with neo-orthodoxy, but with a conservatism that placed the Bible alone as the center of its theology.[405]

The sermon revealed two noteworthy viewpoints embraced by Hobbs throughout his career. First, Hobbs, while affirming traditional conservative Baptist theology, tolerated a degree of diversity in the denomination as long as it did not threaten the unity of the convention. Second, Hobbs embraced a utilitarian approach to seminary education, emphasizing the need for theological students to be "indoctrinated" to those things Southern Baptists believe and practice if they intended on becoming leaders in the denomination.[406]

One significant result of the Elliott Controversy, besides Elliott's dismissal from the faculty, was the vote by the 1962 convention to draw up a new confession of faith. The confession was the brainchild of the established leadership of the convention—in particular, Albert McClellan, Porter Routh, and Hobbs. These men decided that a new confession could work to keep the peace by uniting various factions in the SBC under one statement of faith.[407] Hobbs chaired the committee and took an active role in managing the thinking of the committee. He introduced concepts and phrases and sorted through the scripture basis for each clause in the confession.[408] The SBC adopted the confession at the Kansas City meeting in 1963.[409] This may have been Hobbs's finest hour as a denominational servant.

The committee revised the 1925 confession, making some notable changes. The 1963 statement reasserted a commitment to biblical authority found in the earlier confession, but added a sentence declaring, "[T]he criterion by which the Scriptures are to be interpreted is Jesus Christ."[410] Hobbs later asserted that the sentence was added as a correction to Elliott's "Neo-orthodox" position. He stated further, "I'll stand till Gabriel blows his horn on that statement. Any interpretation that does not agree with the revelation of God in Jesus Christ is the wrong interpretation."[411] Hobbs claimed that the committee spent more time putting the preamble of the confession together than any one article of the confession. Hobbs said on numerous occasions that the preamble, which emphasized soul competency, is as much a part of the confession as any of the seventeen articles. Hobbs believed that the preamble protected the individual conscience and guarded against a creedal faith. Hobbs rejected the notion that the confession should be made a "test of fellowship or orthodoxy."[412]

By 1980, Hobbs's influence in the convention had begun to wane. Efforts by fundamentalists to take control of the convention had begun. They faced resistance from moderates. With the convention in turmoil, Hobbs tried to play the role of peacemaker. At the annual convention meeting in St. Louis, Hobbs, as a senior statesman and past convention president, asked for a point of personal privilege in order to appeal to messengers to move beyond their differences and renew their commitment to evangelism and missions. Before he could complete his remarks, Hobbs was drowned out by a chorus of boos from the audience.[413] A few years later, Hobbs was named as a member of the Peace Committee, established in 1985 to seek to reconcile theological differences in the convention. The twenty-two-member committee spent three years working together but failed to bring peace.[414] Hobbs sought to be a mediator and to build bridges between the disputing parties, but he was unsuccessful.

In recent years, various leaders in the new SBC have appraised Hobbs, often unfairly. Cooperative Baptist Fellowship leaders, on the other hand, have ignored Hobbs, looking to E.Y. Mullins as their primary theological guide.[415] This disregard for Hobbs may be in part because Hobbs was such a thoroughgoing Southern Baptist denominationalist.

In 1990, James Hefley identified Hobbs as a key player among a group of "well-intentioned kingmakers" who sought to thwart the efforts of "activist conservatives in the early 1960s."[416] Neo-Calvinists have criticized Hobbs for leading Southern Baptists away from an earlier commitment to a pristine Reformed theology to an inadequate Arminian outlook.[417] David Dockery and Timothy George might not care for Hobbs's Arminianism, but in the end they affirm him due to Hobbs's theologically conservative outlook.[418] In 2000, several Southern Baptist leaders criticized the 1963 Baptist Faith and Message committee for lacking a professional theologian and further asserted that Hobbs was "duped" by neo-orthodox individuals who heavily influenced the 1963 document.[419]

In the final analysis, we might best remember Hobbs as an influential pastor-theologian who loved the SBC and prized denominational solidarity, and believed that theological tension in the convention was healthy. He accepted those he considered to be to the right and left of him theologically, with the stipulation that they defend their position biblically and try not to impose their position upon the convention and disrupt denominational unity. In the end, Hobbs often engaged in a political strategy of compromise in order to thwart division and promote unity in the convention for the sake of evangelism and missions. These are the marks of an old-time Southern Baptist. And Herschel Hobbs preferred to be known as an old-time Baptist.

Suggested Reading

Dockery, David S. "Herschel H. Hobbs." In *Theologians of the Baptist Tradition*, edited by Timothy George and David S. Dockery. Nashville TN: Broadman & Holman, 2001.

Garrett, James Leo, Jr. "Herschel Harold Hobbs: Pastoral and Denominational Expositor-Theologian." *Southwestern Journal of Theology* 54/2 (Spring 2012): 132–40.

Hobbs, Herschel H. *The Baptist Faith and Message*. Revised edition. Nashville TN: Convention Press, 1996.

———. *Fundamentals of Our Faith*. Nashville TN: Broadman Press, 1960.

———. *My Faith and Message: An Autobiography*. Nashville TN: Broadman & Holman, 1993.

Henlee Barnette
(1911–2004)

Baptist Activist for Love and Justice

Social Justice

Aaron Weaver

HENLEE BARNETTE WAS a pioneer Baptist ethicist whose teaching career, spanning four decades, had an immeasurable influence on the ethical formation of two generations of Southern Baptist pastors and professors. His more than a dozen books and countless articles and columns in denominational publications reached thousands of Southern Baptists in both the pulpit and the pew. He was an activist first and foremost for racial equality and Jim Crow was his target. With a biblical ethic focused on love and justice, Barnette's gospel ministry of activism also led him to champion women's equality, peace, a clean and healthy environment, and the rights of conscientious objectors.

Henlee Hulix Barnette was born 14 August 1911 in a one-room cabin in Taylorsville, North Carolina. Growing up in the Tar Heel State, Barnette, who dropped out of school in the sixth grade, worked long hours as a millworker in the textile town of Kannapolis. While his mother and older sister were committed churchgoers, the Barnette men were not. During a revival, a nineteen-year-old Henlee prayed for his salvation—coincidentally, so did his father at the same service. Henlee was soon baptized and, less than a year later, licensed to preach. Nicknamed "The Bible Preacher" for his extensive quotation of scripture from the pulpit, Barnette enrolled at Wake Forest College at the age of twenty-six where he continued to preach, serving as pastor of two local Baptist churches.

His educational journey took him next to Southern Baptist Theological Seminary in Louisville, Kentucky. There, Barnette was introduced to the social gospel theology of Walter Rauschenbusch—the subject of his dissertation. As a seminarian, Barnette made an intentional effort to live out what he learned in the classroom. This passion for a social theology and action-oriented ethic led him to minister in Louisville's slum area known as the "Haymarket," first as a volunteer and later as superintendent of the Union Gospel Mission (1941–1945). As superintendent, he enlisted dozens of young volunteers to attend to the physical and spiritual needs of the more than 10,000 Haymarket residents.

In 1946, Barnette left Louisville to begin his teaching career in the sociology department of Howard College, a Baptist-affiliated school (now known as Samford University) in Birmingham, Alabama. After just one year, he left Howard for a position at another Baptist school, Stetson College in Deland, Florida. Four years later, Barnette returned to Louisville to teach ethics at his alma mater. He would serve as a professor of Christian ethics at Southern Seminary from 1951 until 1977, and after his "retirement," as a medical ethics professor at the University of Louisville from 1977 to 1992.

Barnette served as an activist in an era when most Southern Baptists frowned upon activism. He believed that Jesus offered fundamental principles that should inform the politics of Christians. Barnette preached, wrote, and taught that Christians as individuals and congregations had a biblical responsibility to cooperate with the state in promoting human welfare and justice in society. Barnette encouraged his students to be actively involved in the political process at all levels, and called on churches to urge its members to do the same.

With all the issues he confronted, Barnette rooted his ethical method in the teachings of Jesus Christ about love, which he affirmed as the ultimate authority for moral concern and action. "Love (*agape*) is the central motif of the Christian faith," wrote Barnette in his widely read book, *Crucial Problems in Christian Perspective*.[420]

This *agape* principle was Barnette's guide to decision-making. He contended that an ethic of love and justice went hand in hand: "Love and justice are inseparable. Agape without justice is sentimental and abstract. Justice socializes love, saving it from being purely personal and sentimental; love humanizes justice, saving it from being rigidly legalistic and unredemptive. Love is the norm of justice, and justice is the instrument of love. In short, justice is love in action in all areas of human existence."[421]

The mission of the church, according to Barnette, is to represent Christ's *agape* ethic to the world, demonstrating the gospel to be both personal and social. "Personal regeneration and public reconstruction are the goals of the gospel," he wrote. "We must work at both of these simultaneously. It is unrealistic to try to transform the world into the Kingdom of God without transformed people."[422] Barnette emphasized the power of the Holy Spirit to bring individuals to a "new life in Christ" and experience the same type of transformation that he had as a young millworker.

Barnette practiced what he preached to his students and readers. His activism extended from city hall to the halls of Congress, and unlike many religious leaders, his activism was not limited to affixing his signature to a statement of support for a candidate or cause. While a professor at Stetson College, Barnette protested a proposal to permit gambling at a horse racetrack, and as a Southern Seminary professor, he campaigned for numerous local Louisville politicians. During his career, Barnette publicly backed several candidates for statewide office and helped organize a group called "Clergy for Carter" in 1976 to aid then Georgia Governor Jimmy Carter's presidential bid. Most notably, Barnette loudly criticized the policies of his own government, marching against segregation and voting restrictions and participating in demonstrations against the war in Vietnam.

Barnette was a significant influence on shaping Southern Baptist attitudes toward race relations, confronting the evil of racial inequality early in his ministry. While a professor in Birmingham in 1946, Barnette and a colleague attended a meeting of the all-Black Birmingham Baptist Ministers' Conference at the Sixteenth Street Baptist Church in order to make new friends and start a dialogue. That meeting soon led to the establishment of an interracial organization for Baptist pastors, and the first gathering of the group featured Benjamin Mays, a civil rights advocate and president of Atlanta's Morehouse College. The presence of White and Black pastors and laymen under one roof was an historic occasion, as well as an act of civil disobedience under Alabama law.

The next year, Barnette stepped up his activism and championed equal pay for Black teachers in a speech to the Jefferson County Negro Teachers Association. This speech did not sit well with his bosses at Howard College, but Barnette pressed on. On Easter Sunday in 1947, Barnette boarded a bus and sat in a rear seat reserved for African Americans. He stayed seated until a second threat from the bus driver forced him to stand.

Two years later at the 1949 meeting of the Florida Baptist Convention, Barnette gave a rousing speech on racial equality to the displeasure of many of his fellow Southern Baptists. The recording secretary even objected to his speech being published in the convention's official report. Barnette gave a similar speech to more than 2,000 Southern Baptist women at the Florida Woman's Missionary Union Convention in Orlando. That speech received mixed reviews within the denomination and attracted much media attention, with one woman telling a reporter that she felt like hitting Henlee with her pocketbook!

Before the Supreme Court issued its landmark *Brown vs. Board of Education* ruling desegregating public schools in 1954, Barnette advocated the integration of Southern Baptist colleges and seminaries. He even outlined a racial equality strategy for the denomination's five seminaries that called for complete integration, recruitment of Black students, and support for religion undergraduate programs at African-American schools. Barnette, who boldly endorsed the excommunication of unrepentant racist congregants, was known for his warm welcome to Black students as well as his lobbying efforts for a full-time African-American professor on the Southern Seminary faculty, in addition to the creation of a Black church studies program.

During spring 1961, Barnette helped bring Martin Luther King, Jr. to Southern Seminary to deliver the prestigious Julius Brown Gay lectures. King's visit came at a tumultuous time, mere days following the United States invasion of Cuba at the Bay of Pigs and the launching of the Student Nonviolent Coordinating Committee. The city of Louisville was in the middle of its own civil rights struggle and racial tensions were palpable. Protestors were demonstrating to integrate public facilities and Black students were engaging in sit-ins at Whites-only restaurants.

In his address "The Church on the Frontier of Racial Tension," King declared the nation's racial crisis to be much more than a political problem—it was a moral problem, too. The church must learn "to live together as brothers or we will perish as fools," King told the packed crowd of 1,400.[423] The civil rights leader also attended a combined meeting of Barnette's ethics classes for a question-and-answer session with 500 students.

Although the seminary neglected to mention King's visit in their publications, his appearance on the campus of the Southern Baptist Convention's flagship seminary resulted in extensive media coverage. This coverage captured the attention of grassroots Southern Baptists and prompted a severe backlash across the denomination. While the seminary's faculty, staff, and students welcomed King, many Southern Baptist leaders and pastors expressed their anger. Churches threatened to withhold financial support to the seminary, and six congregations in Alabama made good on their threat. An Alabama layman even raised $50,000 for a mass mailing to all Southern Baptist churches in an effort to get Southern Seminary President Duke McCall fired. Three months after the controversial visit, the seminary's trustees issued statements distancing the school from King and his civil rights efforts.

Despite the intense backlash, Barnette continued on with his activism for civil rights and racial equality. He served as a founding member of the Kentucky Christian Leadership Conference, a state affiliate of King's civil rights group, the Southern Christian Leadership Conference. In fact, Barnette co-authored the KCLC's constitution with King's brother and Louisville pastor, A.D. Williams King. In 1964, three years after King's appearance on the Southern Seminary campus, Barnette joined him again—this time at the state capital in Frankfurt at a march for desegregated housing. The following year, Barnette took part in "Operation Selma" at Louisville's Broadway Temple A.M.E. Zion Church. There, he spoke and helped raise funds for the now historic 1965 march in Alabama from Selma to Montgomery.

Barnette focused his advocacy on open housing in the mid-1960s, writing columns for local newspapers and also raising funds. When King was assassinated in 1968, Barnette organized a memorial at the seminary. He summed up his core conviction regarding the pursuit of racial justice in a column for *Home Missions*, the popular publication of the SBC's domestic missions entity. "It is the mission of the church to participate in God's purpose of tearing down the walls of hostility and achieving of the one new humanity under the lordship of Christ (Eph. 2:20)," Barnette wrote.[424] This is what he aimed to do—tear down the walls of hostility within his denomination, community, state, and nation.

Like King, Barnette became an outspoken opponent of the Vietnam War. Although not a pacifist, Barnette began to emphasize peacemaking in his writings and activism during the Korean War. He called on Christians to pray for peace and for churches to teach peacemaking and emphasize diplomacy over war and multilateral disarmament over an arms race. In 1954, he testified before a congressional committee in Washington, D.C. in support of strengthening the United Nations in pursuit of a "warless world." He also joined the chorus of clergy who were questioning the feasibility of classic Just War Theory in an age of "weapons of mass destruction."

For Barnette, the war in Vietnam was deeply personal. His son Wayne was a draft resister who left the U.S. for Sweden, and his son John was a fighter pilot flying missions in North Vietnam. Barnette ardently advocated for the conscientious-objector claims like those of Wayne and urged the government to grant amnesty to the thousands of young Americans who refused to aid the war. Barnette again spoke out against his own denomination, which, despite its professed support for freedom of conscience, had failed to offer support to its own Southern Baptist conscientious objectors in the Vietnam War and during previous military campaigns. Southern Baptist pastors who condemned the civil disobedience of draft resisters and/or insisted that Christians not question the decisions of political leaders in the realm of foreign affairs were guilty of idolatry, according to Barnette, for making the state absolute and ultimate.

Throughout his career, many Southern Baptists recognized Barnette as the SBC's leading expert on environmental issues. He was almost exclusively concerned with the environmental crisis during the first years of the 1970s, as environmentalism emerged as a (temporarily) bipartisan issue in American politics. In 1970, Barnette helped a group of students at Southern Seminary form an "Ecoclub." Serving as the group's faculty sponsor, Barnette and the Ecoclub collected papers, cans, and other items to be recycled. He also led his students to participate in the nation's first-ever Earth Day on 22 April 1970, and ensured that Earth Day was observed in the seminary's chapel. The following semester, Barnette taught a course on the ecological crisis, the first of its kind at any SBC seminary. From 1970–1972, Barnette lectured on and researched environmental issues, taking a sabbatical to study with renowned environmentalist Howard Thomas Odum at the University of Florida. *The Church and the Ecological Crisis* was the final product of Barnette's sabbatical. Published by the evangelical publisher Eerdmans, this helpful book was crammed full of succinct ethical strategies for environmental action. In his book, Barnette charted a middle ground, situating himself between environmental doomsayers like Paul Ehrlich, who proposed radical action, and those who denied the need for any environmental concern. Barnette also differed with another popular scholar, Lynn White, who blamed Western Christianity for the ecological crisis. Barnette argued that the exploitation of nature has characterized most nations and people who have ever inhabited the earth, not just Christians in the Western hemisphere.

While environmental theologians wrote primarily for other theologians, Barnette offered an accessible and concise ecological theology for his fellow Christians. His eco-theology rested on the basic belief that God is the creator and sustainer of the universe. The covenant between God and humanity extended to the rest of God's creation, Barnette stressed. Consequently, he viewed environmental abuse as sin. Barnette understood the biblical view of humans as that of caretakers or "stewards" of the Earth. The first requirement of stewardship, Barnette argued, is faithfulness to God's command to responsibly exercise care for God's creation. He championed a "holistic" environmental ethic that urged reverence for all life and included a biblical sense of adoration of nature—an attitude he believed to be especially reflected in the Book of Psalms.

His eco-theology centered upon environmental action. Barnette prescribed a long list of "personal ecotactics," such as recycling and lifestyle choices to limit pollution. However, he insisted that personal ecotactics must be extended to collective social ecotactics, such as political action. He called on churches to place environmental issues on the top of their agenda and implored both individual Christians and congregations to call for greater government regulation of polluting industries and businesses. In addition to political action, Barnette also encouraged churches to begin educational environmental programs, host seminars, participate in environmental organizations, and take part in community clean-up projects. He pressed churches to redefine their theology to "see love in terms of willing the welfare of all God's creatures and things" and embrace an understanding of stewardship that "transcends giving a tithe faithfully and sees a responsibility to the whole earth."[425]

From his fight for racial equality in the Jim Crow South to his efforts to wage peace in a hawkish denomination, Henlee Barnette modeled Christian activism for his fellow Southern Baptists. He did so armed with a biblical message rooted in the agape love ethic of Jesus Christ. His influence on multiple generations of Southern Baptists is significant indeed. Perhaps most importantly, Barnette offered an example to the nation's largest Protestant denomination—a denomination with a long history of making resolutions—of how to make its words meaningful through an ethic of action.

Suggested Reading

Barnette, Henlee. *The Church and the Ecological Crisis*. Grand Rapids MI: Eerdmans Publishing Co., 1972.

———. *Crucial Problems in Christian Perspective*. Philadelphia PA: Westminster Press, 1970.

———. *Exploring Medical Ethics*. Macon GA: Mercer University Press, 1982.

———. *Introducing Christian Ethics*. Nashville TN: Broadman Press, 1961.

———. *A Pilgrimage of Faith: My Story*. Macon GA: Mercer University Press, 2004.

Gardner Taylor
(1918–2015)

Poet Laureate of Preaching

Preaching

Kelly Pigott

Gardner Taylor can preach. One discovers this immediately when listening to him. His words form deep in his chest and stroll out in a bass tone with perfect diction. His presence at the pulpit demands attention. He has a way of captivating his listeners with storytelling and brilliant metaphors. Then he reaches out his hand and invites the audience to dance with him as his prose takes on a cadence. Literary devices become his instruments. He promenades the audience through sweeping ideas, until they are gently placed back into their pews, feeling both comforted and disturbed, because the Word has been spoken to them through a prophet.

Taylor's natural gift for speaking was passed onto him from his parents and perfected with years of practice. But he learned to preach as he struggled alongside the men, women, and children in his community. This came during a time when the United States was painfully working out what Abraham Lincoln meant when he redefined the phrase "all men are created equal" at Gettysburg by applying it to slaves.

Growing up in Louisiana, Gardner Calvin Taylor heard firsthand stories about the hardships of slavery. Both grandfathers were slaves, and his father, Washington Monroe Taylor (b. 1870), pastored one of the largest African-American churches in Baton Rouge, Mt. Zion Baptist Church, when many parishioners bore the literal scars of oppression on their backs. As his father said, "You could almost still hear the echo of hounds baying to the trail of runaway slaves."[426]

Though uneducated, Washington Taylor read voraciously and demonstrated a love for the English language, which he passed onto his son. Tragically, Washington Taylor died in 1931 when Gardner was only twelve.[427] To support the family and pay off debts, his mother, Selina Gesell Taylor, taught at Perkins Road School. Selina proved to be an able educator and a strict disciplinarian. She made sure that her son took advantage of the limited educational opportunities available for people of color in the Deep South.

Despite demonstrating a very high IQ when tested, Gardner Taylor struggled in school. Before there were laws against such things, teachers occasionally called out grades at an assembly. When a Professor Paige read Taylor's average, he commented loud enough for others to hear, "a good mind going to waste...."[428] Though a bit unconventional, his chiding worked. Taylor graduated McKinley High School as the valedictorian of his class and the captain of the football team.

He continued his education at the nearby Leland College (A.B., 1937) and aspired to be a lawyer. Despite the fact that Leland was unaccredited, the University of Michigan Law School accepted Taylor. In a recent interview, Taylor reflected on this moment in his life when no African American had ever passed the bar in Louisiana. He recalled a family member saying with dismay, "Where you going to practice, in the middle of the Mississippi River?"[429]

Despite his family's misgivings, Taylor's brilliance and tenacity made a career in law a very real possibility; however, during his senior year at college he experienced a theophany that he has described in several interviews. Dr. J. A. Bacoats, the president of Leland College, hired Taylor as his chauffer and often allowed the senior to borrow the car. Taylor recalls coming back to campus one day when an oncoming Model-T Ford crossed the highway and sped straight for him. He attempted to get out of the way by veering toward a ditch, but the other car crashed, killing the occupants—two White men. This was spring 1937 in South Louisiana, where a quick lynching for people of color still occurred. At the inquest, Taylor described being in shock, not knowing what to expect. However, two White men, a farmer and a Baptist preacher, came forward as witnesses to the event and testified that Taylor was not at fault, prompting the young man's dismissal. Afterwards, Taylor felt a "consuming feeling" that he wanted to go into the ministry. He abandoned law and followed in the footsteps of his father by becoming a preacher. Dr. Bacoats encouraged Taylor to enroll in his alma mater, Oberlin Graduate School of Theology.

Taylor preached his first sermon at his home church, Mt. Zion, in 1937. He travelled to Oberlin and began his theological training. While there, Taylor honed his preaching skills by accepting every opportunity that came his way. It was no coincidence that he became more interested in politics at this time as well. His family's struggle for freedom experienced early in his life greatly shaped Gardner Taylor's prophetic call, and liberation from oppression became a dominant theme of his preaching.

While at Oberlin, Taylor met his wife, Laura Bell Scott, a student at Oberlin College. After a few years of courtship, they married in 1941 and had one daughter, Martha. Laura, like Garland Taylor's mother, was an educator. In 1960, she helped establish Concord Elementary School in Brooklyn, where she served as principal for thirty-two years without pay. Gardner Taylor always spoke fondly of his wife as his "dearest of friends" and "harshest of critics."[430] She died in 1995. Gardner Taylor then married Phyllis Strong, a church member, in 1996.

Taylor's first pastorate was at Bethany Baptist Church in Elyria, Ohio (1938–1941). After he graduated, he moved to New Orleans, Louisiana, to pastor Beulah Baptist Church (1941–1943). He then moved back to Baton Rouge where he became the pastor of his home church, Mt. Zion (1943–1947). These early pastorates became crucial to his growth as a minister and pulpiteer. He recalled, "I preached to salvage their innate dignity in a society which totally sought to crush them."[431]

Taylor's leadership at these churches fostered strength and growth. He had many gifts that contributed to this success. Towering above them all was his powerful preaching. His reputation grew considerably, so that at the age of twenty-nine he was invited to preach at Concord Baptist Church in Brooklyn, a 6,000-member congregation and one of the most prestigious churches in the National Baptist Convention. That same year, he also spoke at the Baptist World Alliance meeting in Copenhagen, Denmark. When he returned from overseas, Concord offered him the job of senior pastor. In 1948, Taylor accepted, and he remained there until his retirement in 1990.

During Taylor's tenure, Concord added 9,000 members. In addition, the church started the Concord Elementary School and the Concord Nursing Home. It even helped establish the Concord Credit Union to cater to the financial needs of African Americans. Taylor effectively led the church through many crises, not the least of which was a devastating fire that destroyed the sanctuary in 1952. An architect told Taylor that it would cost at least a million dollars to replace the building. Although he had a sizeable church, Taylor felt devastated. He believed the amount far too much for his congregation to afford. His wife consoled him by convincing her husband that the architect did not know what he was talking about, and that it would not cost any more than $750,000. Taylor laughs as he recalls the event, because he believed her, and it gave him the confidence to rally his church to collect the funds to pay for a building that wound up costing over two million dollars.[432]

Firmly established in his pulpit in Brooklyn, Taylor focused his attention on the plight of African Americans. As a result, his preaching turned more and more prophetic. He befriended Martin Luther King, Jr., and even invited the young pastor to preach at Concord in 1951. The two men shared a common vision of taking a more active approach to civil rights. While many leaders cautioned patience, Taylor and King felt that they had been patient enough.

A showdown occurred within the National Baptist Convention (NBC) as the two men decided to challenge the established leadership and their seemingly more conservative approach to civil rights. The incumbent president, Joseph H. Jackson, pastor of Olivet Baptist Church in Chicago, sought reelection. King had grown disgruntled with Jackson's leadership, and the feud between the two had reached a tinderbox state. Taylor joined King in an attempt to gain leadership of the convention by agreeing to run for president against Jackson. A contentious election in 1960 reinstated Jackson after events led to a court suit, even though Taylor had overwhelmingly won the popular vote.

In 1961, Taylor ran against Jackson again. During one of the convention meetings, members of the "Taylor Team" rushed the platform in an attempt to force Jackson off the stage so that Taylor could assume control. In the pushing and shoving that ensued, a Jackson supporter named Arthur G. Wright fell and fractured his skull, dying a couple of days later. In the sober aftermath, Jackson was reinstated as president, and the bid to control the NBC was extinguished.[433]

The event became a watershed moment for Taylor and the civil rights movement. Despite attempts by some to label this as a feud between a "conservative" and "activist" approach, the underlying agendas were far more complicated and nuanced. Granted, Jackson felt King and Taylor's activism was too extreme. But egos, vague parliamentary procedures, disagreements about strategy, differing priorities, and the like were but a few of the many layers to this unfortunate event.

In November 1961, L.V. Booth of Zion Baptist Church in Cincinnati, Ohio, invited several leaders to a meeting to discuss the possibility of forming a rival organization, which led to the creation of the Progressive National Baptist Convention (PNBC). Although Taylor did not attend the initial meeting, he became a major voice in the newly formed convention, serving as its second president from 1966–1969. The PNBC became a powerful ally in the non-violent, activist approach to the Civil Rights Movement.

While Taylor downplays the relationship, by some accounts, Taylor's preaching influenced King. Indeed, the two fought side-by-side in many of the most tumultuous battles of the 1950s and 1960s in an attempt to show a united front in both the North and South. In retrospect, Taylor reflects with somber tones about the relationship. "I did not realize—I should have, I've felt guilty about that—I did not realize the pressures this man was under."[434]

Taylor's activism in civil rights led him to several other key positions. In New York he was appointed to the Board of Education in 1958. He became the first African American to serve as president of the Protestant Council of Churches. He also served on the board of directors of the Urban League and was a member of the New York City Commission on Inter-Group Relations.[435] In the 1960s, he was arrested for picketing a construction site to raise awareness about prejudicial hiring practices.[436]

Some aspects of civil rights came slowly. Taylor admits that he had a gradual "conversion" when it came to the rights of women during the latter part of the 1960s. It reached a pinnacle during the Anita Hill-Clarence Thomas incident. "I reached the conclusion that Black women have been so put upon that they have developed a kind of psychological scar tissue, so that they've learned to take in stride things that ought to outrage them."[437]

Though a significant leader in the Civil Rights Movement, Gardner Taylor's legacy will most likely be his gift of preaching. He has influenced a countless number students. Formally, he taught preaching at such distinctive locations as Colgate Rochester Divinity School, Union Theological Seminary, and Harvard Divinity.

The informal title that has often been granted Taylor is "Poet Laureate of Preaching." Formally, *Time* magazine declared him the "Dean of the Nation's Black Preachers." *Ebony* magazine twice declared him as one of the greatest preachers in American history. Baylor University honored him as one of the twelve greatest preachers in the English-speaking world. Taylor has also collected a plethora of honorary degrees, and in 2000, President Clinton awarded him the Presidential Medal of Freedom.

As further proof of his gift, Yale invited Taylor to be the Lyman Beecher lecturer in 1976. At this event, Taylor declared,

> ...I confess that preaching has often seemed to me such a clumsy and unclear form of communication. At its lowest elevations it seems many times to be a dull and unexciting rehashing of old matters. At its impassioned heights, it seems to approach a vulgarity of intensity and a making public of sentiments and experiences which if they have happened at all seem altogether too private, and precious to be paraded before a crowd of strangers....

At the end of the lecture, Taylor confesses that a preacher often finds him or herself like Ezekiel, standing before a valley of dry bones and asking of God, "Can these bones live?" The only answer a pastor can give is the same one that Ezekiel offered: "Lord, thou knowest." "Thus ought there to be," Taylor says, "some central hush in the preacher's utterance, for he or she stands in the midst of life and death matters, with God very much in the midst of it all."[438]

After Taylor retired as a pastor, he devoted much of his time in the classroom in an attempt to pass on such hard-won wisdom to yet another generation. "Preaching," Taylor confesses, "that's all I know anything about." Indeed.*

Suggested Reading

George, Timothy, James Earl Massey, and Robert Smith, Jr., editors. *Our Sufficiency Is of God: Essays on Preaching in Honor of Gardner C. Taylor*. Macon GA: Mercer University Press, 2010.

Taylor, Edward L., editor. *The Words of Gardner Taylor*. 5 volumes. Valley Forge: Judson Press, 1999–2001.

Taylor, Gardner C. *How Shall They Preach?: The Lyman Beecher Lectures and Five Lenten Sermons*. Elgin IL: Progressive Baptist Publishing House, 1977.

Thomas, Gerald Lamont. *African-American Preaching: The Contribution of Dr. Gardner C. Taylor*. Volume 7. New York: Peter Lang, 2004.

---

* Gardner Taylor died on April 5, 2015, while this book was in editorial production with the publisher.

List of Contributors

Randall Bradley
The Ben H. Williams Professor of Music
Baylor University

Bonnie Oliver Brandon
Freelance Writer, Associate Minister, and Executive Assistant to the Pastor
Mt. Zion Baptist Church, Memphis, Tennessee

Scott Bryant
University Chaplain and Vice President for Spiritual Development
East Texas Baptist University

Karen O'Dell Bullock
Fellow and Professor of Christian Heritage
Director of the Ph.D. Program
B. H. Carroll Theological Institute

Terry Carter
Associate Dean, Pruet School of Christian Studies
W. O. Vaught Professor of Christian History and Ministry
Chair, Department of Christian Ministry and Chair, Department of Christian Missions
Ouachita Baptist University

Brad Creed
Provost and Executive Vice President
Professor of Religion
Samford University

Michael Dain
Assistant Professor of Religion
Religion Coordinator
Wayland Baptist University, Lubbock Campus

Keith Durso
Online Adjunct Instructor of Religion
Ottawa University and St. Leo University

Pamela R. Durso
Executive Director
Baptist Women in Ministry
Atlanta, Georgia

John Inscore Essick
Associate Professor of Church History
Baptist Seminary of Kentucky

Jerry Faught
Professor of Religion
Wiley College

Bruce Gourley
Executive Director
Baptist History and Heritage Society

J. David Holcomb
Professor of History and Political Science Director
Honors Program Coordinator, London Studies Program
University of Mary Hardin-Baylor

List of Contributors

Glenn Jonas
Charles Howard Professor of Religion
and Chair of the Department of
Religion
Campbell University

Sheila Klopfer
Religion Department Chair
Co-Director Christian Scholars
Program
Georgetown College

Melody Maxwell
Assistant Professor of Christian Studies
Howard Payne University

Kendal P. Mobley
Visiting Assistant Professor of Religion
Johnson C. Smith University

Gregory L. Nichols
Lecturer in Baptist and Anabaptist
Studies
International Baptist Theological
Seminary
Amsterdam, The Netherlands

Kelly Pigott
University Chaplain
Associate Professor of Church History
Hardin-Simmons University

Michael D. Sciretti, Jr.
Minister of Spiritual Formation
Freemason Street Baptist Church
Norfolk, Virginia

Delane Tew
Associate Professor of History
Samford University

Todd von Helms
Chaplain, St. David's School
Raleigh, North Carolina
Adjunct Professor
Dallas Baptist University

Aaron Weaver
Communications Manager
Cooperative Baptist Fellowship

Doug Weaver
Professor of Religion
Baylor University

Michael E. (Mike) Williams, Sr.
Professor of History
Dallas Baptist University

Mark Wilson
Director of Civic Learning Initiatives
College of Liberal Arts
Auburn University

Notes

[1] Ernest A. Payne, *Thomas Helwys and the First Baptist Church in England*, 2nd ed. (London: The Baptist Union, 1966) 2.

[2] *Oxford Dictionary of National Biography*, s.v. "Helwys, Thomas (c.1575–c.1614)" (New York: Oxford University Press, 2004) 271.

[3] Payne, *Thomas Helwys*, 2.

[4] "Helwys, Thomas (c.1575–c.1614)," 271.

[5] The Scrooby congregation migrated first to Amsterdam before settling in Leiden. From Leiden, a minority of the congregation known as the "Pilgrims" chose to sail for America in 1619.

[6] Pope A. Duncan, "A History of Baptist Thought 1600–1660" (Th.D. diss., Southern Baptist Theological Seminary, 1947) 97.

[7] John Robinson, *Of Religious Communion, Private and Public* (1614) 41.

[8] See Robinson, *Of Religious Communion*, 41, and G. Hugh Wamble, "The Concept and Practice of Christian Fellowship: The Connectional and Inter-Denominational Aspects Thereof, Among the 17th-Century English Baptists" (Th.D. diss., Southern Baptist Theological Seminary, 1955) 58–59.

[9] Thomas Helwys, *A Short Declaration of the Mystery of Iniquity*, in Joe Early, Jr., *The Life and Writings of Thomas Helwys* (Macon GA: Mercer University Press, 2009) 305.

[10] Ibid., 209.

[11] Ibid., 156.

[12] For more on these Baptists and their prison writings, see Keith E. Durso, *No Armor for the Back: Baptist Prison Writings, 1600s–1700s* (Macon GA: Mercer University Press, 2007).

[13] Roger Williams, founder of Providence Plantations and hence the Rhode Island colony, has been extensively studied by historians. Recent recommended works about Roger Williams include: John M. Barry, *Roger Williams and the Creation of the American Soul: Church, State, and the Birth of Liberty* (New York: Viking, 2012); James P. Byrd, Jr., *The Challenges of Roger Williams: Religious Liberty, Violent Persecution, and the Bible* (Macon GA: Mercer University Press, 2002); and Edwin Gaustad, *Roger Williams: Lives & Legacies* (Oxford and New York: Oxford University Press, 2005). The text of the 14 March 1663 "Patent for Providence Plantations" is available online from the Lillian Goldman Law Library of Yale Law School at http://avalon.law.yale.edu/17th_century/ri03.asp (accessed 7 March 2014).

[14] For a biography of John Clarke, see Wilbur Nelson, *The Hero of Aquidneck: A Life of Dr. John Clarke* (New York: Fleming H. Revell, 1938); for a summary of John Clarke, see Walter B. Shurden, "John Clarke: Ill News from New England," http://centerforbaptiststudies.org/resources/illnewes.htm (accessed 7 March 2014).

[15] The text of the 15 July 1663 "Rhode Island Charter" is available online from the Lillian Goldman Law Library of Yale Law School at http://avalon.law.yale.edu/17th_century/ri04.asp (accessed 7 March 2014).

[16] See Joseph E. Early, ed., *The Life and Writings of Thomas Helwys* (Macon GA: Mercer University Press, 2009).

[17] For more information about the Anne Hutchinson controversy, see Eve LaPlante, *American Jezebel: The Uncommon Life of Anne Hutchinson, the Woman Who Defied the Puritans* (New York: HarperOne, 2005).

[18] John Clarke, *Ill News from New England: or A Narrative of New-England's Persecution Wherein Is Declared That While Old England Is Becoming New, New England Is Becoming Old* (London: Henry Hills, 1652; repr. Baptist Standard Bearer, Inc., 2004) 23.

[19] *Collections of the Rhode Island Historical Society, Vol. IV* (Providence: Knowles, Vose & Company, 1838) 213.

[20] *Records of the Colony of Rhode Island and Providence Plantations in New England*, vol. 1 John Russell Bartlett, ed., (Providence: Rhode Island, 1856) 111. Accessed 7 March, 2014.

[21] Sanford Hoadley Cobb, *The Rise of Religious Liberty in America: A History* (New York: MacMillan, 1902) 430. The Touro Synagogue National Historic Site commemorates America's oldest synagogue in Newport, Rhode Island.

[22] Clarke, *Ill News*, 33.

[23] For a summary of the 1651 jailing, court hearing, and Obadiah Holmes whipping, see ibid., 27–70; and Mabel Thacher Rosemary Washburn, "Craw-ford Ancestry," *The Journal of American History* 12/1 (January–March 1918): 365–67.

[24] Clarke, *Ill News*, 10.

[25] Clarke, *Ill News*, 6, 98–113.

[26] For a discussion of the influence of Williams upon Locke, see Barry, *Roger Williams*, 315, 390.

[27] See 1663 Rhode Island Charter at http://avalon.law.yale.edu/17th_century/ri04.asp (accessed 7 March 2014). "The Avalon Project."

[28] Stanley J. Lemons, "History & Significance: Rhode Island Colonial Charter: 1663–2013," http://livelyexperiment.org/history-significance/ (accessed 7 March 2014).

[29] C. E. Barrows, "Dr. John Clarke," *The Baptist Quarterly* 6 (1872): 483–502.

[30] See the John Clarke Society at http://johnclarkesociety.org/ (accessed 7 March 2014).

[31] See Lemons, "History & Significance"; Maureen Moakley, *Rhode Island Politics and Government* (University of Nebraska Press, 2001); and "The Rhode Island Charter and Roger Williams's Legacy," Roger Williams University, http://pdq.rwu.edu/news/rhode-island-charter-and-roger-williams%E2%80%99s-legacy (accessed 7 March 2014).

[32] Michael Mullet, "Radical Sects and Dissenting Churches, 1600–1750," in *A History of Religion in Britain: Practice and Belief from Pre-Roman Times to the Present*, ed. Sheridan Gilley and W. J. Sheils (Oxford: Basil Blackwell Ltd., 1994) 205; cited by David A. Copeland, *Benjamin Keach and the Development of Baptist Traditions in Seventeenth-Century England* (Lewiston NY: The Edwin Mellen Press, 2001) 32.

[33] See Copeland, *Benjamin Keach*, 155ff.

[34] Thomas Crosby, *The History of the English Baptist: From the Reformation to the Beginning of the Reign of King George I*, 4 vols. (London: printed and sold by the author, 1738–1740) 4: 69–209.

[35] Copeland, *Benjamin Keach*, 36–37.

[36] H. Leon McBeth, *The Baptist Heritage: Four Centuries of Baptist Witness*, vol. 1 (Nashville TN: Broadman Press, 1987) 94.

[37] J. Barry Vaughn, "The Glory of a True Church: Benjamin Keach and Church Order Among Late 17th-Century Particular Baptists," *Baptist History and Heritage* 30/4 (1 October 1995): 47–57. *ATLA Religion Database with ATLASerials*, EBSCO*host* (accessed 19 August 2013).

[38] Vaughn, "The Glory of a True Church," 53.

[39] Ibid., 55.

[40] Ibid.

[41] Ibid., 67.

[42] Copeland, *Benjamin Keach*, 156.

[43] Benjamin Keach, *The Breach Repaired in God's Worship* (London, 1671; Seventeenth Century British Baptist Materials, Publication 669, Microfilm 950, reel 10) vi.

[44] Copeland, *Benjamin Keach*, 157.

[45] Benjamin Keach, "Epistle Dedicatory," *The Articles of Faith of the Church of Christ or Congregation Meeting at Horsely-down*, 1697), quoted in Vaughn, "The Glory of a True Church," 68.

NOTES

[46] George Whitefield ultimately connected those affected by the English, American, and Welsh revivals. In Britain the events were known as the Evangelical Revival; in the American colonies they were considered the Great Awakening. See Mark A. Noll, *The Rise of Evangelicalism: The Age of Edwards, Whitefield, and the Wesleys* (Downers Grove: InterVarsity Press, 2003) 18. Anne Dutton's primary social-spiritual network was the English Calvinistic Methodist wing of the Evangelical Revival represented by Whitefield.

[47] Thomas Gibbons, *Memoirs of Eminently Pious Women, of the British Empire. A New Edition, In Three Volumes* (London: Ogles, Duncan, and Cochran, 1815).

[48] Joseph Ivimey, *A History of the English Baptists, Vol. IV* (London: Isaac Taylor Hinton, Warwick Square; and Holdsworth & Ball, St. Paul's Church-Yard, 1830) 510.

[49] John Cudworth Whitebrook, *Ann Dutton: A Life and Bibliography* (London: A.W. Cannon and Co., 1921) 3.

[50] H. Wheeler Robinson, *The Life and Faith of the Baptists*, rev. ed. (London: Kingsgate Press, 1946; 1st ed., 1927; rept. Wake Forest NC: Chanticleer, 1985) 55–56.

[51] For a portrayal of Dutton as a key lay supporter of the Evangelical Revival, see Diane Susan Durden [O'Brien], "Transatlantic Communications and Literature in the Religious Revivals, 1735–1745" (Ph.D. diss., University of Hull, 1978) 85.

[52] Private spiritual direction takes place when one who is struggling through a transcendence crisis receives guidance and direction from another who is perceived to be holy, wise, loving, experienced, knowledgeable, and sensitive to the Spirit, with the aim of healing and freeing the soul through a deeper understanding and surrender to the Divine in daily life.

[53] *A Brief ACCOUNT of the Gracious Dealings of GOD with a Poor, Sinful, Unworthy Creature, Relating to The Work of Divine Grace on the Heart, in a saving Conversion to CHRIST and to some Establishment in Him. PART 1. By A.D.* (London: printed by J. Hart. and sold by J. Lewis and E. Gardner, 1743), 37. The desert fathers and mothers sometimes called it "guard of the heart." Although not nearly as developed, this practice also appears in Puritan spirituality. Anne Dutton practiced this art and it found a place in her spiritual direction. See Michael D. Sciretti, Jr., "Anne Dutton As a Spiritual Director," in *Women and the Church*, ed. Robert B. Kruschwitz. *Christian Reflection: A Series in Faith and Ethics* 33 (2009): 30–36.

[54] *Brief Account I*, 38.

[55] Ibid., 43–44.

[56] *A Brief ACCOUNT of the Gracious Dealings of GOD with a Poor, Sinful, Unworthy Creature, Relating to A Train of special Providences attending Life, by which the Work of Faith was carried on with Power. Part II. By A.D.* (London: printed by J. Hart. and sold by J. Lewis and E. Gardner, 1743), 30.

[57] Ibid.

[58] In the first edition of her first work, her name appeared on the title page and at the end of the preface. Dutton would never place her name on the title page of any of her works again; at most, she would place her initials. Her most common signature was "One who has tasted that the Lord is gracious."

[59] John Lewis to Thomas Prince, Sr., 20 August 1743, Davis MSS, Massachusetts Historical Society. Unlike Lewis's handling of most contributors to the evangelical magazine, Dutton's name was always concealed during the early years of the Evangelical Revival.

[60] By 1765, Anne Dutton had witnessed the publication of over fifty of her works. She was clearly the most prolific Baptist woman in the eighteenth century. This conclusion is drawn from an examination of W.T. Whitley, ed., *A Baptist Bibliography, 1526–1837*, 2 vols. (London: Kingsgate Press, 1916–1922); and Edward C. Starr, ed., *A Baptist Bibliography*, 25 vols. (Rochester NY: American Baptist Historical Society, 1947–1976).

[61] *A Brief Account II*, 144.

[62] For a study that has demonstrated how this worked in the Christian tradition with other mystics, see

Christopher Rowland, with Patricia Gibbons and Vicente Dobroruka, "Visionary Experience in Ancient Judaism and Christianity," in *Paradise Now: Essays on Early Jewish and Christian Mysticism* (Atlanta: Society of Biblical Literature, 2006) 41–56.

[63] In his work *The Evangelical Conversion Narrative*, D. Bruce Hindmarsh offers an arresting comparison: "If Catherine of Siena was a Third Order Dominican, then Anne Dutton must be reckoned something of a Third Order Baptist mystic." See Hindmarsh, *The Evangelical Conversion Narrative: Spiritual Autobiography in Early Modern England* (New York: Oxford University Press, 2005) 299.

[64] I am following the scholarship of Bernard McGinn in using a broad understanding of mysticism. Bernard McGinn, *The Presence of God: A History of Western Christian Mysticism: Volume One, The Foundations of Mysticism: Origins to the Fifth Century* (New York: Crossroad, 1995) xvii.

[65] For example, she frequently uses images such as "a cloud of darkness" and "the dark night," phrases used by the author of *The Cloud of Unknowing* and St. John of the Cross, respectively. Her spiritual theology addresses how to move through these "clouds" and "dark nights" through simple faith. Much of her ministry of spiritual direction is concerned with communicating this wisdom to souls in despair.

[66] For a discussion of Calvinistic mysticism, see Jean-Daniel Benoît, *Calvin in His Letters: A Study of Calvin's Pastoral Counselling, Mainly from His Letters*, trans. Richard Haig. Courtenay Studies in Reformation Theology 5 (Oxford: Sutton Courtenay Press, 1991) 73. I am adding to Benoît's work, suggesting further evidence that Calvinist mysticism is selfless service to God solely for God's glory.

[67] "Letter 30," Anne Dutton to J(ames) E(rskine), Esq., *Letters on Spiritual Subjects, and Divers Occasions, Sent to Relations and Friends. By One Who Has Tasted That the Lord Is Gracious. Wherefore Comfort Yourselves Together, and Edify One Another, Even As Also Ye Do, I Thess. v.11* (London: printed by J. Hart and sold by John Lewis and Ebenezer Gardner, 1743) 157. See also *A Letter to Such of the Servants of Christ, Who May Have Any Scruple about the Lawfulness of Printing Any Thing Written by a Woman: To Shew, That Book-Teaching Is Private, with Respect to the Church, and Permitted to Private Christians; Yea, Commanded to Those, of Either Sex, Who Are Gifted for, and Inclin'd to Engage in this Service* (London: printed by J. Hart and sold by J. Lewis, 1743).

[68] See especially vol. 1 for a sampling of her spiritual-direction letters; vol. 2 for her important theological work, *Walking with God*, which displays her contemplative theology; and vol. 3 for all three parts of her spiritual autobiography, *A Brief Account of the Gracious Dealings of GOD*.

[69] See C.C. Goen, *Revivalism and Separatism in New England, 1740–1800* (Middletown CT: Wesleyan University Press, 1987) 8–35.

[70] Stearns's experience was not uncommon, as numerous individuals who separated from their parish church eventually adopted the Baptist position of believers-only baptism. See Goen, *Revivalism and Separatism*, 208–57.

[71] Morgan Edwards, "Materials Towards a History of the Baptists in the Province of North Carolina," vol. 4 (typescript, 1772), 2–11.

[72] See John Sparks, *The Roots of Appalachian Christianity: The Life and Legacy of Elder Shubal Stearns* (Lexington: University Press of Kentucky, 2001) 199–290.

[73] The obvious difference is that Stearns and his colleagues would be together constantly for three or four days at a time, while modern revival services are for a few hours in the evening for three or four days in a row.

[74] William H. Brackney, *A Genetic History of Baptist Thought* (Macon GA: Mercer University Press, 2004) 214.

[75] Alvah Hovey, *A Memoir of the Life and Times of the Reverend Isaac Backus* (n.p., 1859) 39.

NOTES

[76] Ibid., 71.

[77] Ibid.; Stanley J. Grenz, "Isaac Backus," in *Baptist Theologians*, ed. Timothy George and David S. Dockery (Nashville TN: Broadman Press, 1990) 68–69.

[78] Hovey, *A Memoir of the Life*, 151.

[79] William G. McLoughlin, *Soul Liberty: The Baptists' Struggle in New England, 1630–1833* (Hanover: Brown University Press, 1991) 262.

[80] Isaac Backus, *An Appeal to the Public for Religious Liberty, Against the Oppression of the Present Day* (Boston: 1773), quoted in McLoughlin, *Soul Liberty*, 263.

[81] Ibid., 252.

[82] Anson Phelps Stokes, *Church and State in the United States: Volume I* (New York: Harper & Brothers Publishers, 1950) 8.

[83] Hovey, *A Memoir of the Life*, 216.

[84] Isaac Backus, *A Declaration of the Rights, of the Inhabitants of the State of Massachusetts-Bay, in New England*, in *A Documentary History of Religion in America to the Civil War*, ed. Edwin S. Gaustad (Grand Rapids MI: William B. Eerdmans Publishing Company, 1990) 268.

[85] Stokes, *Church and State*, 310.

[86] Brackney, *A Genetic History*, 214.

[87] Ibid., 216.

[88] McLoughlin, *Soul Liberty*, 11.

[89] Ibid., 256–57.

[90] Stokes, *Church and State*, 310.

[91] E.F. Clipsham, "Taylor, Dan," *The Blackwell Dictionary of Evangelical Biography: 1730–1860*, ed. Donald M. Lewis (Oxford: Wiley-Blackwell, 1995).

[92] Adam Taylor, *Memoirs of the Rev. Dan Taylor: Late Pastor of the General Baptist Church, Whitechapel, London, with Extract from His Diary, Correspondence, and Unpublished Manuscripts* (London, 1820) 5.

[93] Frank W. Rinaldi, *The Tribe of Dan, The New Connexion of General Baptists 1770–1891: A Study in the Transition from Revival Movement to Established Denomination* (Milton Keynes, UK: Paternoster Press, 2008) 3.

[94] Leon McBeth, *The Baptist Heritage: Four Centuries of Baptist Witness* (Nashville TN: Broadman Press, 1987) 161.

[95] Taylor, *Memoirs*, 74.

[96] Rinaldi, *The Tribe of Dan*, 5.

[97] McBeth, *The Baptist Heritage*, 155.

[98] A. Taylor, *Memoirs*, 72.

[99] "Articles of Religion of the New Connection, 1770," in William L. Lumpkin, *Baptist Confessions of Faith* (Valley Forge: Judson Press, 1969) 343.

[100] A. Taylor, *Memoirs*, 324–27, provides a chronological list of Dan Taylor's publications, circular letters, and the many ordinations in which he participated.

[101] Ibid., 80.

[102] Dan Taylor, *Fundamentals of Religion in Faith and Practice: or An Humble Attempt to Place Some of the Most Important Subjects of Doctrinal, Experimental, and Practical Divinity in a Clear and Scriptural Light* (Leeds: printed for the author, 1775) 1.

[103] Ibid., 4.

[104] Dan Taylor, *The Consistent Christian, or Truth, Peace, Holiness, Unanimity, Steadfastness, and Zeal Recommended to All Professors of Christianity*, 2nd ed. (London: printed for the author) 11.

[105] Taylor, *Memoirs*, 7.

[106] Ibid., 273.

[107] Taylor, *Fundamentals of Religion*, 213.

[108] Ibid, 267.

[109] Rinaldi, *The Tribe of Dan*, 38.

[110] Keith S. Grant, *Andrew Fuller and the Evangelical Renewal of Pastoral Theology*, Studies in Baptist History and Thought 36 (Eugene OR: Wipf and Stock Publishers, 2013) 37–40.

[111] John Ryland, Jr., *The Work of Faith, the Labour of Love, and the Patience of Hope, Illustrated; in the Life and Death of the Rev. Andrew Fuller*, 2nd ed. (Charleston: Samuel Etheridge, 1818) 4; also Gerald L. Priest, "Andrew Fuller, Hyper-Calvinism, and the 'Modern Question,'" in *"At the Pure Fountain of Thy Word": Andrew Fuller As an Apologist*, ed. Michael A. G. Haykin. Studies in Baptist History and Thought 6 (Waynesboro GA: Paternoster, 2004) 5.

[112] Ryland, *The Work of Faith*, 7.

[113] Ryland, *The Work of Faith*, 14.

[114] Morden, "Andrew Fuller: A Biographical Sketch," in Haykin, 4–5.

[115] Paul Brewster, *Andrew Fuller: Model Pastor and Theologian*, B & H Studies in Baptist Life and Thought, ed. Michael A. G. Haykin (Nashville TN: B&H Publishing Group, 2010) 24–25.

[116] Brewster, *Andrew Fuller*, 12.

[117] Morden, "Andrew Fuller: A Biographical Sketch," in Haykin, 36.

[118] Peter Morden, *Offering Christ to the World: Andrew Fuller (1754–1815) and the Revival of Eighteenth-Century Particular Baptist Life*. Studies in Baptist History and Thought 8 (Waynesboro GA: Paternoster, 2003) 45–51.

[119] Morden, "Andrew Fuller: A Biographical Sketch," in Haykin, 32–39.

[120] Ibid., 35.

[121] "Recollections of Elder John Leland," *Berkshire Historical and Scientific Society* (Pittsfield MA: Sun Printing Co., 1892) 277.

[122] Robert Baylor Semple, *History of the Rise and Progress of the Baptists in Virginia* (Richmond: John O'Lynch, Printer, 1810) 77.

[123] "Leland-Madison Memorial Park - Orange County, Virginia – Religious Freedom on Waymarking.com," http://www.waymarking.com/waymarks/WMF79H_Leland_Madison_Memorial_Park_Orange_County_VA. Accessed 15 March, 2014. For more on the meeting between Leland and Madison, see J. Bradley Creed, "John Leland, American Prophet of Religious Individualism" (Ph.D. diss., Southwestern Baptist Theological Seminary, 1986) 84–94. A more recent analysis is by Mark S. Scarberry, "John Leland and James Madison: Religious Influence on the Ratification of the Constitution and on the Proposal of the Bill of Rights," *Penn State Law Review* (Winter 2008): 733–800.

[124] L. F. Greene, ed., *The Writings of the Late Elder John Leland, Including Some Events in His Life, Written by Himself, with Additional Sketches* (New York: Arno Press and New York Times, 1969) 177.

[125] Quoted in H. Leon McBeth, *The Baptist Heritage: Four Centuries of Baptist Witness* (Nashville TN: Broadman Press, 1987) 266.

[126] Greene, "The Virginia Chronicle," *The Writings*, 114.

[127] Brad Creed, "John Leland and Sunday Mail Delivery: Religious Liberty, Evangelical Piety, and the Problem of a 'Christian Nation,'" *Fides et Historia* (Summer/Fall 2001): 1–11.

[128] C. A. Browne, "Elder John Leland and the Mammoth Cheshire Cheese," *Agricultural History* 27 (1944): 145–53.

[129] Greene, "The Yankee Spy," *The Writings*, 221.

[130] Greene, "The Virginia Chronicle," *The Writings*, 118.

[131] Timothy George, *Faithful Witness: The Life and Mission of William Carey* (Birmingham: New Hope, 1991) 3–4. This volume also includes the entire *Enquiry* of Carey on pages E1–E57.

[132] Ibid., 23–24.

NOTES

[133] S. Pearce Carey, *William Carey* (London: The Wakeman Trust, 1993) 23–27.

[134] H. Leon McBeth, *The Baptist Heritage* (Nashville TN: Broadman Press, 1987) 185.

[135] George, *Faithful Witness*, E56–E57.

[136] Eustace Carey, *Memoir of William Carey, D.D.* (Boston: Gould, Kendall, and Lincoln, 1836) 50.

[137] Pearce Carey, *William Carey*, 89–90.

[138] George Smith, *The Life of William Carey: Shoemaker and Missionary* (London: J.M. Dent and Sons, 1909) 43–44.

[139] Terry G. Carter, ed., *The Journal and Selected Letters of William Carey* (Macon GA: Smyth and Helwys, 2000) 3–59. The journal is provided in its entirety.

[140] George, *Faithful Witness*, 96–103.

[141] Mary Drewery, *William Carey: A Biography* (Grand Rapids: Zondervan Publishing House, 1979) 77–78.

[142] Carter, *The Journal and Selected Letters*, 84–85. There are several letters written by Carey describing the difficult situation.

[143] Ibid., 281. Carey to Sisters, 5 October 1795; Carey to Sisters, 10 April 1796; and Carey to Fuller, 16 November 1796.

[144] Smith, *The Life of William Carey*, 87–92.

[145] E. Carey, *Memoir of William Carey*, 297.

[146] George, *Faithful Witness*, 140–41; Carter, *The Journal and Selected Letters*, 154. Carey to Ryland, 17 August 1800.

[147] Pearce Carey, *William Carey*, 204–207.

[148] Carter, *The Journal and Selected Letters*, 146–47. Carey to Ryland, 17 August 1800; Smith, *The Life of William Carey*, 209–10.

[149] Smith, *The Life of William Carey*, 279–80.

[150] Carter, *The Journal and Selected Letters*, 140. Carey to Ryland, 17 July 1806.

[151] George, *Faithful Witness*, 159.

[152] Carter, *The Journal and Selected Letters*, 245, 281, 288. Carey to Sisters, 5 October 1795; Carey to Jabez, 6 October 1815; and Carey to Sisters, 25 October 1827.

[153] Carter, *The Journal and Selected Letters*, 292–94. There are multiple letters from Carey explaining his interests in nature, agriculture, birds, and the organizations and awards he received. These included an honorary doctorate from the University of Rhode Island, a gold medal from the Danish King, and honors from the Linnaean Society, the Geological Society, and the Horticultural Society of London.

[154] George, *Faithful Witness*, E57.

[155] Albert J. Raboteau, *Slave Religion: "The Invisible Institution" in Antebellum South* (New York: Oxford University Press, 1978) 4.

[156] Leroy Fitts, *The Lott Carey Legacy of African-American Mission* (Baltimore: Gateway Press, inc., 1994) x.

[157] Leroy Fitts, *Lott Carey: First Black Missionary to Africa* (Philadelphia: Judson Press, 1978) 11.

[158] Fitts, *The Lott Carey Legacy*, 3–4.

[159] Ibid., 4.

[160] Ibid.

[161] Ibid.

[162] Daryl Grigsby, *In Their Footsteps: Inspirational Reflections on Black History for Every Day of the Year* (IL: Acta Publications, 2007) January 31; and Fitts, *The Lott Carey Legacy*, 4–5.

[163] Fitts, *The Lott Carey Legacy*, 5.

[164] Ibid., 5. Grigsby, *In Their Footsteps*, January 31.

[165] Fitts, *Legacy of Lott Carey*, 5.

¹⁶⁶ Ibid., 6.
¹⁶⁷ Ibid., 7–8.
¹⁶⁸ Bill Leonard, *Baptist Ways: A History* (Philadelphia: Judson Press, 2003) 270; Fitts, *The Lott Carey Legacy*, 8; and Leroy Fitts, *A History of Black Baptists* (Nashville TN: Broadman Press, 1985) 45, 110–11.
¹⁶⁹ Fitts, *The Lott Carey Legacy*, 9.
¹⁷⁰ Ibid., 10–14.
¹⁷¹ Ibid., 14.
¹⁷² Ibid., 18, 20.
¹⁷³ Ibid., 22–23, 28, 34, 38, 58.
¹⁷⁴ Rosalie Hall Hunt, *Bless God and Take Courage: The Judson History and Legacy* (Valley Forge: Judson Press, 2005) 12.
¹⁷⁵ Nathan A. Finn, "Until All Burma Worships the Eternal God, Adoniram Judson, the Missionary 1812–1850," in *Adoniram Judson: A Bicentennial Appreciation of the Pioneer American Missionary*, ed. Jason Duesing (Nashville TN: B&H Publishing Group, 2012) e-book, location 2152.
¹⁷⁶ Francis Wayland, *Memoir of the Life and Labors of the Rev. Adoniram Judson, D.D.* (Boston: Phillips, Sampson, and Company, 1853) 351.
¹⁷⁷ H. Leon McBeth, *The Baptist Heritage: Four Centuries of Baptist Witness* (Nashville TN: Broadman Press, 1987) 470.
¹⁷⁸ *"Jeder Baptist ein Missionar."*
¹⁷⁹ H. Luckey, *Gerhard Oncken und die Anfang des Deutschen Baptismus* (Kassel: J.G. Oncken Verlag, 1958) 42.
¹⁸⁰ The full name of the organization is the "Continental Society for the Diffusion of Religious Knowledge over the Continent of Europe." It was founded in 1819 in London by Robert Haldane and Henry Drummond.
¹⁸¹ William L. Wagner, *New Move Forward in Europe: Growth Patterns of German-Speaking Baptists in Europe* (South Pasadena: William Carey Library, 1978) 32.
¹⁸² He became a citizen of Hamburg in 1828, which did not grant him permission to preach but removed the threat of being banished from Hamburg as a foreigner.
¹⁸³ J.H. Cooke, *Johann Gerhard Oncken: His Life and Work* (London: S.W. Partridge & Co., 1908) 56–57.
¹⁸⁴ The full name of the school was Hamilton Literary and Theological Institution, today known as Colgate University in Hamilton, New York. Barnas Sears became the fifth president of Brown University in Providence, Rhode Island.
¹⁸⁵ There were baptistic beginnings in France starting in 1891. See Ian Randall, *Communities of Conviction: Baptist Beginnings in Europe* (Schwarzenfeld, Germany: Neufeld Verlag, 2009) 38–40.
¹⁸⁶ The first German to be baptized in the United States happened in 1842. By 1882, the German Baptists in the United States numbered approximately 10,334. For more details on the German movement in the U.S., see McBeth, *The Baptist Heritage*, 407.
¹⁸⁷ J.H. Rushbrooke, *The Baptist Movement on the Continent of Europe: A Contribution to Modern History* (London: Carey Press, 1915) 28.
¹⁸⁸ Ibid., 143.
¹⁸⁹ Ian M. Randall, "'Pious Wishes': Baptists and Wider Renewal Movements in Nineteenth-Century Europe," *Baptist Quarterly* 38/7 (July 2000): 316–17.
¹⁹⁰ Randall, *Communities of Conviction*, 56.
¹⁹¹ The list could be expanded to include the non-European countries of Turkey, Australia, and Cameroon.

NOTES

[192] The *Bund* (union) began as a German association, which included representatives from Prussia. One year later it was reorganized as the "Union of Associated Churches of Baptized Christians in Germany and Denmark," with fifty-six representatives present.

[193] For more on Oncken's Statement of Faith and an English translation, see W.L. Lumpkin, *Baptist Confessions of Faith* (Valley Forge: Judson Press, 1969) 401–407.

[194] This was the "Norwalk Rail Accident," which killed forty-eight and is considered to be the first major railroad bridge disaster in U.S. history.

[195] Two of his children died in infancy, his youngest son died in a fire at the age of eight, and one of his daughters died in 1873 at the age of twenty-nine.

[196] Significant portions of this chapter are synthesized from the author Michael E. Williams, Sr.'s *Isaac Taylor Tichenor, The Creation of the Baptist New South* (Tuscaloosa: University of Alabama Press, 2005). Used by permission, University of Alabama Press.

[197] Walter B. Shurden, "The Turn toward Denominational Cooperation," in Michael E. Williams, Sr. and Walter B. Shurden, *Turning Points in Baptist History: A Festschrift in Honor of Harry Leon McBeth* (Macon GA: Mercer University Press, 2008) 69, 70; Rosalie Beck, "Baptist Missions and the Turn toward Global Responsibility," in Williams and Shurden, *Turning Points in Baptist History*, 105; Carol Crawford Holcomb, "Baptist Missions and the Turn toward Denominational Organizations," in Williams and Shurden, *Turning Points in Baptist History*, 124, 125; and H. Leon McBeth, *The Baptist Heritage: Four Centuries of Baptist Witness* (Nashville TN: Broadman Press, 1987) 368–69.

[198] Williams, Sr., *Isaac Taylor Tichenor*, 13–39.

[199] Ibid., 40, 51–52, 57–66.

[200] Ibid., 70–96.

[201] *Annual, SBC, 1882*, 29; *Alabama Baptist*, 1 June 1882; and Home Mission Board minutes, 22 May 1882, 113, 114, on microfilm at the Southern Baptist Library and Archives, Nashville, Tennessee.

[202] *Annual, SBC, 1883*, I, II.

[203] Williams, Sr., *Isaac Taylor Tichenor*, 105–12; Jesse C. Fletcher, *The Southern Baptist Convention: A Sesquicentennial History* (Nashville TN: Broadman & Holman, 1994) 92–93; Home Mission Board Minutes, 25 September 1882, 124; Glenn T. Miller, "Baptist Businessmen in Historical Perspective," *Baptist History & Heritage* 13 (1978): 58; *Annual, SBC, 1882*, 46; *Annual, SBC, 1883*, iv; *Annual, SBC, 1887*, xxxii; and *Annual, SBC, 1892*, ii, xiii.

[204] Williams, Sr., *Isaac Taylor Tichenor*, 103–104, 129ff; *Annual, SBC, 1903*, 154; and J. B. Hawthorne, "I. T. Tichenor, D.D.: An Oration Delivered before the SBC in Savannah, Georgia," *Baptist Argus*, 30 July 1903, 3–4.

[205] John Franklin Loftis, "Factors in Southern Baptist Identity as Reflected in Ministerial Role Models, 1750–1925" (Ph.D. diss., Southern Baptist Theological Seminary, 1987) 138.

[206] *Annual, SBC, 1883*, xi.

[207] Williams, Sr., *Isaac Taylor Tichenor*, 203.

[208] Baptist General Convention of Texas, *Proceedings*, 1919; see the eulogy titled, "In Memoriam," 95.

[209] Buckner preferred to be called "R. C.," as was custom in his era. The children of the orphanage preferred to call him "Father Buckner." The log cabin in which he was born was later purchased and moved to the Dallas Buckner Orphans' Home and placed next to the chapel in honor of Buckner's eightieth birthday. See J. B. Cranfill and J. L. Walker, *R. C. Buckner: Life of Faith and Works* (Dallas TX: Buckner Orphans' Home, 1914) 7–15.

[210] J. H. Spencer, *A History of Kentucky Baptists from 1769–1885*, vol. 1 (Cincinnati: printed by the author, 1885) 419–21. See also Joseph H. Borum's *Biographical Sketches of Tennessee Baptist Ministers* (Memphis: Rogers and Company, 1880) 61–64.

[211] Walker, *Buckner*, 41.

[212] The Kentucky region in which the Buckner family lived was anti-slavery by conviction, and Buckner respected many Black preachers who were members of his church as a boy and young man. Uncle Charlie Denton was one of these whose influence upon Robert's life was profound. See Karen O'Dell Bullock, *Homeward Bound: The Heart and Heritage of Buckner* (Dallas TX: Buckner Children's Home, 1993) 45–46. See also Walter Prescott Webb, ed., "Dickson Colored Orphanage," in *The Handbook of Texas*, vol. 1 (Austin: The Texas State Historical Association, 1952) 501.

[213] Robert and Vienna had six living children: three daughters and two sons, Joe Dudley (1871) and Hal Frieland (1878), both of whom administrated the home after their father died in 1919. Two sisters also helped with the work.

[214] Robert Andrew Baker, *The Blossoming Desert: A Concise History of Texas Baptists* (Waco TX: Word Books, 1970) 7, 33.

[215] *Proceedings*, General Association, 1868–1870. He served as Superintendent of Missions from 1877–1892.

[216] B. F. Fuller, *History of Texas Baptists* (Louisville KY: Baptist Book Concern, 1900) 68. Benajah Harvey Carroll was the pastor of First Baptist Church, Waco, taught Bible in Baylor University's Religion Department, organized the Baylor Seminary in 1905, and served as a leader in the General Association and, after its merger in 1886, in the BGCT. Under Carroll's leadership, the seminary was chartered as Southwestern Baptist Theological Seminary in 1908, and relocated to Fort Worth in 1910. See McBeth, *Baptist Heritage: Four Centuries of Baptist Witness* (Nashville TN: Broadman, 1987) 669–71.

[217] Cranfill and Walker, *R. C. Buckner*, 89.

[218] The cabin had been the home of John Neely Bryant, built in 1841, and was the first house within the radius of one hundred miles of where the Dallas Courthouse now stands. See Jerrilyn Armstrong, ed., *Texas Baptist Family Album: 1885–1985* (Dallas TX: Baptist General Convention of Texas, 1985) 4; Fuller's *History*, 298; and Cranfill and Walker, *R. C. Buckner*, 91.

[219] Fuller, *History*, 299.

[220] See Karen O'Dell Bullock, "Life and Contributions of Robert Cooke Buckner: Progenitor of Social Christianity Among Texas Baptists 1860–1919" (Ph.D. diss., Southwestern Baptist Theological Seminary, 1991) 108–38.

[221] Ibid., 129–33. Buckner Home shared with the Dickson Orphanage groceries, funds, and hearings at BGCT sessions.

[222] Ibid., 147–52.

[223] Ibid., 154–59. Texas Baptists supplied all textbooks, materials, slate pencils, globes, blackboards, and erasers. Dozens of teachers through the years came from Texas Baptist colleges, like Baylor.

[224] The Baptist Women's Missionary Training School in Louisville, Kentucky, associated with the Southern Baptist Theological Seminary, organized three years later.

[225] This building is now the women's Bernard Residence Hall on the Southwestern Seminary campus.

[226] Bullock, "Life and Contributions of Buckner,"170–82. The oldest children's hospital in America is the Children's Hospital of Philadelphia, opened in 1855, before the Civil War. Buckner traveled both to St. Louis and Philadelphia to interview and engage nurses for the hospitals in Texas.

[227] This is the same year that Buckner called for State Reformatories, one for girls and another for boys, to be built in Texas. They opened in 1887.

NOTES

[228] Texas Baptists' eulogy, "*In Memoriam,*" published in the BGCT *Annual*, 1919.

[229] Today, Buckner Orphans' Home is Buckner International. Its work encompasses the globe as it cares for the whole family. See Buckner International and the scope of its ministries at http://www.buckner.org/.

[230] Charles Spurgeon, *C.H. Spurgeon Autobiography, Volume 1: The Early Years* (Carlisle PA: Banner of Truth, 2011) 88.

[231] Charles Spurgeon, *Lectures to My Students: Complete and Unabridged* (Grand Rapids: Zondervan, 1954) 48.

[232] Darrel W. Amundsen, "The Anguish and Agonies of Charles Spurgeon," *Christian History* 10/1 (1991): 24, 25.

[233] Spurgeon, *Lectures to My Students*, 201, 203.

[234] Irwin T. Hyatt, Jr., *Our Ordered Lives Confess: Three Nineteenth-Century American Missionaries in East Shantung* (Cambridge MA: Harvard University Press, 1976) 93; Regina Sullivan, *Lottie Moon: A Southern Baptist Missionary to China in History and Legend* (Baton Rouge: Louisiana State University Press, 2011) 9; and Lottie Moon and Keith Harper, *Send the Light: Lottie Moon's Letters and Other Writings* (Macon GA: Mercer University Press, 2002) x.

[235] Lottie Moon, "The Woman Question Again," *Woman's Work in China*, November 1883, 48.

[236] Lottie Moon to Henry Tupper, 10 May 1879, in Moon and Harper, *Send the Light*, 90.

[237] Lottie Moon to *Foreign Mission Journal*, 15 September 1887, in Moon and Harper, *Send the Light*, 224.

[238] Ibid.

[239] Unnamed author, *Arkansas Baptist*, 31 July 1890, cited in Sullivan, *Lottie Moon*, 112.

[240] Jessie Pettigrew to James Gaston, 28 October 1912, in Moon and Harper, *Send the Light*, 446.

[241] *San Francisco Chronicle*, 15 January 1913, 5.

[242] Una Roberts Lawrence, *Lottie Moon* (Nashville TN: Sunday School Board of the Southern Baptist Convention, 1927) 308.

[243] Catherine Allen, *The New Lottie Moon Story*, 2nd ed. (Birmingham AL: Woman's Missionary Union, 1997) 276.

[244] See Sullivan, *Lottie Moon*, 155–59.

[245] W. W. Adams to WMU, 1 December 1947; cited in Sullivan, *Lottie Moon*, 158.

[246] See Elizabeth Flowers, "The Contested Legacy of Lottie Moon: Southern Baptists, Women, and Partisan Protestantism," in *Through a Glass Darkly: Contested Notions of Baptist Identity*, ed. Keith Harper (Tuscaloosa: University of Alabama Press, 2012) 118; and Sullivan, *Lottie Moon*, 155–56.

[247] Allen, *The New Lottie Moon Story*, 293.

[248] Flowers, "The Contested Legacy," 116–24. See also Sullivan, *Lottie Moon*, 161–62.

[249] Lynn Madison Barrett, "A Cool Drink of Water," *Royal Service*, December 1974, 16. See also Flowers, "The Contested Legacy," 129.

[250] J. Duane Bolin, "Honoring the Real Lottie Moon," *Associated Baptist Press*, 10 June 2013. Available at http://abpnews.com/opinion/commentaries/item/8567-honoring-the-real-lottie-moon.

[251] Al Mohler, cited in Emily Griffin and Garrett Wishall, "Lottie Moon's Legacy Explored at Southern," *Baptist Press*, 22 October 2009. Available at http://www.bpnews.net/bpnews.asp?ID=31520.

[252] Ibid.

[253] Portions of this chapter originally appeared in "'The Heaven-Appointed Doctrine…the Social Equality of the Races and Classes': The Life, Legacy, and Writings of E. C. Morris," *Whitsitt Journal* 16/2 (Fall 2008): 3–11.

[254] Todd E. Lewis, "Elias Camp Morris (1855–1922)," *The Encyclopedia of Arkansas History and Culture* http://encyclopediaofarkansas.net/encyclopedia/entry-detail.aspx?entryID=433 (accessed 22 April 2014).

[255] "The College," http://www.arkansasbaptist.edu/?page_id=26 (accessed 26 April 2014). At Arkansas Baptist College website, no author listed.

[256] E. C. Morris, *Sermons, Addresses and Reminiscences, and Important Correspondence, with a Picture Gallery of Eminent Ministers and Scholars* (Nashville TN: National Baptist Publication Board, 1901) 144, http://docsouth.unc.edu/church/morris/morris.html (accessed 25 April 2014).

[257] Lewis, "Elias Camp Morris."

[258] N. H. Pius, *An Outline of Baptist History: A Splendid Reference Work for Busy Workers, A Record of the Struggles and Triumphs of Baptist Pioneers and Builders* (Nashville TN: National Baptist Publishing Board, 1911) 91–92, http://docsouth.unc.edu/church/pius/pius.html (accessed 22 April 2014).

[259] Lewis, "Elias Camp Morris."

[260] Morris, *Sermons, Addresses and Reminiscences*, 7.

[261] Ibid., 24, 53, 54.

[262] Ibid., 37.

[263] Ibid., 39, 40.

[264] Ibid., 69.

[265] Ibid., 71.

[266] Ibid., 37–38, 156.

[267] Peggy Harris, "Preservation Plea: Historic Baptist Church in Arkansas Could Become a Black-Heritage Center," 23 August 2008, http://www2.hickoryrecord.com/content/2008/aug/23/preservation-plea-historic-baptist-church-in-arkan/lifestyles/ (accessed 11 October 2008).

[268] Russell H. Dilday, Jr., "E. Y. Mullins: The Bible's Authority Is a Living, Transforming Reality," in *The Unfettered Word: Southern Baptists Confront the Authority-Inerrancy Question*, ed. Robison B. James (Waco: Word Books, 1987) 114.

[269] E. Y. Mullins, *The Axioms of Religion* (1908), ed. C. Douglas Weaver (Macon GA: Mercer University Press, 2010) 65.

[270] Ibid., 62–63.

[271] E. Y. Mullins, "Baptist Life in the World's Life," *Review and Expositor* 25/3 (July 1928): 312.

[272] Bill J. Leonard, *God's Last & Only Hope: The Fragmentation of the Southern Baptist Convention* (Grand Rapids: Eerdmans, 1990) 31, 38, 51.

[273] Dores R. Sharpe, *Walter Rauschenbusch* (New York: Macmillan, 1942) 284. There have been two other major biographies of Rauschenbusch: Paul M. Minus, *Walter Rauschenbusch: American Reformer* (New York: MacMillan, 1988); and most recently, Christopher H. Evans, *The Kingdom Is Always but Coming: A Life of Walter Rauschenbusch* (Grand Rapids: Eerdmans, 2004). Evans's work is the most comprehensive. Additionally, I am indebted to three very fine articles about Rauschenbusch. The first comprises the introductory chapter of Walter Rauschenbusch's *The Righteousness of the Kingdom*, ed. Max L. Stackhouse (Nashville TN: Abingdon, 1968). Stackhouse discovered this manuscript in the Rauschenbusch papers, edited the work, and then published it. His introductory chapter called "The Continuing Importance of Walter Rauschenbusch" (13–59) is a very good interpretation of the life and theology of Rauschenbusch. A second important biographical interpretation is found in Stanley Hauerwas, *A Better Hope: Resources for a Church Confronting Capitalism, Democracy, and Postmodernity* (Grand Rapids: Brazos, 2000) 71–107. Hauerwas naturally concentrates on Rauschenbusch's ethical thought. Finally, an interesting article that focuses on the

NOTES

preaching of Rauschenbusch is found in Clyde M. Fant, Jr. and William M. Pinson, Jr., eds., *20 Centuries of Great Preaching, Vol. VII* (Waco: Word, 1971) 127–43.

[274] Minus, *Walter Rauschenbusch: American Reformer*, 50. See also Evans, *The Kingdom Is Always but Coming*, 45–73.

[275] Minus, *Walter Rauschenbusch: American Reformer*, 50. Minus devotes an entire chapter to Rauschenbusch as pastor.

[276] Sharpe, *Walter Rauschenbusch*, 65–66. Sharpe indicates that the deafness was the result of a relapse of Russian grippe, a highly contagious upper respiratory disease.

[277] Walter Rauschenbusch, 1888–1891 Diary, as cited in Minus, *Walter Rauschenbusch: American Reformer*, 69.

[278] Ibid., 70.

[279] See Minus, *Walter Rauschenbusch: American Reformer*, 83–101, for a discussion of Rauschenbusch's intellectual development on this issue. In this chapter, Minus discusses Rauschenbusch's participation in an organization he helped form called "The Brotherhood of the Kingdom." Organized by Rauschenbusch and several like-minded friends, it met regularly for fellowship and discussion on social issues. See also Evans, *The Kingdom Is Always but Coming*, 104–11.

[280] Minus., 157–65.

[281] Walter Rauschenbusch, *Christianity and the Social Crisis* (New York: Macmillan, 1907) xv.

[282] Ibid., 281.

[283] Ibid., 143, xiii.

[284] Ibid., 143–210. In this chapter Rauschenbusch provides thirteen specific reasons the Church lost sight of its original mission during the Middle Ages.

[285] Ibid., 339, 340, 407ff. Rauschenbusch more fully discusses his views on socialism and the contradiction between Christianity and capitalism in Walter Rauschenbusch, *Christianizing the Social Order* (New York: Macmillan, 1912).

[286] *Journal and Messenger*, 14 November 1907, as cited by Minus, *Walter Rauschenbusch: American Reformer*, 162; and I. M. Haldeman, "Rauschenbusch's Christianity and the Social Crisis," pamphlet, 1911, as cited by Minus, *Walter Rauschenbusch: American Reformer*, 163.

[287] See Walter Rauschenbusch, *Prayers of the Social Awakening* (Boston: Pilgrim Press, 1910); *Christianizing the Social Order* (New York: MacMillan, 1912); *Unto Me: The Religious Quality of Social Work* (Rochester: Pilgrim Press, 1912); *Dare We Be Christians* (Boston: Pilgrim Press, 1914); *The Social Principles of Jesus* (Philadelphia: American Baptist Publication Society, 1916); and *A Theology for the Social Gospel* (New York: MacMillan, 1918).

[288] Minus, *Walter Rauschenbusch: American Reformer*, 177–78. See also Evans, *The Kingdom Is Always but Coming*, 271–94.

[289] Walter Rauschenbusch, "Be Fair to Germany: A Plea for Open-Mindedness," *Congregationalist*, 15 October 1914, as cited by Minus, *Walter Rauschenbusch: American Reformer*, 178–79, and from a private letter written by Rauschenbusch, 7 March 1917, as cited by Minus, *Walter Rauschenbusch: American Reformer*, 181.

[290] Minus, *Walter Rauschenbusch: American Reformer*, 189ff. Minus concludes that in addition to stress from public scorn over his feelings about the war, Rauschenbusch also encountered serious stress from theological conservatives who relentlessly criticized his theological conclusions. These factors together contributed to a decline in his physical health.

[291] Ibid., 177. The scripture reference is Matthew 13:57.

[292] Kendal P. Mobley, *Helen Barrett Montgomery: The Global Mission of Domestic Feminism* (Waco: Baylor University Press, 2009) 2.

[293] W. T. Whitley, *Third Baptist World Congress, Stockholm, July 21–27, 1923. Record of Proceedings*. Introduction by J. H. Shakespeare (London: Kingsgate Press, 1923) 99.

²⁹⁴ Helen Barrett Montgomery, "Her Own Story," in *Helen Baptist Montgomery: From Campus to World Citizenship* (New York: Fleming H. Revell, 1940) 34.
²⁹⁵ Mobley, *Helen Barrett Montgomery*, 63–66.
²⁹⁶ Conda Delite Hitch Abbott, *Envoy of Grace: The Life of Helen Barrett Montgomery* (Valley Forge: American Baptist Historical Society, 1997) 9.
²⁹⁷ Mobley, *Helen Barrett Montgomery*, 245–57.
²⁹⁸ Whitley, *Third Baptist World Congress*, 99.
²⁹⁹ See George W. Truett, "Baptists and Religious Liberty," http://www.bjconline.org/index.php?option=com_content&task=view&id=4454 (accessed 29 November 2013).
³⁰⁰ George W. Truett, *On Preachers and Preaching: Address of Dr. George W. Truett, Pastor of the First Baptist Church, Dallas, Texas* (n.p., [1934]) 6, TC 1940. This and some of the following citations contain a "TC" reference, which refers to the George W. Truett Collection, located at the A. Webb Roberts Library (AWRL), Southwestern.
³⁰¹ George W. Truett, "Preaching," lecture notes, 1899, [2], TC 1912.
³⁰² George W. Truett, "The Preacher As a Soul-Winner" (address, Southwestern Baptist Theological Seminary, Fort Worth, Texas, 3 November 1914) 4, TC 1915.
³⁰³ Ibid., 4–5.
³⁰⁴ Reinhold Niebuhr, "The Montgomery Savagery," *Christianity and Crisis* 21/10 (1961): 103.
³⁰⁵ George W. Truett, *President's Address: 6th Baptist World Congress* (audio recording, Baptist World Alliance, 1939) located at the AWRL.
³⁰⁶ To read the sermon, see George W. Truett, *The Baptist Message and Mission for the World Today* (Nashville TN: Sunday School Board, 1939).
³⁰⁷ Truett, *On Preachers and Preaching*, 8–9, TC 1940.
³⁰⁸ *George W. Truett: A Tribute*, DVD (Waco TX: Mason Jar Documentaries, n.d.).
³⁰⁹ George W. Truett, "Bible Preaching and Preachers," *Baptist Standard*, 7 February 1901, 1.
³¹⁰ George W. Truett, *We Would See Jesus*, ed. J. B. Cranfill (New York: Fleming H. Revell Company, 1915) 86.
³¹¹ Truett, *We Would See Jesus*, 74.
³¹² This essay is adapted from the author Mark Wilson's book, *William Owen Carver's Controversies in the Baptist South* (Macon GA: Mercer University Press, 2010).
³¹³ W. O. Carver, "Characteristics of the Creation Story in Genesis," *Western Recorder* (13 October 1921): 1–3.
³¹⁴ W. O. Carver, "Christianizing Evolution," *Review and Expositor* 23/1 (Winter 1926): 82–87.
³¹⁵ Newspaper clipping, box 23, folder 23, William Owen Carver Papers, Southern Baptist Historical Library and Archives, Nashville, Tennessee.
³¹⁶ W. O. Carver, "The Baptist, His Creed, and His Fellowship," *The Christian Index*, 7 May 1925, 10.
³¹⁷ W. O. Carver, "Southern Baptists and the World Council of Churches," box 24, folder 60, Carver Papers.
³¹⁸ W. O. Carver, "William Heth Whitsitt: The Seminary's Martyr," *Review and Expositor* 51/4 (October 1954): 449–69.
³¹⁹ See http://en.wikipedia.org/wiki/1870_in_the_United_Kingdom (accessed 19 April 2014).
³²⁰ Charles Darwin's *Origin of the Species* (1859) had introduced doubts about the veracity of the Creation account in Genesis, for example. In Baptist life, the old Arian questions had resurfaced among the General Baptists when the eighteenth and nineteenth-century influences of Matthew Caffyn (1628–1714) and William Viddler (1758–1816) were resurrected. These and other concerns regarding "doctrinal decay" lay at the heart of the Down Grade Controversy, which erupted in 1887 with Spurgeon's *Sword and Trowel* avowal that heresy was being preached from some pulpits among

NOTES

General Baptists, that attendance at mid-week prayer meetings was declining, and that some pastors were becoming worldly to the point of bringing "entertainment" into their services. See the first article of "The Down Grade" in the March 1887 *Sword and Trowel* at http://www.reformedreader.org/spurgeon/dgc02.htm, and the second article from April 1887 at http://www.reformedreader.org/spurgeon/dgc03.htm. For a succinct summary of the Down Grade Controversy, see also Leon McBeth, *Baptist Heritage: Four Centuries of Baptist Witness* (Nashville TN: Broadman Press, 1987) 302–307.

[321] McBeth, *Baptist Heritage*, 302–307. See also Clifford's impact in Paul R. Dekar, *For the Healing of the Nations: Baptist Peacemakers* (Macon GA: Smyth and Helwys Publishers, 1993).

[322] Bernard Green, *Tomorrow's Man: A Biography of James Henry Rushbrooke* (Didcot, Oxford: The Baptist Historical Society, 1997) 12–13. When Harry was three years old, his family moved to rural Essex where his father became the station-master at Thorpe-le-Soken, a village located near Frinton-on-Sea. Here Harry received most of his education, impressing his schoolmasters to such a degree that they offered him Latin and Greek studies in addition to his other coursework and prepared him for the university. His testimonials were glowing: the local Vicar; the pastor of the Baptist church, which Harry sometimes attended; the Anglican Churchwarden; community farmers; and others noted his fine intelligence, attention to detail, steady habits, courteous behavior, and sensitivity to those who had no means by which to sustain themselves.

[323] Ibid., 15. Rushbrooke's Praed Street Chapel congregation built for him a larger preaching hall, called the Westbourne Park Baptist Chapel, in 1877. During these years of discipleship, one of Rushbrooke's closest friends was Thomas Phillips, pastor of Bloomsbury Central Baptist Church and then Principal of Cardiff Baptist College in Wales. For a list of the other names, see H. F. Bonsall and E. H. Robertson, *The Dream of an Ideal City: Westbourne Park 1877–1977* (London: Westbourne Park Street Church, 1978).

[324] J. MacQuarrie, *Twentieth-Century Religious Thought* (Norwich: SCM Press, 1963) 88–89.

[325] Ian Randall, "Tomorrow's Man: J. H. Rushbrooke," in *Baptist Quarterly* 37/3 (July 1997): 105–107.

[326] Bernard Green, *Tomorrow's Man: A Biography of James Henry Rushbrooke* (Didcot, Oxford: The Baptist Historical Society, 1997) 184.

[327] Bernard Green, *European Baptists and the Third Reich* (Didcot, Oxford: The Baptist Historical Society, 2008) 123.

[328] Bernard Green, *Crossing the Boundaries: History of the European Baptist Federation* (Didcot, Oxford: The Baptist Historical Society, 1999) 74. Figures of inflation calculated using "This Money," the British exchange online inflation calculator, by year and amount; see at http://www.thisismoney.co.uk/money/bills/article-1633409/Historic-inflation-calculator-value-money-changed-1900.html (accessed 16 January 2014).

[329] See Green, *Tomorrow's Man*, 184; one of the thirteen Baptist seminaries was still functioning in 1944.

[330] From the speech of German Baptist layman Eberhard Schroeder, who gave a testimony of the difficulty of these events at the 1947 BWA Congress in Copenhagen, Denmark; see BWA *Congress Report*, 1947, 124–28.

[331] For an explanation of Rushbrooke's involvement, see Green, *European Baptists and the Third Reich*, 124–40, 207–09.

[332] See Green, *Tomorrow's Man*, 12, 149–203.

[333] Karen A. Johnson, *Uplifting the Women and the Race: The Educational Philosophies and Social Activism of Anna Julia Cooper and Nannie Helen Burroughs*, Garland Studies in African-American History and Culture (New York: Routledge, 2000) 45–46.

[334] Ibid., 52.

[335] Ibid.

³³⁶ Evelyn Brooks Higginbotham, *Righteous Discontent: The Women's Movement in the Black Baptist Church, 1880–1920* (Cambridge MA: Harvard University Press, 1993) 202. See also Dormetria La Sharne Robinson, "Nannie Helen Burroughs: The Trailblazer," *American Baptist Quarterly* 23/2 (June 2004): 157.

³³⁷ Earl L. Harrison, *The Dream and the Dreamer: An Abbreviated Story of the Life of Dr. Nannie Helen Burroughs and Nannie Helen Burroughs School* (Washington, D.C.: Nannie H. Burroughs Literature Foundation Publisher, 1956) 9.

³³⁸ Karen E. Smith, "Nannie Helen Burroughs (1879–1961): A Voice for Social Justice and Reform," in *Twentieth-Century Shapers of Baptist Social Ethics*, ed. Larry L. McSwain and William Loyd Allen (Macon GA: Mercer University Press, 2008) 43.

³³⁹ Ibid.

³⁴⁰ Higginbotham, *Righteous Discontent*, 154.

³⁴¹ Martia Bradley, "The Work and Witness of Southern Negro Baptist Women from 1865 until 1935," *Quarterly Review* 37/1 (October–December 1976): 56.

³⁴² Quoted in Higginbotham, *Righteous Discontent*, 150.

³⁴³ Ibid., 158.

³⁴⁴ "National Baptist Convention, Eighth Annual Assembly of the Women's Convention," 1908, Nannie Helen Burroughs papers, Library of Congress, quoted in Johnson, *Uplifting the Women*, 121.

³⁴⁵ Johnson, *Uplifting the Women*, 90.

³⁴⁶ Ibid., 91.

³⁴⁷ "Nannie Helen Burroughs School: Private School Review," http://www.privateschoolreview.com/school_ov/school_id/5846 (accessed 5 May 2014).

³⁴⁸ Quoted in Prathia LauraAnn Hall, "The Religious and Social Consciousness of African-American Baptist Women" (Ph.D. diss., Princeton University, Princeton NJ, 1997) 66.

³⁴⁹ Sharon Harley, "Nannie Helen Burroughs: 'The Black Goddess of Liberty,'" *Journal of Negro History* 81/1–4 (Winter–Autumn 1996): 68.

³⁵⁰ Quoted in Hall, "The Religious and Social Consciousness," 226.

³⁵¹ Higginbotham, *Righteous Discontent*, 225.

³⁵² Johnson, *Uplifting the Women*, 100.

³⁵³ Harrison, *The Dream and the Dreamer*, 37–38.

³⁵⁴ Robert J. Hastings, *Glorious Is Thy Name: B. B. McKinney, the Man and His Music* (Nashville TN: Broadman, 1986) 18.

³⁵⁵ Paul R. Powell, *Wherever He Leads I'll Go: The Story of B. B. McKinney* (New Orleans: Insight, 1974) 17.

³⁵⁶ William J. Reynolds, "The Contributions of B. B. McKinney to Southern Baptist Church Music," *Baptist History and Heritage* 21/3 (1 July 1986): 41–49. *ATLA Religion Database with ATLASerials*, EBSCO *host* (accessed 20 August 2013) 42.

³⁵⁷ In the years that followed, two children were born to the McKinneys: Baylus Benjamin, Jr. (1920) and Eugene Calvin (1922).

³⁵⁸ Indicative of the esteem with which Holcomb held McKinney was his giving McKinney unlimited time away from the office for revivals and conferences, a privilege he held until his death. Reynolds, "The Contributions of B. B. McKinney," 45.

³⁵⁹ This collection contained three songs with words and music by McKinney and three songs with McKinney's music and Lizzie DeArmond's words. Reynolds, "The Contributions of B. B. McKinney," 42.

³⁶⁰ Coleman had published his first songbook in 1909, and in subsequent years published thirty-three different publications including hymnals, songbooks, and collections for men's voices and women's voices.

NOTES

[361] Those for whom McKinney's editing was cited include *Coleman's New Quartet Book* (1925), *Coleman's Male Choir* (1928), and *Coleman's Songs for Men* (1932). Reynolds, "The Contributions of B. B. McKinney," 42. *Coleman's Songs for Men* is still in print; see Amazon.com.

[362] A carbon copy of this resignation, dated 4 June 1930, is in the archives, Roberts Library, Southwestern Baptist Theological Seminary, Fort Worth TX. Reynolds, "The Contributions of B. B. McKinney," 43.

[363] While McKinney was a proponent of gospel music in the churches and not a defender of choirs, in the previous decade Reynolds had assumed a more elevated view of church music, openly espousing hymn-based congregational songs and classically oriented choral repertoire. Hastings, *Glorious Is Thy Name*, 111–12.

[364] For a thorough discussion of the relationship between Reynolds and McKinney, see Hastings, *Glorious Is Thy Name*, 46–47. This account quotes Leila McKinney as having said, "Reynolds got McKinney fired from the seminary." It also offers analysis from Clifford A. Holcomb, retired staff member of the Church Music Department, Baptist Sunday School Board, who reportedly spoke with all four men involved in the incident. In the late 1940s, both men taught in an associational music school in January 1947, and they were intentionally assigned adjacent rooms with an adjoining door. Apparently, they used this opportunity to smooth over their differences.

[365] Reynolds, "The Contributions of B. B. McKinney," 43.

[366] The two men had become friends shortly beforehand when they worked together during two revivals in which McKinney was the singer. Reynolds, "The Contributions of B. B. McKinney," 44.

[367] Ibid.

[368] This book was the first in which two of McKinney's most beloved hymns, "Wherever He Leads I'll Go" and "Holy Spirit Breathe on Me," were published. Ibid.

[369] Ibid., 44–45.

[370] The book was released in cloth and limp bindings, round and shape notes, a special choir edition, a deluxe pulpit edition, a home edition, and with orchestration for thirteen instruments. The book contained sixty responsive readings. Reynolds, "The Contributions of B. B. McKinney," 46.

[371] Some sales records of the *Broadman Hymnal* are not available, making it impossible to know exactly how many hymnals have been sold. Likely, the most widely distributed hymnal of all time is *Hymns Ancient and Modern*, first published in 1861 and still available today; however, *Hymns Ancient and Modern* has gone through numerous revisions while the *Broadman Hymnal* has never been revised.

[372] Reynolds, "The Contributions of B. B. McKinney," 46.

[373] William M. Tillman, Jr., "Baptists and the Turn toward Racial Inclusion: 1955," in *Turning Points in Baptist History: A Festschrift in Honor of Harry Leon McBeth*, ed. Michael E. Williams, Sr. and Walter B. Shurden (Macon GA: Mercer University Press, 2008) 269–72.

[374] William M. Pinson, Jr., "Biography," in *An Approach to Christian Ethics* (Nashville TN: Broadman Press, 1979) 14–22.

[375] Aaron Weaver, "The Impact of Social Progressive T. B. Maston on Southern Baptist Life in the Twentieth-Century," *Texas Baptist History* 29 (2009): 50; and William M. Tillman, Jr., *Baptist Prophets: Their Lives and Their Contributions* (Brentwood TN: Baptist History & Heritage Society, 2006) 22.

[376] William M. Tillman, "T. B. Maston (1897–1988): Mentor to Southern Baptist Prophets," in *Twentieth-Century Shapers of Baptist Social Ethics*," ed. Larry L. McSwain and Wm. Loyd Allen (Macon GA: Mercer University Press, 2008) 80.

[377] T. B. Maston, *Biblical Ethics: A Guide to the Ethical Message of the Scriptures from Genesis to Revelation* (Macon GA: Mercer University Press; rept. 1988) 287, 288; T. B. Maston, *Christianity and World Issues* (New York: The MacMillan Company, 1957) 327; and T. B. Maston, *Why Live the Christian Life?* (Nashville TN: Broadman Press, 1974) 157. Emphasis is Maston's.

[378] See Pinson, Jr., *An Approach to Christian Ethics*, 14–22; and Tillman, "T. B. Maston (1897–1988)," 78.

[379] Maston, *Christianity and World Issues*, 91–116; and Weaver, "The Impact of Social Progressive T. B. Maston," 51. See T. B. Maston, *Of One: A Study of Christian Principles and Race Relations* (Atlanta: Home Mission Board, 1946); and T. B. Maston, *The Bible and Race: A Careful Examination of Biblical Teachings on Human Relations* (Nashville TN: Broadman Press, 1959).

[380] Jace Jones, "To Race Relations," in Pinson, Jr., *An Approach to Christian Ethics*, 64.

[381] Ibid.

[382] Maston, *Why Live the Christian Life?*, 145.

[383] Tillman, "T. B. Maston (1897–1988)," 79.

[384] T. B. Maston, *The Bible and Race* (Nashville TN: Broadman Press, 1959) 49.

[385] Jones, in Pinson, Jr., *An Approach to Christian Ethics*, 65.

[386] Tillman, "T. B. Maston (1897–1988)," 79; and Jones, in Pinson, Jr., *An Approach to Christian Ethics*, 65.

[387] T. B. Maston, *To Walk As He Walked* (Nashville TN: Broadman Press, 1985) 11.

[388] David S. Dockery, "Herschel H. Hobbs," in *Theologians of the Baptist Tradition*, ed. Timothy George and David S. Dockery (Nashville TN: Broadman & Holman, 2001) 217.

[389] Walter B. Shurden, "In Defense of the SBC: The Moderate Response to Fundamentalism," *The Theological Educator* 30 (1985): 13. See also "The Pastor As Denominational Theologian in Southern Baptist History," *Baptist History and Heritage Journal* (July 1980): 21.

[390] H. Leon McBeth, *The Baptist Heritage* (Nashville TN: Broadman Press, 1987) 676; James Leo Garrett, Jr., *Baptist Theology: A Four-Century Study* (Macon GA: Mercer University Press, 2009) 468–73, cf. 481–86; and Messenger Staff, "Hobbs Selected As Most Influential Oklahoma Baptist of the 20th Century," *Baptist Messenger*, 16 December 1999, 1, 5.

[391] Herschel H. Hobbs, *My Faith and Message* (Nashville TN: Broadman & Holman, 1993) 107, 129, 142–45. In the end, Hobbs did not nominate Lee due to some unusual circumstances that developed.

[392] Bob L. Blackburn and Alvin O. Turner, *First Family: A Centennial History of the First Baptist Church of Oklahoma City* (Oklahoma City: SafeSport Publishing, 1990) 140–44.

[393] William H. Brackney, *The A to Z of the Baptists* (Lanham MD: Scarecrow Press, 2009) 284.

[394] Theodore Lott, "The Baptist Hour," *Encyclopedia of Southern Baptists*, vol. 1 (Nashville TN: Broadman Press) 115–16. Harold Bennett, "Foreword," in Hobbs, *My Faith and Message*, xv. Hobbs claimed that the Baptist Hour was broadcast over 600 stations.

[395] See J. Donald Baker, *Mr. Baptist Hour* (Jefferson City MO: LeRoi Publishers, 1974). See also John Steven Gaines, "An Analysis of the Correlation between Representative Baptist Hour Sermons by Herschel H. Hobbs and Selected Articles of *The Baptist Faith and Message*" (Ph.D. diss., Southwestern Baptist Theological Seminary, 1991).

[396] Hobbs, *My Faith and Message*, 231–32.

[397] James Leo Garrett, Jr., "Herschel Harold Hobbs: Pastoral and Denominational Expositor-Theologian," *Southwestern Journal of Theology* 54/2 (Spring 2012): 135.

[398] Hobbs, *My Faith and Message*, 61, 74; Herschel H. Hobbs and E.Y. Mullins, *The Axioms of Religion* (Nashville TN: Broadman Press, 1978); and Herschel H. Hobbs, *The Baptist Faith and Message* (Nashville TN: Convention Press, 1971) 7–10.

[399] Bennett, "Foreword," in Hobbs, *My Faith and Message*, xvi.

[400] Hobbs, *My Faith and Message*, 216.

[401] Ralph Elliott, *The Message of Genesis* (Nashville TN: Broadman, 1961).

[402] K. Owen White, "…Death in the Pot," *Baptist Standard*, 10 January 1962, 6. White, pastor of First Baptist, Houston, offered perhaps the most recognized criticism of Elliott.

[403] *Annual*, Southern Baptist Convention, 1962, 65, 68.

NOTES

[404] Jerry L. Faught, *The Resurgence of Fundamentalism in the Southern Baptist Convention: A History from 1960–1979* (Lewiston NY: Mellen Press, 2014) 128–50.

[405] *Annual*, Southern Baptist Convention, 1962, 65, 68.

[406] Hobbs, *My Faith and Message*, 240.

[407] Ibid., 236, 240–43.

[408] Herschel H. Hobbs, interview by Ronald Tonks, Herschel H. Hobbs Papers, Southern Baptist Historical Library and Archives, Nashville, Tennessee, 272.

[409] SBC, *Annual*, 1963, 269–81.

[410] Hobbs, *My Faith and Message*, 243–44; and Hobbs, *The Baptist Faith and Message*, 26.

[411] Herschel H. Hobbs, interview with Dennis Wiles, June 1990, 227. A transcript of this interview can be found in Dennis Wiles, "Factors Contributing to the Resurgence of Fundamentalism in the Southern Baptist Convention, 1979–1990" (Ph.D. diss., Southwestern Baptist Theological Seminary, 1992) appendix 2.

[412] Hobbs, *My Faith and Message*, 241–42.

[413] Terry Mattingly, "Old Baptists, New Baptists: A Reporter Looks at the Battle to Control the SBC," *Southwestern Journal of Theology* 28 (Summer 1986): 6–7.

[414] Jesse C. Fletcher, *The Southern Baptist Convention: A Sesquicentennial History* (Nashville TN: Broadman & Holman, 1994) 284.

[415] James Leo Garrett, Jr., "From Denominational Statesman to Rejected Leader; From Neglected Author to Recovered Author?" *Southwestern Journal of Theology* 54/2 (Spring 2012) 147–49.

[416] James C. Hefley, *The Truth in Crisis: The Controversy in the Southern Baptist Convention*, vol. 5 (Richmond: Hannibal Books, 1990) 21.

[417] Dockery, "Herschel H. Hobbs," 226. Hobbs held to only one point of Dortian Calvinism (perseverance).

[418] David S. Dockery, "Southern Baptists and Calvinism: A Historical Look," in *Calvinism: A Southern Baptist Dialogue*, ed. E. Ray Clendenen and Brad J. Waggoner (Nashville: Broadman & Holman, 2008) 38–39; and Timothy and Denise George, eds., *Baptist Why and Why Not Revisited* (Nashville TN: Broadman & Holman, 1997) 11–22.

[419] Report of the BGCT Seminary Study Committee, *BGCT Book of Reports 2000*, Baptist General Convention of Texas, assets.baptiststandard.com/archived/2003/210/pages/decision.html (accessed 1 April 2014).

[420] Henlee Barnette, *Crucial Problems in Christian Perspective* (Philadelphia PA: Westminster Press, 1970) 133.

[421] Ibid., 18.

[422] Henlee Barnette, "The Glorious Gospel," *Southwestern Journal of Theology* 34/3 (Summer 1992): 5.

[423] Henlee Barnette, "The Southern Baptist Theological Seminary and the Civil Rights Movement: The Visit of Martin Luther King, Jr., Part Two," *Review and Expositor* 93 (Winter 1996): 79.

[424] Henlee Barnette, "The Cross Is for Real, Man," *Home Missions* 40/4 (April 1969): 22.

[425] Henlee Barnette, *The Church and the Ecological Crisis* (Grand Rapids MI: William B. Eerdmans Publishing Company, 1972) 83.

[426] Gerald Lamont Thomas, *African-American Preaching: The Contribution of Dr. Gardner C. Taylor* (New York: Peter Lang, 2004) 82. I am indebted to this source for much of Taylor's biographical information.

[427] One of the difficulties about finding biographical information about Taylor is that much of it comes from oral history. In the introduction of Edward L. Taylor, ed., *The Words of Gardner Taylor* (Valley Forge: Judson Press, 1999), 1, Taylor indicates that Gardner Taylor was thirteen when his

father died. In an earlier account found in Taylor's own words [Gardner Taylor, "Why I Believe There Is a God," in *Why I Believe There Is a God: Sixteen Essays by Negro Clergymen* (Chicago: Johnson Publishing Co., 1965) 104], Gardner indicates he was twelve.

[428] Thomas, *African-American Preaching*, 86.

[429] Reverend Gardner C. Taylor, "Religion and Ethics Newsweekly," PBS, 18 August 2006, http://www.pbs.org/wnet/religionandethics/2006/08/18/august-18-2006-reverend-gardner-c-taylor/1786/ (accessed 8 April 2014).

[430] G. C. Taylor, "Why I Believe There Is a God," 106.

[431] Thomas, *African-American Preaching*, 95.

[432] Michael Eric Dyson, "Gardner Taylor: Poet Laureate of the Pulpit," *Christian Century*, 4–11 January 1995, 14.

[433] Wallace Best, "The Right Achieved and the Wrong Way Conquered," *Religion and American Culture* 16/2 (Summer 2006): 203–205. Also Sandy Dwayne Martin, "The Formation of the Progressive National Baptist Convention," *Baptist History and Heritage* (Spring 2011): 18–27.

[434] G. C. Taylor, "Religion and Ethics Newsweekly," (accessed 8 April 2014).

[435] "Dr. Taylor to Join Education Board," *New York Times*, 25 March 1958, 19.

[436] Brian Purnell, *Fighting Jim Crow in the County of Kings: The Congress of Racial Equality in Brooklyn* (Lexington KY: University of Kentucky Press, 2013) 226–27.

[437] Dyson, "Gardner Taylor: Poet Laureate," 14.

[438] Gardner C. Taylor, *How Shall They Preach?* (Elgin IL: Progressive Baptist Publishing House, 1977) 42ff.

Index

Abemarle Female Institute, 115
Adams, John, 41, 63
Adams, Sam, 41
African-American Baptist State Convention (AR), 122
Agricultural and Mechanical College (Normal, AL), 123
Alabama A & M (Auburn University), 95, 96
American Baptist, 159
American Baptist Foreign Mission Society, 92, 147
American Baptist Hospital Association, 105
American Baptist Missionary Union, 93
American Baptist Publication Society, 125, 144, 148
Anabaptist Movement, 88
Annie Armstrong Offering, 119
Antioch Baptist Church (TX), 104
Appeal to the Public for Religious Liberty, An, 40
Approach to Christian Ethics, An, 185
(American) Civil War, 93
American Colonization Society, 77
Andover Seminary, 80
Answer to a Deceitful Book, An, 19
Anthony, Susan B., 145
Archway Road Free Church, 164
Arkansas Baptist College, 122
Arkansas Times, 122
Arminianism, 194
Armstrong, Annie, 97
Articles of Religion, 46, 47
Ashmore, Joan, 1
Axioms of Religion, 130, 131, 132, 134, 191

Backus, Isaac, 38-43, 64
Bacoats, J. A., 204, 205
Bainfield, Francis, 6
Baptist Beliefs, 130
Baptist Board of Foreign Missions, 82
Baptist Faith and Message (1925), 132
Baptist Faith and Message (1963), 191, 192, 193, 194
Baptist Foreign Mission Convention, 171
Baptist General Association (TX), 101, 102
Baptist General Convention of Texas (BGCT), 103, 106, 186

Baptist Hymnal, The, 182
Baptist Messenger, 189
Baptist Missionary Society, 52, 54, 55, 56, 68, 71, 93
Baptist Pastor's Conference, 158
Baptist Recovery of Europe Plan, 166
Baptist Recovery Committee, 166
Baptist Union, 111, 112, 165, 167
Baptist Vanguard, 122
Baptist Women's Missionary Training School, 105
Baptist World Alliance, 123, 131, 145, 165, 205
Baptist World Alliance Congress, 153, 167
Baptist World Alliance World Emergency Relief Committee, 166
Barber, Edward, 6
Barrett Family, 143
Barrett Memorial Sunday School Class, 145
Barnette Family, 200
Barnette, Henlee, 195-202
Battle of Shiloh, 95
Baylor University, 150, 208
Berquist, Millard, 191
Bethany Baptist Church (OH), 205
Beulah Baptist Church (LA), 205
Bible and Race, The, 186
Biblical Ethics, 185
Birmingham Baptist Ministers' Conference, 197
Bloody Tenet of Persecution, 40
Boardman, George Dana, 84
Booth, W. V., 207
Board of Commissioners for Foreign Missions, 80, 81
Book of Common Prayer, 1, 2, 3, 18
Booth, William, 111
Bradford Academy, 80
Bradford Congregational Church, 80
Breach Repaired, The, 19
Brief Discourse, 19
Brine, John, 50
British Red Cross, 162
Broadman Hymnal, The, 180
Broadman Press, 191
Broadway Temple AME Zion Church, 199
Brown v. Board of Education, 157, 198

Brown University (Rhode Island College), 40, 79, 80, 149
Bryan, William Jennings, 158
Buckner, Robert Cooke, 100-07,
Buckner Family, Robert Cooke, 101
Buckner Home Baptist Church, 102
Buckner Home School, 104
Buckner's Orphan Home, 102, 103
Bunyan, John, 54, 108
Burroughs Family, 169
Burroughs, Nannie Helen, 169-75
Bush Conservatory of Music, 178

Caldwell Female Institute, 115
Calvin, John; Calvinism; Calvinists, 17, 18, 24, 27, 28, 29, 42, 46, 50, 56
Carey, Dorothy Plackett, 67, 68, 69, 71
Carey, Dorothy Rumohr, 71
Carey, Edmund, 66
Carey, Felix, 70, 71
Carey, Grace Hughes, 71
Carey, Jabez, 71
Carey, Jonathan, 71
Carey, Lott, 73-78
Carey, Mihala, 74, 76
Carey, Peter, 66
Carey, William, 55, 66-72
Carey, Jr., William, 71
Carnegie, Andrew, 100
Carroll, B. H., 102
Carson-Newman College, 183
Carter, President Jimmy, 197
Carver, W. O., 130, 152-61
Cattell, Thomas, 25
Celebrating Grace Hymnal, 182
Centenary Translation, 143, 148, 149
Centennial Baptist Church, Helena,(AR), 121, 122, 127
Central Committee on United Study of Foreign Missions, 146
Charleston Baptist Association, 35
Children's Bureau Bill, 106
Child's Instructor, The, 17, 21
Christian Banner, The, 170
Christian Life Commission of Texas, 186
Christian Religion in Its Doctrinal Expression, The, 130-31
Christianity and World Issues, 185, 186
Christianity at the Crossroads, 131
Christ's Coming and His Kingdom, 129
Christianity and the Social Crisis, 138, 139, 140, 141

Christianizing the Social Order, 141
Church Musician, The, 181, 182
Church Music Week, 181
Church and the Ecological Crisis, The, 201
Christian, William A., 74
Civic Righteousness and Social Service Committee, 106
Civil Rights Movement, 121, 190, 207, 208
Clarke, John, 8-15
Clifford, John, 162, 163, 164, 165
Clinton, President Bill, 208
Coleman, Robert H., 178, 179, 180, 181
Colgate Rochester Divinity School, 208
College Lane Baptist Church, 25
College Women's Club, 145
Collins, Hercules, 6
Commentary on Ephesians and Colossians, 130
Committee on Christian Literature for Women and Children in Mission Fields, 147
Concord Baptist Church (NY), 205
Concord Credit Union, 206
Concord Elementary School (NY), 205, 206
Concord Credit Union, 206
Congress of English Speaking Peoples of the World, 123
Continental Congress, 41
Continental Society, 87-88
Cooperative Baptist Fellowship (CBF), 183, 193
Cooperative Program (SBC), 98
Courtney, John R. , 71
Crane, William C., 76, 77
Crandall, John, 12
Cranmer, Thomas, 1
Crawford, T. P., 116
Crosby, Thomas, 16
Crucial Problems in Christian Perspective, 196
Crystal Palace, London, 110

Dallas Baptist Association Pastor's Conference, 104
Danville Female Seminary, 115
Dauphin Way Baptist Church (AL), 189
Davies, Horton, 18
Davis, W. Hersey, 191
Declaration of Faith of English People Remaining in Holland, 4
Delane, Thomas, 6
Denison University, 149
Dickens, Charles, 162
Dickson Negro Orphanage, 103

Index

Dockery, David, 189
Domestic Mission Board (also Domestic and Indian Mission Board), 93, 94, 96, 101
Down Grade Controversy, The, 111, 162
Durham, Allen Pinckney, 177
Dutton, Anne Williams, 24-30
Dutton, Benjamin 26, 27

Earth Day, 201
East Alabama Male College, 95
East Waco Baptist Church (TX), 150, 155
Ebony, 208
E. C. Morris Foundation, 127
Ecumenical Missionary Conference. 146
Edwards, Jonathan , 54
Ehrlich, Paul, 201
Elliott, Ralph, 191, 192
Elliott Controversy, 193
Emancipation Proclamation, 169
Endicott, John, 12
Enquiry, An, 55, 68
Evangelical Revival, 24, 26, 27, 48, 51
Eve, John, 51, 52
Evolution Theory: Plain Words for Plain Folks, The, 159
Executive Committee (BGCT), 106
Exeter Hall, (London), 110

Falls Creek Baptist Assembly, 179
Federal Council of Churches of Christ, 123
First African Baptist Church of Richmond (VA), 78
First Baptist Church of Charlottesville (VA), 115
First Baptist Church of Dallas (TX), 128, 150, 153, 155, 189
First Baptist Church of Montgomery (AL), 94, 95
First Baptist Church of Newport (RI), 11, 14
First Baptist Church of New York City (NY), 140
First Baptist Church of Oklahoma City (OK), 190
First Baptist Church of Providence (RI), 10, 14
First Baptist Church of Richmond (VA), 75, 76
First Great Awakening, 38, 62
Florida Baptist Convention, 198

Florida Woman's Missionary Union Convention, 8
Ford, Henry, 100
Following the Sunrise, 147
Foreign Mission Board, 93, 114, 115, 116, 117, 119, 128, 129
Foreign Mission Journal, 116
Franklin College, 149
Freedom and Authority in Religion, 130
Freedom of the Will, 54
Freeman, Alice, 144
Ft. William College, 70
Fuller, Andrew, 50-56, 67, 68, 109
Fuller Family, 53
Fullerism, 55
Fundamentals of Religion, 48
Fundamentals, The, 131
Fundamentalist-Modernist Conflict, 131

Gambrell Street Baptist Church, 187
Gano, John, 35
Garnett, Ellis, 178
Garrett, James Leo, 189, 190
General Baptists, 16, 17,l 21, 44, 45, 46, 47, 50
General Baptist Academy, 45
General Baptist Magazine, 45
General Committee of Baptists of Virginia, 59
General Convention of Baptists in North America, 123
George, Timothy, 194
Gilbert, C. J. 177
Gill, John, 50, 109
Gladstone, William E., 162
Glory of Christ, The, 25
Golden Jubilee Celebration, 146
Gold Refined, 19
Gospel Worthy of All Acceptation, The, 54
Grace Abounding to the Chief of Sinners, 54
Graves, Allen W., 181
Great Commission, 67, 68
Great Gransden Church, 26
Great Queen Street Methodist Chapel, 87
Green, Bernard, 165
Griggs, A. R., 103
Haldeman, I. M., 140
Hall, Gordon, 81
Hall, Robert, 52
Hamburg Altona Baptist Church, 91
Hamburg Mission School, 91
Hammonds, Phyllis, 127

Hampstead Garden Suburb Free Church, 164
Harnack, Adolf von, 164
Harriet Beecher Stowe Literary Society, 170
Harris, Howell, 26, 29
Hart, Oliver, 35
Hartwell, J. B., 116
Hauerwas, Stanley, 188
Harvard College, 19
Harvard Divinity School, 208
Hasseltine, John, 80
Haysville Baptist Church, 150
Hefley, James, 194
Hell's Kitchen, 136, 138
Helwys, Edward, 1
Helwys, Joan, 3
Helwys, Thomas 1-7, 9, 44, 164
High Calvinism, 50, 51, 52, 53
History of Infant Baptism, A, 44
History of New England with Particular Reference to the . . . Baptists, 38, 42
Hobbs, Herschel H., 189-94
Holcomb, Thomas Luther, 179
Hollins Institute, 115
Holmes, Obadiah, 12, 13, 42
Home-Finding State Conference Address, 106
Home Mission Board, 96, 97
Home Mission Society, 93, 96
Home Missions, 200
Horsley-down Particular Baptist Church, 19
Hough, George and Phoebe, 82
Hovey, Alvah, 129
Howard College (also Samford University), 196, 198
Hubmaier, Balthasar, 645
Hussey, Joseph, 25
Hutchinson, Anne, 10
Hyper-Calvinism, 67

Ill Newes from New England, 13
Indian Mission Association, 93, 97
Ivimey, Joseph, 24

Jackson, Joseph H., 206, 207
Jefferson, Thomas, 42, 63
Jefferson County Negro Teachers Association, 198
John Clarke Society of Early American Democracy, 15
Johns Hopkins University, 129

Joint Committee for Women's Union Christian Colleges in Foreign Fields, 147
Jordan, L. G., 170
Journal and Messenger, 140
Judson, Adoniram, 79-86
Judson, Anne Hasseltine, 80-84
Judson Family, 79-85
Judson, Emily Chubbuck (Fannie Forrester), 85
Judson, Sarah Boardman, 84

Keach, Benjamin, 16-22
Keach Family, 16, 17
Kebel College, 162
Kentucky Christian Leadership Conference, 199
Kettering Baptist Church, 53
King Charles II, 8, 9, 14
King James I, 1, 6, 9
King, Jr., Martin Luther, 127, 198, 199, 206, 207
King, A. D. Williams, 199
Kobner, Julius, 90, 91
Korean War, 200

Ladies Aid Society, 101
Lake Avenue Baptist Church (NY), 143, 144, 145
Langford, Joseph, 76
Leatherwood, Mattie C., 181
Lee, R. G. 190
Lehmann, Gottfried W. 89, 90
Leland College, 204
Leland, John, 42, 58-65
Leland, Sallie Devine, 61
Lemons, Stanley J., 14
Let Us Sing, 180
Lewis, John, 26
Lincolnshire General Baptist Association, 45
Literary Digest, 14
Livingstone, David, 111
Livingstone Park Seminary, 144
Locke, John, 13
London Missions Society, 81
London Confession, 1689, 21

London Weekly Papers, The, 26, 29
Lott Carey Foreign Mission Convention, 73, 77
Lottie Moon Christmas Offering, 118, 119

Index

Louisiana College, 177
Luter, Jr., Fred, 183
Lyman Beecher Lecture, 208
Lyle Avenue Mission, 143

MacLeish, Martha Hillard, 147
MacMillan Publishers, 139
Madison, James, 40, 59, 60, 63
Marlow, Isaac, 19, 20
Marshall, Daniel, 33
Marshall, Martha Stearns, 33, 34
Marshman, John, 69
Martin, T. T., 159
Maryland Baptist, 129
Mason, Caroline Atwater, 48
Maston Family, 184
Maston, T. B., 183-88
Married Women's Property Act, 162
Mary Hardin-Baylor College, 177
Mays, Benjamin, 197
Maze Pond Church, 26
McBeth, H. Leon, 87, 189
McCall, Duke, 199
McCall, Emmanuel, 183
McClellan, Albert, 192
McIntosh, W. H., 96
McKinley High School (LA), 204
McKinney, B. B., 176-82
McKinney Family, 176, 177
McLaughlin, William, 39, 41, 43
McNeely, Edwin, 178
Memorial and Remonstrance, 40
Metropolitan Tabernacle Church, 110, 162
Midland Baptist College, 164
Midwestern Baptist Theological Seminary, 191
Mile End Green Church, 19
Minister's Relief Board, 103
Minus, Paul, 138
Modern Question Concerning Repentance and Faith, 52, 54
Monroe Baptist Association, 144
Montevallo Mining Company, 95
Montgomery, Helen Barrett, 144-49
Montgomery, William A., 144
Moon Family, 115
Moon, Lottie, 114-20
Morehouse College, 197
Morgan, J. P., 100
Morris, E. C., 121-27
Morris, Fannie Ella, 122
Mt. Lebanon Academy, 177

Mt. Lebanon Baptist Church (LA), 177
Mt. Zion Baptist Church (LA), 203, 205
Muller, George, 111
Mullins, E. Y., 128-35
Mullins, Isla Mae Hawley, 128
Munter, Jan, 3
Murton, John, 6

Narration of the Wonders of Grace, A, 26
National Association for the Advancement of Colored People (NAACP), 186
"National Baptist Catechism," 126
National Conference of Charities and Corrections, 105
National Baptist Convention, 121, 122, 123, 124, 125, 126, 170, 171, 172, 173, 205
National Baptist Foreign Mission Board, 170
National Baptist Publication Board, 123
National Training School for Women and Girls, 172
Neo-Calvinists, 194
Newell, Samuel, 81
Newgate Prison, 6
Newton Centre Baptist Church, 120
New Connection of General Baptists, 44, 45, 46, 47
New Hampshire Confession of Faith, 130
New Hope Baptist Church (TX), 103
New Lights, 38, 39
New Park Street Baptist Church, 109
New South Movement, 95
New York City Commission on Inter-Group Relations, 207
New York State Constitution, 145
New York State Federation of Women's Clubs, 145
Newton Theological Institution, 129, 149
Nicholls, Clarke, 67
Niebuhr, Reinhold, 152, 188
Niebuhr, Richard, 188
Nineteenth Street Baptist Church, 170, 174
Northamptonshire Association of Particular Baptist Churches, 52, 55
Northern Baptist Convention, 125, 147, 148
Northern Baptist Home Mission Society, 94
Nott, Samuel, 81

Oberlin College, 205
Oberlin Graduate School of Theology, 205
Odum, Howard Thomas, 201

Of One: A Study of Christian Principles and Race Relations, 186
Oklahoma Baptist Convention, 179
Oklahoma Baptist University, 179
Oncken, Johann Gerhard, 87-92

Pal, Krishna, 70
Palmer, Wait, 32
Parliament, 8, 13
Particular Baptist(s), 17, 19, 20, 48, 50, 51, 67, 68, 111, 162
Pasteur Institute, 105
Peabody, Lucy Waterbury, 144
Peace Committee (SBC), 193
Peck, John Mason, 93
Pegg Scholarship, 164
Perkins Road School, 204
Philadelphia Baptist Association, 35, 40
Pietism, Pietistic Revivals, 89
Pilgrim's Progress, 54, 66, 108
Pinson, Bill, 185
Pinson, J. T., 102
Political Equality Club, 145
Porter, John W., 159
Praed Street Baptist Chapel, 162
Preacher's Institute, 163
Preaching Value of Missions, The, 149
Presidential Medal of Freedom, 208
Progressive National Baptist Convention, 173, 207
Protestant Council of Churches, 207
Puritans, Puritanism, 2, 5, 7, 8, 13, 31, 108

Queensbury Street Baptist Church, 164
Queen Victoria, 163

Rauschenbusch, Walter, 100, 130, 136-42, 196
Reconstruction Era, 93, 170
Religious Herald, 130
Religious Messenger, The, 102, 103
Review and Expositor, 130, 157, 158
Reynolds, I. E., 177, 178, 179
Rhode Island General Assembly, 14
Rice, Luther, 81, 82
Richmond African Baptist Missionary Society, 76
Richmond College, 157
Ridgecrest Assembly, 177, 181
Rights of Conscience Inalienable, The, 60
Rippen, John, 109

Ritchschlian School, 164
Roberts, John, 18
Robertson, A. T., 191
Robinson, John, 2, 3
Rochester Free Academy, 144
Rochester Theological Seminary, 136, 138, 143
Rochester Women's Educational and Industrial Union, 145
Rockefeller, Sr., John D., 100
Routh, Porter, 192
Royal Surrey Gardens Music Hall, 110
Rushbrooke, J. H., 162-68
Rushbrooke Family, 163, 164
Ryland, Jr., J. H., 52, 53, 67
Ryland, Sr., J. H. 67

Safford, Anna, 115
Salvation Army, 111
Sandy Creek Baptist Association, 34, 35, 36, 37
Sandy Creek Baptist Church, 33, 34, 35
Scarborough, L. R., 146, 178
Scottsville Baptist Church, 115
Sears, Barnas, 89
Second German Baptist Church (NY), 136, 137
Second Great Awakening, 80, 101
Second London Confession, 1689, 111
Separatists, Separatism, 2, 4, 7, 9, 32, 39
Serampore College, 70
Sermons, Addresses, and Reminiscences, 123
Seventeenth Alabama Regiment, 95
Sharpe, Dores, 136
Shockoe Tobacco Warehouse, 7
Short, Charles, 69
Short, Kitty Plackett, 68, 69
Short Declaration of the Mystery of Iniquity, 5, 6
Shurden, Walter B., 93, 189
Siegel-Myers School of Music, 178
Sims, W. Hines, 181
Sister Grove Association, 197
Sixteenth Street Baptist Church (AL), 197
Smyth, John, 1, 2, 4, 5, 6, 9, 44
Sober Appeal for Right and Justice, 20
Sober Reply to Mr. Steed's Epistle Concerning Singing, 19
Social Christianity Movement, 100
Social Gospel Movement, 100, 138, 142, 161, 180
Soham Baptist Church, 51, 52

Index

Songs of Victory, 180
Southern Baptist Convention (SBC), 93, 94, 96, 98, 115, 119, 129, 131, 157, 160, 180, 183, 190, 191, 193, 194, 196, 199, 200
Southern Baptist Theological Seminary, 95, 97, 127, 128, 130, 157, 161, 189, 191, 195, 197, 198, 199, 200, 201
Southwestern Baptist Theological Seminary, 105, 177, 178, 183, 184, 187
Southern Christian Leadership Conference, 199
Spurgeon, Charles Haddon, 108-13, 162
Spurgeon Family, 109, 111
Spurgeon, James, 108
State University (KY), 123
Stearns, Sally, 33
Stearns, Shubal, 31-37
Stetson College, 197
Stokes, Anson Phelps, 43
St. Mary's Gate Church, 164
St. Michael's Church, 164
Students Non-Violent Coordinating Committee, 198
Studying Adult Life and Work Lessons, 191
Sunday School Board (SBC), 130, 179, 181
Sutcliffe, John, 52, 53, 66
Sword and the Trowel, 111

Taylor, Abraham, 52
Taylor, Dan, 44-49, 54
Taylor Family, Gardner, 203, 204, 205
Taylor, Gardner, 203-09
Taylor, Joseph Judson, 159
Teague, Collin, 76
Texas A & M University, 128
Texas Baptist, 103
Texas Baptist Women Mission Workers, 104, 105
Texas Baptist Sanatorium, 105
Texas Child Labor Law, 106
Texas Christian University, 183
Texas Prisoner's Aid Association, 106
Texas Prison Board, 106
Theology for the Social Gospel, 141
Thomas, John, 68, 69
Tichenor, Isaac Taylor, 93-99
Tillman, 184, 186, 187
Time, 208
To Walk As He Walked, 188
Toy, Crawford, 116
Tolland, C. N., 32

Travis Avenue Baptist Church (TX), 179, 180
Treasury of David, 112
Trent, Robbie, 181
Triennial Convention, 56, 76, 85, 93
Truett, George W., 150-56
Tuberculosis Sanatorium, 105
Tupper, Henry, 116
Tuskegee Institute, 170
Twentieth-Century Shapers of Baptist Social Ethics, 187

Udney, George, 69
Union Gospel Mission, 196
Union Theological Seminary, 208
United Nations, 200
United Nations' Declaration of Human Rights, 9, 15
University of Florida, 201
University of Louisville, 196
University of Michigan Law School, 204
University of Rochester, 136, 145
U. S. Bill of Rights, 9, 15, 41, 59, 60
U. S. Constitution, 9, 15, 41

Vardaman, James W., 153
Virginia Union University, 169

Wake Forest College, 195
Walking with God, 28
Wall, William, 44
Wallace, Martha, 55
Ward, William, 56, 69, 77
Warr, John
Warren Association, 38, 40
Washington Colored High School (M Street High School), 170
Watts, Isaac, 19
Wayland, Francis, 85
Wednesday Morning Club, 145
Wellesley College, 144, 149
Wellesley Preparatory School, 144
Western Women in Eastern Lands, 146
Whilden, Lula, 115
Whinnel, Thomas, 19, 20
White, Lynn, 201
White House Conference on Dependent Children, 106
Whitefield, George, 26, 27, 29, 31, 32, 33, 34, 44, 51, 62, 109
Whitsitt, W. H., 129, 130, 161
Whitsitt Controversy, 129

Whitewright Baptist Church, 150
Why is Christianity True?, 130
Why Live the Christian Life?, 186
Willesdon District Council, 163
Williams, Roger, 8, 9, 13, 42, 43, 64
Willingham, R. H., 129
Winchester, Elhanan, 61
Witter, William, 12
Woman's American Baptist Foreign
    Missions Society, 146, 147
Woman's Ethical Club, 145
Women's Foreign Missions Committee, 171
Women's Missionary Union, 97, 117, 119
WMU Training School, 130
World Council of Churches, 160
World Day of Prayer, 147
Worship and Theology in England, 18
Wright, Arthur G., 206
World War I, 103, 165, 177'
World War II, 165, 179

Yale University, 193, 208
Young Men's Bible Class, 163

Zion Baptist Association (TX), 103
Zion Baptist Church (OH), 207
Zwingli, Ulrich, 18

www.ingramcontent.com/pod-product-compliance
Lightning Source LLC
Chambersburg PA
CBHW031807220426
43662CB00007B/556